LETTERS FROM HOME

LIFT YOUR MISSIONARY & UNIFY YOUR FAMILY

Robert E. Quinn

Praise for
Letters from Home

"Robert and his daughter Shauri have done a magnificent job in bringing new insights to preparing and strengthening missionaries. Their vision of the work and their letter-writing section have opened new vistas for strengthening the missionary and family together. Brother Quinn's experience as a mission president has provided significant understanding of the challenges that missionaries face and the way to face them with faith. This is a groundbreaking book that will bless the lives of all who receive it and take it into their lives. I recommend this book for all preparing and serving missionaries and their parents. It is absolutely a must-read so as to bless the missionary and his family and friends. I simply loved the book, and it motivated me to action.

Ed J Pinegar, author of *Gethsemane, Golgotha and the Garden Tomb, What Every Future Missionary & Their Parents Need To Know*, and the bestselling Christmas story *The Christmas Code*.

"Most of us have framed our weekly letters to our missionaries and family members in faraway places as newsletters. Bob Quinn has framed this weekly ritual differently. By becoming missionaries ourselves, our letters can be written to inspire and motivate our family members to teach each other how to build the kingdom of God. This is an inspiring book."

Clayton Christensen, missionary and author of *The Power of Everyday Missionaries*

"Bob Quinn is the master at making the complex simple. He never fails to excite and enhance the doing of good. This book is filled with practical suggestions of how to build relationships with family and missionaries that will last beyond the mission and into life and the eternities. The guidance he provides can be applied not only to missionaries, but also to any relationships you want to enhance, build, and make Christlike. You will enjoy and gain tremendously from his thoughts and suggestions gained from experiences."

Lloyd Baird, Organizational Behavior Department Chair, Boston University Questrom School of Business

ROBERT QUINN

with SHAURI QUINN DEWEY

AIR MAIL
REGISTERED

CHESHIRE
10 -PM
29 OCT
1991

LETTERS

FROM HOME

LIFT YOUR MISSIONARY & UNIFY YOUR FAMILY

CFI
An imprint of Cedar Fort, Inc.
Springville, Utah

ISBN 13: 978-1-4621-1876-2

Published by CFI, an imprint of Cedar Fort, Inc.
2373 W. 700 S., Springville, UT, 84663
Distributed by Cedar Fort, Inc., www.cedarfort.com

LIBRARY OF CONGRESS CATALOGING-IN-PUBLICATION DATA

Names: Quinn, Robert E., author. | Dewey, Shauri Quinn, 1971- author.
Title: Letters from home : lift your missionary and unify your family /
   Robert E. Quinn, Shauri Quinn Dewey.
Description: Springville, Utah : CFI, An imprint of Cedar Fort, Inc., [2016]
   | Includes bibliographical references and index.
Identifiers: LCCN 2016013019 (print) | LCCN 2016015098 (ebook) | ISBN
   9781462118762 (perfect bound : alk. paper) | ISBN 9781462126347 (epub,
   pdf, mobi)
Subjects: LCSH: Mormon missionaries--Correspondence. | Letter
   writing--Religious aspects--Church of Jesus Christ of Latter-day Saints.
Classification: LCC BX8661 .Q46 2016 (print) | LCC BX8661 (ebook) | DDC
   266/.9332--dc23
LC record available at https://lccn.loc.gov/2016013019

Cover design by Shawnda T. Craig
Cover design © 2016 by Cedar Fort, Inc.
Edited and typeset by Sydnee Hyer

Printed in the United States of America

10 9 8 7 6 5 4 3 2 1

Printed on acid-free paper

Contents

Acknowledgments

This book spans a quarter of century in its creation. It began the day my first child left on his mission, continued throughout my other children's service, and was further developed as the same letters were sent weekly to the sisters and elders serving with Delsa and I in Adelaide, Australia. The seed of an idea, planted decades ago, at last comes to fruition in the form of this book.

Over those twenty-five years, many people have impacted the final product. We are lucky to have friends all over the world who volunteered to read the manuscript, provide valuable feedback, and help us to share this message. These friends committed many hours and took us in new directions with their insights. I am deeply indebted to Michael McIlwaine, Laura Padilla, Corey Garff, Angela Cheney, Kirk Blad, Stephanie DeFilippis, Ed Morreall, Joanna Prestwich, Kerri Nelson, Mindy Barnes, Jennifer Wellesley, Heather Wimmer, Heather Aeschilman, Blake Carter, Jordan Collet, Shelley Beard, Brooke Gale, Helen Kirk, Phil Howes, Judy Howes, and Kristen Jowers. Kristen in particular not only sent her feedback, but also shared one of her own personal letters to her missionary children which we decided to put in the book. Thank you.

There are a few other people who contributed in important ways to the development of this book. Ryan Elder talked us through the marketing and design of our book. Aleta Luke shared some of her treasured missionary homecoming photos with us for the cover of the book as well as our website. The images she captured convey the genuine joy of a missionary reunion. Ramona Faititi and Quentin Daniels are beloved missionaries of mine who graciously allowed us to share some of their personal family letters and stories.

Rodger Dean Duncan and Ed Pinegar went the extra mile. They read the manuscript and gave support at every turn.

Of all the contributions to this book, the most central has been that of my family. Without them, there would be no letters, and there would be no book. Each of them contributed to this book in important ways.

Ryan was my first child to leave and it was the pain of losing him that started me thinking about a different way to write letters. Kristin and Travis were the last two children to serve missions and their commitment to the final letter-writing process, and the content from their very authentic and open letters is what fueled a large part of the challenges you find in the second part of this book. They inspired me then and continue to do so.

My wife, Delsa, is always inspirational in her commitment to me and to my family. She throws herself in heart and soul and makes every project not only possible, but better. There is no greater support, partner, and example in my life.

Shauri, Shawn, Amy, Lisa, and Garrett all shared their stories and were part of the letter-writing project as well. They each added a unique and important voice. Finally, my son-in-law James spent many hours helping us to edit this book, re-reading multiple versions to make sure that the copy and message were what we hoped it would be. His gift for words, and the gift of his time are much appreciated.

And so, I dedicate this book to my family. Like Nephi, we wrote on these pages the things of our souls. We learned from each other, we communed with each other and we came to better know the Lord together through our shared experiences. I hope this book will serve as a record and a reminder for them, their children, and their children's children. I am grateful to be part of an eternal family.

Preface

A few months after my daughter Kristin and my son Travis left on their missions, my wife, Delsa, said, "I now have what every mother wants but never gets." I could not imagine what she was talking about, so I asked. She replied, "I know what each of my children is thinking and feeling." With children who ranged from uncommunicative teenagers to busy young adults starting families, this was no small miracle.

My wife, Delsa, and I have six wonderful children. From oldest to youngest, they are Shauri, Ryan, Shawn, Kristin, Travis, and Garrett. Kristin and Travis were our last two to serve missions.

I rejoiced each time one of my children decided to serve a mission, knowing the benefits they would reap from their service. I also worried about the dangers they might face; I knew I would not be there to protect them. I felt the pain of separation and great loneliness. Like Nephi, "mine eyes water[ed] my pillow by night, because of them; and I [cried] unto my God in faith, and I [knew] he [would] hear my cry" (2 Nephi 33:3). Having my children serve missions softened my heart and turned my normal prayers into prayers of real intent.

My professional friends would often comment on the length of missions and would suggest that I must miss my children terribly. I often replied that I felt closer to them while they were on their missions than I did when they were home. How was that possible?

In a particularly lonely moment after my son Ryan left on his mission, I had an epiphany. The only connections we have with our children on their missions are the letters we exchange. If I changed the way I wrote, and opened myself to the Spirit, I could be a mouthpiece for the Lord. I realized that this is one of the few ways in which a parent can truly help their child during this difficult, soul-stretching journey. We couldn't be physically close, but we could draw closer spiritually and emotionally through our letters.

The letter-writing project described in this book started with my letters but evolved over a ten-year stretch and became a family project. By the time my fourth and fifth children (Travis and Kristin) were serving their missions, every family member at home was involved in the project at some level. We were all communicating in disciplined ways about the deepest concerns of our lives. Since we did this regularly, even though we were geographically distant, I felt like I was with my missionaries all the time. And I was. During that period, we were not only close to our two missionaries, we were also close to God and to one another. Our communication style changed dramatically, and it blessed all of us in surprising ways. As Delsa expressed, we were getting what I think all of us want (and rarely get): continuous, loving communion with the people closest to us and with God.

Being far from home and facing the rigors of missionary life altered my children. Their routine prayers also became prayers of real intent and they deepened their relationship with God. They became receptive to communication with us, their parents, in a way they weren't before. They paid great attention to the letters they received from home. Here is a statement written by my son Travis when he was a missionary:

> Dad, I really enjoyed your last letter. It was very meaningful to me. When you write about some of my earlier experiences, they bring tears to my eyes. A mission has pushed me in a lot of directions, and many of the experiences are dear to my heart. Thank you all for taking time to write meaningful letters. You'd be amazed how your letters help me to refocus myself.

My daughter Kristin was serving a mission at the same time as Travis. In response to the letters she was receiving from home, she wrote:

> Please know how much I treasure your letters. The first letter you sent, about learning to let us go with gratitude, I have kept it in my scriptures. It is precious to me. I was reading your recent letter where you said, "this kind of opposition usually helps us see how important the thing is that we are desiring, this kind of opposition also helps

us purge ourselves, make ourselves clean in the eyes of the Lord, this kind of opposition teaches us patience." How true that is. It's never been clearer to me than right now. You quoted D&C 122:7–8. As I read it, I remembered the first time I read it and said to myself, "I'm willing to do that. I'm willing to do anything for the Lord." So here I am, having the hardest experience of my life. Am I willing to do anything for the Lord? Yes. And I'll do it as many times as he asks me to. I love you all more than I could possibly ever tell you. Please know that I'm not just doing this for God, but so I can be with all of you forever.

Messages like these from my children made my heart soar. In the mission field, our children become more open. In trying to fulfill a calling beyond their natural capacity, they sensed their own inadequacies and they yearned for help. Leaders at every level in the mission structure can nurture them, but often this is not enough. There is a crucial audience that is perfectly positioned to sense the open windows and fill them with customized messages of revelation. That crucial audience is composed of the missionary's parents, siblings, and friends.

Missionaries have the opportunity to change lives by drawing closer to Christ and speaking by revelation. Transformed into men and women of God, they can return home to build righteous families and lead the future Church with revelatory power.

It is a grand transformation. Yet to get there, they need people who love them to find windows to their soul. They need people who will pray on their behalf for revelation and who will allow God to speak through their letters by the spirit of prophecy, the spirit of revelation, and the power and authority of God.

In this book, I invite you to do just that—write letters by the spirit of prophecy, the spirit of revelation, and the power and authority of God (see Alma 17:1–3). I invite you to teach by letters of love and revelation, as did the Apostle Paul. Because you love your missionary and you love God, you are already well positioned. I pray that this book will assist you in experiencing continuous, loving communion with God and with your missionary who is trying to learn how to effectively invite people to Jesus Christ. It is my hope that reading this book will help you to lift your missionary, unify your family, and move you closer to God.

Visit our Website

You can find lots of additional tools and resources on our website at www.lettersfromhomebook.com. We will post digital copies of the challenge letters you will read at the end of this book. In addition, we plan to post a new challenge letter each month. Please visit the site to use these tools and to share your experiences with us as you embark on your own letter-writing projects.

Chapter One

Lead by Example

The first of our children to leave on a mission was Ryan. I handled his departure in a very masculine way: at his farewell and at the airport, I remained in control of my emotions. This, of course, was ridiculous. The pain of separation was killing me. I was full of feelings and needed to express them. The next day, I missed him more than I could say; after a couple of days, I could stand it no more. I went home in the middle of the workday and went downstairs. I rummaged around until I found a particular video and watched footage of armies of missionaries at the MTC singing the song "Called to Serve."[1] I cried for half an hour.

Those were complicated tears. There was pain because he was gone, and there was joy because he was where he was supposed to be. There was concern for his safety, for his challenges, and for his learning, growth, and development.

It turns out that these intense feelings were important. As the days passed, I noticed a change in me. I was focused on my son. In fact, I was praying continually for my son and they were prayers of real intent. Having my son leave to serve a mission opened a window between God and me.

I had those feelings for each of our children that followed, and those feelings blessed my life in ways I could not have anticipated. Because of those intense feelings, I acted in ways I had not planned. Because of those feelings, I reaped the benefit of eternal intimacy. Because God and I became more intimate, my son and I came to know each other as never before. Let me explain.

Changing Myself

The first few weeks of Ryan's mission, I dutifully wrote him letters. These were the normal letters that most parents of missionaries write. They were full of the mundane news of "we miss you and here is what is happening." After a time, I began to feel those letters were inadequate. I missed Ryan intensely, and I knew he was now trying to meet the greatest challenge of his life. My letters to him, written from my comfort zone, were not what he (or I) needed.

Then it dawned on me. I was praying for Ryan to become one with Christ and to be a powerful missionary, while I was content to stay on my same old track. But if he was going to stretch to live in revelation, then I needed to stretch to live in revelation. I needed to move closer to Jesus Christ. I needed to exercise discipline and make sacrifices. I needed to change myself so Ryan could find support in changing himself. Since I had no direct day-to-day contact with him, the key was in the writing. I needed to craft letters that would make a difference.

First, my purpose in writing these letters needed to be clear. My purpose was to inspire my son to desire to move closer to Jesus Christ and in the process to build a closer relationship with me. This purpose is important. Previously, I was writing because I was a father who loved my son. I was writing to inform and entertain him. Once I clarified my purpose, my letters changed. I had a higher purpose that became a calling from God, and it was one of the most meaningful callings I have ever had. As I fulfilled this calling, I gradually came to love it. I was motivated from within. Writing turned from a duty to a labor of love.

Second, in reading his letters, I needed to be sensitive enough to read between the lines, see into his soul, and recognize his deepest needs. As I prayed for the gift of discernment, reading his letters became even more meaningful. It was as if I were reading scripture and getting revelation. And the revelation was not general: I was receiving promptings about how the Lord could minister to my son through me.

Third, I needed to get out of the traditional parent role and write letters that were brimming with authenticity and vulnerability. I needed to tell him my most important stories and invite him to see into my soul.

Finally, I needed to pray often and fast occasionally in order to write by "the spirit of prophecy, and the spirit of revelation" and the "power and authority of God" (Alma 17:3). As a parent, I was in a position to write to my son as Paul wrote to Timothy.

As this realization dawned on me, I knew I would have to give more time and energy to the letter-writing process—and improving my messages would not be enough. I needed to be, in the words of Gandhi, "the change I wanted to see in the world." I needed to move closer to Jesus Christ, so my son could move closer to Jesus Christ, so his investigators could move closer to Jesus Christ. This was neither a comfortable nor natural process for me, and it may not be for you; it was, and is, a tall order.

A Reflection on Misgivings

Normally I would respond to the above realizations as follows: "That is too much, I am not capable, and I do not have the time." Often when I am asked to do hard things in the Church, I have such a response. This time I did not. I was praying about how to help my son and impressions came. Instead of resisting them, I accepted. Why?

I would be willing to die for my sons or daughters. I decided that if that was the case, I was also willing to sacrifice and do the hard work of self-change during the short time they were on missions. I recognized that the potential was there for my child to grow more spiritually than almost any other concentrated time, but he could do that more effectively with my help. I decided to do the work of leading by example and raising the bar for myself, instead of just asking my son to change.

As I wrestled with my impressions about letter writing, I began to evolve. I read Ryan's letters more deeply, and I prayed to understand his needs. Then I pondered the scriptures and my own spiritual experiences. I prayed my way into greater sensitivity to the revelatory whisperings of the Spirit and recorded my impressions in letters focused on his concerns and struggles. I reduced the writing about day-to-day events, and my letters became more spiritually intimate.

Once I began to repent and change myself, Ryan's letters began to change. I could see that he was now reading my letters very carefully. He was finding more value in them for himself, and he was sharing them with others. In his letters home, Ryan exposed his struggles and his victories more explicitly and he wrote of intimate spiritual experiences. Our spiritual communication gained an enhanced quality it had never had before.

Many years after his mission, Ryan and I were together in a professional setting. Someone asked him a question about our relationship and he responded, "I came to know my father when I was away for two years as a missionary." Ryan then talked about our letter-writing experience, and how in reading my letters, he discovered who I was.

I was so grateful that day to hear Ryan's words. Our relationship changed during his mission because we each changed ourselves. Together we moved closer to Christ, and in the process we became more vulnerable, more trusting, and more bonded. We each helped to more fully convert the other. In the process we became intimate for eternity.

Please ponder the notion of bonding and eternal intimacy. There is an implication of equality. I was not in a superior role giving parental expertise. He wasn't my pupil or disciple. We were in a relationship of authentic, mutual exploration and learning. We were helping each other to become more committed disciples of Jesus Christ. I see this willingness to lead by example in others.

I have a friend named Kristen who has a daughter serving a mission in Russia. She wrote to me and shared her doubts and misgivings as a mother of a missionary. Like most of us, she also had a strong faith and desire to help her missionary. She understood the importance of being the change, and she acted on it. She recounted a captivating story and, with her permission, I share what she wrote to her daughter.

> I have been praying the past few weeks that the Lord would help me—not just to pray for you but to do something to help you by opening my mouth, by ACTING when I am prompted. I have been asking for a desire to be better at sharing the message you two both work so hard every week to share. AND OH HOW THE LORD WILL ANSWER PRAYERS AND REVEAL HIMSELF TO YOU IF YOU JUST ASK HIM!

Notice the level of commitment. She is not offering normal prayers for her child. She is praying that she can change for her child. This is a very authentic form of prayer, the kind that usually gets answered.

In her story, Kristen described going to a restaurant. As she was walking in, she noticed a woman struggling with a baby stroller at the door. She writes:

I darted across the parking lot to help her with the door. She turned and said, "Thank you so much!" and I thought to myself, She has an accent. She was ahead of me in the line, and I was checking her out and I knew by how she was dressed that she was European. She ordered and I thought, Oh, I think she is Russian. The guy at the register asked her, "Where are you from?" She said, "I am from Russia." I thought to myself, OH, I AM ON IT.

She pushed her baby stroller to a table, and then we both were at the drink dispenser getting drinks and our forks. I said, "Did I hear you say you are from Russia?" She said, a bit dismissively, "Yes, I'm Russian." She turned away, so I leaned around to make sure she heard me and I said, "Oh wow, because my daughter is living in Russia right now!"

She WHIPPED her head around and said, "You have a daughter in Russia?"

At this point Kristen had caught the woman's interest. She asked if she could sit with her to eat lunch and the woman agreed. The woman's name was Elena and as fate would have it, she was just in Utah for a few months to have her baby because of the medical care she required. She would be returning to Moscow in a couple of weeks, and she lived in Kristen's daughter's area. They talked for three hours and she asked Kristen all about her daughter and what she did all day. These were Kristen's final words:

Elena said, "Would you give my phone number and my email to your daughter and maybe she would like to come have a visit someday?"

"WELL YES, I WOULD LOVE, LOVE, LOVE TO DO THAT, Elena! Thank you so much!"

SO HERE IS A REFERRAL FOR YOU, MY HARD-WORK-ING, ANGEL DAUGHTER! Her name is Elena—she is a lovely woman who has three children and a great husband.

Kristen tells this story with passion and with the Spirit of testimony. She believes God answered her prayer. She knows He did. Notice what happened here. Reconsider these words:

I have been praying the past few weeks that the Lord would help me—not just to pray for you, but to do something to help you by opening my mouth, by ACTING when I am prompted. I have been asking for a desire to better share the message you two both work so hard every week to share. AND OH HOW THE LORD WILL

ANSWER PRAYERS AND REVEAL HIMSELF TO YOU IF
YOU JUST ASK HIM!

If we did a poll of all of the ward mission leaders in the Church and
asked how successful they have been at getting people to "open their
mouths" and talk with someone about the gospel, most ward mission
leaders would shake their heads in discouragement. Getting members
or even missionaries to "open their mouths" is a major challenge. Yet
here is Kristen, who sends her child to Russia and cares so much about
her child and what her child is doing that Kristen acquires new spiritual desires. She is willing to do things she may not have been willing
to otherwise do. She offers new prayers of real intent, obtains answers,
has new experiences, and passionately rejoices in them. She knows that
God lives.

Kristen's experience had an impact on her daughter in Russia. Her
daughter read the account, and, through tears, immediately wrote back
that the woman her mother met did in fact live in the area to which she
has just been transferred. The daughter's faith was not only lifted by the
miraculous referral, it was also lifted by the fact that her mother loved
her so much that she chose to move closer to Jesus Christ.

In the above case, Kristen was not a parent speaking down to and
instructing her daughter. Instead, she was communicating a message
of such love that it would never be forgotten. Kristen raised the bar in
a very significant way. Because she so loved her daughter, she had an
increased willingness to move closer to God. She was willing to learn
by faith. She was willing to pray for help, accept impressions, trust in
them, act on them, and create learning experiences that elevate her relationship with her God and her daughter.

Eternal Intimacy

I understand Kristen's story because it is my story, and it is the story
of many people who send missionaries off to serve their God. When we
send off missionaries, God tends to get our attention and He gives us
His attention. Impressions come. When we change ourselves by moving
closer to God, our repentance and progress can inspire our missionaries
to move closer to God. The impact is not just for eighteen months or
two years.

One of the blessings is eternal intimacy. Parents spend years wringing their hands and expressing their frustrations over their inability to communicate with their teenage children. I know because I have done plenty of that. When a child goes on a mission, they are far from home and they feel more vulnerable than they ever have before. In such a setting, they become open windows, and they hunger for any inspired word of advice, support, or encouragement that may help them cope. (We do the same at home as we cope with our own loss!) They may not write directly of such needs, but the needs are there.

At church, our teachers and leaders constantly urge us to engage in study and prayer. Yet even when we commit to these spiritual disciplines, we often lack motivation and focus on a daily basis. When Ryan was serving as a missionary, my motivation grew and my behavior changed. Scripture study was no longer about passively moving my eyes across words from ancient texts. My mind and heart focused first on his written words and I looked for his deep yearnings under the words. As his needs became evident, I longed to minister to him. With real intent, I searched those same ancient texts, I listened to latter-day prophets, and I scoured my daily experiences for messages I might not normally detect.

As I wrote and rewrote the messages, treasures emerged and I sent those treasures to Ryan. In the process, I was doing what I wanted him to do: I was moving closer to Christ. And because I was moving closer to Christ, I was moving closer to Ryan. I now sincerely believe that when we engage in such a process, we can expect our child to one day say as Ryan did, "I came to truly know my (parent, sibling, friend) when I was in the mission field."

The Work of Nephi

Sometimes I refer to this kind of letter writing as the Work of Nephi. One of the most powerful chapters in the Book of Mormon includes the "Psalm of Nephi" (2 Nephi 4:15–35). In that passage, Nephi records the death of his parents and the increasing belligerence of his older brothers Laman and Lemuel. In this time of trial, Nephi expresses his depression and then he turns to God and is raised to great spiritual heights. At the outset of this incredible psalm are two important verses (15–16):

> And upon these [plates] I write the things of my soul, and many of the scriptures which are engraven upon the plates of brass. For my soul delighteth in the scriptures, and my heart pondereth them, and writeth them for the learning and profit of my children.
>
> Behold, my soul delighteth in the things of the Lord; and my heart pondereth continually upon the things which I have seen and heard.

These words describe a sacred process. First, Nephi writes the things of his soul. He does not write about the latest football score, the new car, the re-painting of the house, or social happenings. He had other plates upon which he could record the more general events of his time. Instead, he writes about the things at the core of his being. He also copies many of the scriptures into his personal record (see 2 Nephi 11:8). These also seem to be associated with the things at the core of his being. He says his soul delights in scriptures and he both ponders and writes them. Why does he do this? He does it "for the learning and the profit" of his children.

The last phrase is so important. When we are doing something for the learning and profit of our children, we are often willing to do things we would not normally do. Kristen was willing to open her mouth at a restaurant. I was willing to change how I wrote to my children. Nephi was trying to elevate the learning process, not only for his children, but also for all of his posterity. He knows that he and his descendants can "liken all scriptures unto [their own lives]" (1 Nephi 19:23) for their short and long-term benefit.

In writing to our missionaries, we are not only writing to them; we are writing for our posterity hundreds of years into the future. Imagine a great-great-granddaughter trying to decide if she should stay on her mission. She then receives a letter from her mother citing a paragraph that you wrote to your missionary child almost a hundred years before. She reads it, feels bonded to you—whom she has never met—and decides to stay on her mission.

In verse 16, Nephi writes another key line: his soul "[delights] in the things of the Lord" and his heart ponders continually upon the things that he has "seen and heard." Nephi is saying that he loves the things he reads in the scriptures but he also thinks continually about his own personal experiences. He digests his day-to-day events. He ponders on the times he feels the Spirit. Then he integrates the principles in the scriptures with his own personal experiences so as to better understand himself and to better bless his children. By grounding eternal principles in daily experiences, he can testify of the power of God in ways others can understand.

Think of Kristen's letter to her daughter. In her story, the power of God is clearly communicated. While I refer to this kind of writing as the "Work of Nephi," all of the prophets have engaged in this pattern of examining the scriptures, refining themselves, and pondering and writing about the things of their soul. Often their primary audiences were their immediate descendants. From latter-day scripture, we know that Adam and Eve taught their children from the words of God and from their personal experiences (see Moses 5:10–12). Abraham taught Isaac, who taught Jacob, who taught his children-turned-tribes. The Apostle Paul wrote fervently of his conversion and his travels; he is a magnificent example of letter writing. Joseph Smith's letters in the Doctrine and Covenants, at times from the misery of a jail cell, echo this same process (see D&C 121–122).

My testimony is that this type of letter writing is one of the most powerful ways we can bless our children while they serve as missionaries. The more we understand our own relationship with the things of eternity and make our spiritual selves transparent to our children, the more we will bless our posterity for time and eternity. As I wrote letters to my children on missions, I realized I was doing something very similar to what Nephi was doing when he wrote his two books and what Paul was doing when he wrote his epistles. This opportunity is open to all.

I also came to realize something else. When we engage in the process described by Nephi, we become recipients of revealed knowledge and producers of sacred words—words that can better change lives. We thus fulfill our responsibility to become prophets in our stewardship. In contemplating the same verses from 2 Nephi 4, H. Wallace Goddard considers this to be the gift of prophecy:

> Most of us do not imagine that we are called to prophesy. Indeed, it is not our role as rank and file members of the Church to announce the Second Coming of the Lord. But it is our role, even our obligation to announce his coming to our own lives. Each week as I

sat to write to our missionary children, I was discouraged with the prospect of eking out of my notes of the week anything meaningful. But I determined to make the best of it. As I sat to write of the little blessings of the days, I discovered unnoticed miracles and patterns of miracles. By the time I finished writing of the week, I was overwhelmed with awe. "How could he have blessed us so much?" When we open our eyes, we discover that "the mountain [is] full of horses and chariots of fire round about" (2 Kings 6:17) each of us. That is the spirit of prophecy.[2]

If it is our obligation to "announce his coming to our own lives," is there a better audience for our declarations than our own missionary? If we find the work of writing the things of our soul "discouraging" but "determine to make the best of it," are we not prime candidates for revelation? I think we are. I testify with Brother Goddard that writing opened my eyes to the hand of God in my life. It also connected me to my children as never before. I pray that the same blessing of eternal intimacy might be yours.

Note: At the end of each chapter, I include a few reflection questions and a few ideas for family home evening. They are designed to help you create your own family letter project and/or think about how you would like to communicate with your missionary child. Hopefully these will be helpful to you personally and also to your family.

Reflection

How does a mission open a window of opportunity for a parent, sibling, or friend?

_____

_____

_____

What does a missionary most need from a parent, sibling, or friend?

_____

_____

_____

How much am I willing to give to have my missionary come to
know Christ?

_____

_____

_____

What benefits will flow to me and to the people around me if I
write from my soul?

_____

_____

_____

Family Home Evening

Read and ponder Matthew 7:3–5.

Read the 2007 talk, "O Remember, Remember" by President
Henry B. Eyring, in which he beautifully explains the process
and the blessings of recording our promptings.

Select three paragraphs in this chapter that will stimulate a positive
discussion in your family. Read each one as a family and share
your impressions.

Chapter Two

Family communication is a challenge. When I look at Church videos of family home evenings, I see children sitting reverently, listening to parents, and willingly contributing to the conversation. When I reflect on our family home evenings, I remember six active and often uncooperative children with thirty-second attention spans. Our experiences were usually chaotic and discouraging, and moments of real communication were rare. Letter writing turned into an important second chance.

As I mentioned in chapter one, my son Ryan made the comment that he came to really know me on his mission. I would read his letters with care and seek prayerfully to understand his needs. Then I would search my own soul and seek to connect to him as my equal. In doing this, I would often draw on my own most important and intimate experiences. I sometimes shared stories he had never heard. Other times I would share stories he had heard but now he was ready, for the first time, to ponder.

In telling those stories to help him, I was revealing me. I was sharing the victories and challenges of my youth, my mission, my adult life, and the victories and challenges I continued to confront each day. Writing to Ryan was like bearing a powerful testimony in a sacrament meeting at church.

In testimony meeting, not all testimonies are equal. Sometimes people speak from their heads and I listen. Other times, people speak from the core of their souls and they reveal the intimate realities of their present relationship with the living God. When that happens, I don't just listen; I become both cognitively and emotionally engaged. I feel the Holy Ghost bearing witness to what I am hearing. As He does this,

He also calls things to my memory. My perception and understanding are enlarged. Interestingly, if I glance around the room, others are usually intensely engaged. God is speaking through a mind of firmness and a heart of real intent (see Jacob 3:2; 2 Nephi 31:13).

My letters to Ryan were like a revelatory testimony. I wrote them from the core of my soul. His letters were written from the core of his soul. The walls were down and communication was open. Through our letters, we were connecting at a deeper level, a level we experience on sacred occasions when the Spirit is present.

If I had just recited canonized scriptures and written doctrine, my missionary would have been only partially instructed. When I likened the scriptures unto myself (1 Nephi 19:23) and told my own stories (2 Nephi 4:15), the scriptures came alive for me and for him. I call these personal accounts my "core stories."

A core story is a defining moment in one's life, large or small. When we examine our defining moments, we usually find God. To hear someone's core story is to hear the essence of that person's prophetic witness. When a person tells a core story, they feel some degree of the power of God that was originally manifest when they had the experience, and we, in turn, tend to feel that power as we listen to the authentic voice of the storyteller.

The Power of Core Stories

Core stories have power for people of God and they have power for people of the world. Core stories are an important way to communicate in our spiritual, personal, and professional lives. In my current role as a professor of management and organizations, I teach executives across the globe.

I was going to Hong Kong to teach a three-day workshop. Everyone warned me that my material was not culturally transferable. Both the content and the process were "too American." Colleagues told me the Asian participants would come expecting to take notes while I lectured and that they were unlikely to participate in discussions or learning exercises. I was very concerned—even panicked—as the plane approached Hong Kong. In the middle of the panic, I returned to my core assumptions, clarified my purpose and my motives, and had an insight.

The next day I walked into the class of about thirty business people. Instead of introducing the course or doing anything I was supposed to do,

I stood quietly for a time, looked around, and said, "I will tell you a story." They were surprised by such an introduction, but they were listening.

I told them that once I attended an academic conference in the United States where one of the speakers was from the University of Chicago. He gave a lecture on ethnomethodology, or the techniques for living with a village or group and making and recording anthropological observations. It seemed a little dry. In the middle of his lecture, he stopped. He said he wanted to tell us about his work. He studied Laotian immigrants in the city of Chicago. He went into their neighborhood and he observed what they did and he recorded their life stories. At this point, he also mentioned that his hobby outside of work was improvisational acting.

The professor also told us that when he did his work he often got pulled out of his professional role. Since he was the American the Laotians knew best, he was the one they asked to intervene on their behalf when they were in trouble. The professor said that meant he was always talking to police, landlords, and other authority figures. These experiences had something in common: he was always unsuccessful. The police always made the arrest and the landlords always threw the person out of the apartment.

One day he was asked to talk to a landlord. He went to the door and got ready to knock, but he could foresee the entire interaction, including the unsatisfactory conclusion. The Laotian man he was representing was standing next to him. They had spent many hours in interviews together and the professor knew him well. Suddenly the professor decided to take a risk. The landlord came to the door and looked at the professor and the Laotian man, and he got ready for an argument. But the professor surprised the landlord by bowing and introducing himself as the man he was representing. He then gave an account that went roughly like this:

> I come from the village where the sun rises. There I lived happily with my wife and my baby until the night the fire-spitting dragons came over the hill. We ran in terror. As we ran, my wife and baby turned to ashes. When the dragons left, we knew that the curse came upon our village because we did not do the ritual of the season when the frogs came up from the pond.

The professor then bowed and looked at the landlord. The landlord stared at him, and then he looked at the Laotian man. He turned back to the professor and said, "Okay, he can stay."

15

After telling the story in Hong Kong, I turned to the class and I said, "That is my case study. Your job is to analyze it. We will begin now." People looked at each other. There was not a sound. I stood there for two minutes as the discomfort of the participants became intense. Finally I said, "This could be a long three days." They burst into laughter.

One woman raised her hand and offered her analysis. I thanked her, made a comment, and invited more discussion. The case was very hard for them, as it is for people all over the world. People do not know how to make sense of such a strange case. It took a half hour to unpack it.

Under normal assumptions, the landlord looks at the Asian man and sees a thing. He sees the other half of a financial transaction. But after hearing that person's core story, the landlord sees a human being. Why? In hearing the man's core story, the landlord met the man. He was no longer a transaction. He was a fully human being. The relationship between the landlord and the tenant changed.

As I finished debriefing that case in Hong Kong, I said, "That which we consider most unique about ourselves is that which we have most in common with humanity. That which we often seek to hide from the world is that which holds the most potential to bond us."

I told them they paid a great deal of money to come to the program and they deserved a great deal of growth. Yet growth requires an investment other than money. If we were going to grow during the week, we needed to understand something about the process of community building. I then explained that in a few minutes I was going to send them out of the room in their new groups and ask them to tell the three core stories that most communicate the essence of who they are. I modeled the process by telling some intimate stories about myself. I told of growing up in a difficult relationship with a stepfather, another about an intimate interaction with a son, and a third about a life crisis that turned our family upside down for a time. I explained how each one helped to shape my identity.

I then gave them a few minutes to prepare, and I sent them out. An hour later they returned on fire. They were exhilarated by the fact that they had formed deep and supportive relationships. They were ready to take on anything.

I have since done this exercise all over the world. It always transforms the class. As people share who they really are, they see commonalities.

The sense of isolation evaporates and the feeling of bonding and trust increases. They begin to value authenticity. The need to be "onstage" goes down. Learning accelerates.

What I have learned over the years is that what I do tends to scare people. In other countries they express the fear by saying, "That is American." What they mean is, "We do not do that here." They are right that they don't do that where they come from, but they are wrong that it is American. Americans feel the same way they do. The fear of intimacy is universal, but the great power and potential of intimacy is also universal.

Braver, Stronger, and More Complete

I thought of an illustration of the power of core stories and the fear to tell them. It was an account shared by Virginia Pearce in her wonderful book on the love of God:

> I was speaking on a program with Emma Lou Thayne. She is a wise and gifted writer. On this particular day, she shared with a group of seminary students a tender and personal story of her daughter's battle with an eating disorder. She openly discussed her own struggle as a mother, trying to help her daughter. It was touching. Afterwards I said to Emma Lou, "I am in awe of your willingness to be so personal about your own difficulties. I don't know that I could do that."
>
> I will never forget her answer. She turned to me squarely, but with understanding. Her gentle response went something like this: "Virginia, our stories are what make the difference, and if we can tell them honestly we can hope to help each other. In the end, we have nothing to offer each other but our stories. When I open-heartedly offer my stories to you, both of us feel less alone. We both feel braver, stronger, and more complete." [3]

Telling a story about struggling with a daughter who has an eating disorder does not seem to be a story about God. But I suspect it is. In the deepest struggles of our life, we find God. When we share our stories, the Holy Ghost often helps us see the connections between the story of the other person and our own crucial experiences. Feelings of faith, hope, and charity are ignited. We bond because we feel the pure love of Christ unfold. In a business setting, like the one I described earlier, we would not think to explain the process in terms of the Holy Ghost, yet that is what I think happens. When we share our core stories, we invite each other into our lives and we find God in real time.

In our society there is a great fear of intimacy. If we model intimacy and authenticity to our missionary through our letters, that missionary will draw closer to us, and they may also learn to teach from the depths of his or her soul, bringing others to Christ.

Lost Opportunity

I once ran the above storytelling exercise with a particularly reticent group of executives. Afterwards, one of them raised his hand and we had the following exchange.

> Executive: "When I went in the room, I could only think of one story. Then as I listened to others, more and more important stories came to me. I really wanted to tell all those stories but I could only tell three."
>
> Me: "How often do you get to tell the other stories on that list?"
> Executive: "Never."
> Me: "What is the implication of that fact?"

The man lowered his head and went silent. So did the rest of the class. At that moment we were all seeing one of the tragedies of life. The fear of intimacy keeps us from becoming "braver, stronger, and more complete."

Once I shared this observation with Ed Pinegar, a noted LDS author. He was quiet for a time, and then he spoke from his heart: "Because the fear of man makes us weak, we lose the empowerment of the Holy Spirit."

Core Stories at Church

In an enlightening article, "The How and Why of Faith-Promoting Stories," Elder Bruce R. McConkie gave advice on how to give a "perfect" talk, but his counsel can be easily related to letter writing. Elder McConkie said, "Perhaps the perfect pattern in presenting faith-promoting stories is to teach what is found in the scriptures and then to put a seal of living reality upon it by telling a similar and equivalent thing that has happened in our dispensation and to our people *and—most ideally—to us as individuals.*" [4] By teaching from the scriptures, we provide a witness that eternal principles were true in the distant past. By sharing our current faith-promoting stories, we provide a witness that those same eternal principles operate in the present. We thus put the "seal of living reality" on what we teach. Our stories move God from the realm of abstract discussion to the here and now, and they have the power to connect us to each other and to God. (For more on this, see Challenge 22 in Part II of this book.)

Connecting to Each Other

While I was serving as the mission president of the Australia Adelaide Mission, our missionaries began to have great success with African immigrants. In one ward, they brought forty African immigrants to church. While this sounds wonderful, the members found it disruptive. Their seats were taken. The Primary teachers were not prepared for the influx of new children. These Africans were strangers. In short, the members actually complained about the success of the missionaries!

I asked the missionaries to turn the Africans from strangers into "fellowcitizens with the saints" in "the household of God" (Ephesians 2:19). I suggested that they talk to the bishop and find a way for the Africans to tell their core stories. The bishop agreed with the suggestion of the missionaries, and he asked these investigators to share their spiritual experiences in sacrament meeting. The missionaries helped these non-members to prepare talks in which they told of their core stories with God.

One woman, for example, told of watching from the bushes as her family was gunned down. Pregnant and with a small child as well, she walked across the continent to a refugee camp only to be turned away and be told that she would have to walk an equal distance to another camp. In the desert, and without water, she and her fellow travelers came to the end of their capacity. They fell to their knees and begged for help. Suddenly it started to rain in the desert. As she spoke of the rain, she spoke also of her unshakable faith in the living God and declared her ability to withstand the challenges of settling in a new country where people saw her as a stranger. From that moment, she was accepted as a precious sister in the ward.

As others told their stories, they were also accepted. Core stories are powerful because they carry the "seal of living reality." They declare that God is real right now and the Holy Ghost confirms this truth. They promote faith, hope, and charity. They make us all "braver, stronger, and more complete." As Brian Zahnd once said, "An enemy is someone whose story you haven't heard."

Our Daily Core Stories

Whenever I teach this principle, there are two predictable responses. First, people declare that they have no core stories. Yet if they listen to others tell their core stories like the above executive did, they often begin to recall experiences worth sharing. We all have core stories. They emerge when we ponder. If we prayerfully read the experiences of the prophets in the scriptures, for example, the Spirit often connects that experience to some memory of our own. In a testimony meeting, if we hear several powerful testimonies, often our own memories are stirred and an account comes to mind. By paying attention to the core stories of others, we can find our own core experiences.

For many it is a stumbling block to initially think about their core stories in terms of God or spirituality. On your first pass, a simple way to get thinking about your core stories is to simply list the ten best and the ten worst things that ever happened to you. Each of them is a core story. (You might also think of stories that changed you or the life path you were traveling in some way.) With these 20 stories in mind, you can then find a hundred. Looking back on your list, you can often see the hand of God in them even if it is not at first apparent. Sometimes the connection to God only comes when you share them with others because as you share them, you feel the Holy Ghost. Sometimes God is part of the story, and sometimes He is part of the telling of the story.

The second, related response is based on the assumption that a core story must be big and dramatic. One of the beauties of becoming a missionary to your missionary is that your attention begins to focus on the hand of God in your own everyday life. You begin to discover that you have core experiences every day. This happened to me. I began to search each day for the moments for which I felt most grateful and then I recorded the one of greatest impact. Here are two illustrations of simple core stories that come from my gratitude journal.

> **A Small Event:** Today I am grateful for a very small event. We have been hit by snow and extreme cold. The battery in my car died, so yesterday I went to Sears for a new battery. It was around 4:30 PM. There was a line of about twelve people in front of me. There were so many battery problems that Sears was flooded all day. The Sears people were trying to be civil but they were overwhelmed. Each transaction at the cash register was taking 15–20 minutes.

The woman who came in behind me started talking. She was just there to pick up her car that was already finished, but it was clear it would be a very long time before she would get it. She was trying hard to stay positive, as was the woman in front of me. I was also trying to stay positive.

After a long period, the woman behind me told me she was starting to feel stressed because she was supposed to pick up her little girl. As this stress built, I could feel her emotions changing. She wanted to stay positive but the situation was getting the best of her.

More time passed. Finally I was at the front of the line. The man at the desk noticed the woman behind me and realized she was just picking up her car. He asked me if I would be willing to let her go ahead of me. I said I would. She went to the counter. After a time, he gave her the key and she ran towards the door.

As she got to the door she stopped in her tracks. She turned, she looked at me, and she waved as she mouthed the words "Thank you." I waved back and she ran out the door. That little wave was an act that required her to stop in the midst of her stress-driven rush. It was a conscious choice to do something that was not required. It was a conscious choice to express gratitude.

That spontaneous act of gratitude then filled me with gratitude at a time when it was hard to feel gratitude. I am grateful for the force that operated inside that woman and invited her to choose to stop and wave. The force behind that little act is the force that gives life and light to the universe.

A Surprise in the Hallway: When I write a gratitude entry, I sometimes ask, "When in the last 24 hours did I feel the love of God wash over me?" Sometimes there is not an obvious answer, so I list the ten most meaningful moments of the previous day. I select and write about one. As I write, I discover the love of God was flowing during the episode. This morning I made such a list and my attention was drawn to a very small conversation that took place in the hallway at church.

One of the speakers in sacrament was a young mother. She began by making apologies and, based on this behavior, I assumed it would be an uninteresting talk. I glanced around and noticed that a lot of people dropped their attention level. But I disciplined myself to do a good thing. I reached down, picked up my notebook, and started looking for key phrases. Doing this forced me to pay attention.

A few minutes into her talk, I realized that she was communicating precious notions. She was giving a very good talk. As I wrote notes, I felt inspired by the Spirit. I felt gratitude for what she was saying and for how difficult it must have been for her to prepare and give this talk. That thought really filled me with gratitude and I made a mental note to catch her and thank her for her talk.

Later in the morning, I did stop her and convey sincere appreciation. She received this well, and then said something that really surprised me. She said, "Thank you for paying attention. I looked out and saw you really listening and I thought, *Bob Quinn is paying attention to me; what I am saying must matter.* And that really helped me to keep going."

This message stopped me in my tracks. I did not realize that she was paying attention to my paying attention to her. I did not realize that we were in a relationship of mutual influence. The thought humbled me. I was so grateful that paying attention was of assistance to her. I remembered the many lessons I have given and the power of listening and resolved to better remember that sitting in the audience I play a role in the quality of the talk that is given.

I am grateful for church and thousands of little lessons that unfold in hallways and classrooms. I am grateful when I find the love of God in small events of the day, events I would not examine if I did not keep a gratitude journal. Writing in my journal is a form of prayer that identifies the love of God and makes me more aware and open to it.

These are not dramatic experiences like causing the Red Sea to part or calling down fire from heaven. These are everyday experiences. By keeping a gratitude journal, I change my consciousness. Not only am I recording a moment I would normally forget, but also, in writing about it, I begin to see the hand of God where I normally would not have noticed it. This awareness of God in the details of my life changes how I feel about God, about life, and about me. By reflecting on the things that I have "seen and heard" and writing "the things of my soul" (2 Nephi 4:15–16), I find that my life is full of core stories and I can tell them with a passion that makes them valuable to others.

The interesting thing is that my missionary, on a given week, might write of some particular concern. With inspiration, the above stories could be linked to almost any concern and used to teach some principle like gratitude, kindness, patience, listening, humility, positivity, love, communication, and so on.

My core stories of the week can be linked to the deepest needs of my missionary or to the core stories that my missionary shares with me. When I do so, my missionary will read and feel the originality and the authenticity of my story. My missionary will see a connection to his or her celebration or challenge. My missionary will feel supported in the struggle to move closer to God because my missionary will know that I am working to move closer to God. A triangle of divine intimacy will intensify.

The above two accounts suggest that all of us have core stories occurring all the time. Yet it is not natural to do what Nephi did. It isn't natural to reflect on the scriptures, reflect upon the things we have seen and heard (our daily experiences), and write what we learn from God (revelatory impressions) for the profit and learning of our children. On the other hand, when we have a child serving a mission, we feel an urgent, genuine desire for that child to prosper. It is a time when our love for our missionary can drive us to overcome the natural man and draw closer to God.

Conclusion

When we are moved by the Spirit to tell our core stories, we tell them with passion and authenticity. our words become more congruent with our feelings and they take on a transformational resonance. We call this speaking or writing by the Spirit. When we do so, we attract attention to the Spirit, and the Spirit places the "seal of living reality" on our message.

By paying attention to our past and present experiences, we can often find the hand of god. When we do, we feel grateful, and gratitude ignites faith, hope, and charity. When we bathe in the pure love of Christ, we gain the heart, mind, and voice of Jesus Christ. We become qualified to minister in Christ. When we write to others, the words of Christ can flow through our fingers and onto the page. The reader can then be filled with faith, hope, and charity and find the capacity to do what they are called to do. We can help them become "braver, stronger, and more complete."

Reflection

Identify a core story (childhood, baptism, mission, etc.) and write it down. Once you've written down one, consider your top 5–10 and write those as well.

_____

_____

What is the core story of your day yesterday or so far today?

_____

_____

What would happen if you made a list of your core stories and added to it each day?

_____

_____

What would happen if next week in church, you recorded the core stories told by others and then used them to surface your own core stories?

_____

_____

Family Home Evening Ideas

Discuss key points from 2 Nephi 4.

Explain the concept of a core story.

Share an example of a core story from this chapter.

Explore the power of sharing core stories.

Explore when it is appropriate and inappropriate to share core stories.

Have each member identify the need of a missionary, identify their own core story, and write a short letter to the missionary.

Read your letters to each other.

Discuss how you can better minister to your missionary by writing the things of your souls.

Chapter Three

INVITE YOUR FAMILY

As my first three children (Shauri, Ryan, and Shawn) served missions, I wrote to them each week. The letter-writing process was a source of purification, revelation, and love. As the next two (Kristin and Travis) prepared to serve, I saw the possibility for a new arrangement.

My daughter Kristin and my son Travis were scheduled to leave on missions at about the same time. About five months before they were to leave, the whole family was coming home for Christmas. I notified them that on successive days I would like to hold two family home evenings. My plan was to invite them to join me in writing meaningful letters. I told them that we would spend an hour and a half one evening and an hour and a half the next. To say that this proposal was greeted with caution would be an understatement. How could we possibly meet for *that* long?

Once we had all gathered and the revolt was temporarily quieted, I shared my proposal. I suggested that Kristin's and Travis's letters home should be copied, scanned, and distributed via email to the rest of the family. (This process should be much easier now that missionaries actually write to you via email!) Each of us at home would be assigned a different day of the week to write back so that Kristin and Travis would receive a letter every day. That letter would be focused on their missionary concerns and it would be written for their "learning" and "profit" (2 Nephi 4:15; see also 1 Nephi 19:23). They would get love and support and hopefully some revelation from reading and pondering each letter.

After making this brief proposal, the other children expressed many concerns. Some were logistical, but most had to do with doubts about the ability to write or a lack of desire to commit to the work. During that first half hour, we explored each concern. Some we resolved and some we did not.

I asked them to spend the final hour writing a letter to Kristin and Travis even though neither of them had left on their missions yet. I challenged them to write with spiritual power. The next night, we would share our letters and then reevaluate our concerns. I assured them that the letters could be quite short, that there was no such thing as doing it wrong, and that all I wanted them to do was to write down something sacred from their personal lives that might be of value to the two missionaries as they prepared for their mission service. With some reluctance, they gave it a try.

The next evening, we read our letters. There was no discussion until everyone was finished. At the end, there was a feeling that something very important had just happened. One daughter-in-law, the one who had not served a mission and who felt intimidated the night before, wrote of her love for her brother and how she felt when he was away on his mission. It was a powerful testimony. Others also struggled. Most tended to focus on an experience they had on their own missions. Again there was much power.

An hour later, my two oldest sons approached me and said that they thought this family home evening was the most powerful experience we had ever shared.

Despite this meaningful experience, many concerns remained. Delsa, for example, encouraged everyone to participate, but she privately worried that she had nothing to say. She could not imagine producing 104 "meaningful" letters in two years. Nevertheless, because of her intense commitment to her children, she kept trying. Some time later, she gave a talk in which she said the following:

> Trying to be a supportive wife and mother, I encouraged everyone to agree to write a weekly letter of this kind. What none of them knew was that I was screaming inside. I was so filled with doubt. I do not like to write. I find it extremely painful. But now I was going to have to do this on a weekly basis. I was going to have to change myself.
>
> I decided that during the four months before they were supposed to leave that I would practice. I would pray about what to write, find scriptures about the subject, and try to think of experiences I could

share and then I would begin writing. I have never enjoyed writing or been trained in it, so after writing my first draft, I would ask Bob to read it and give me feedback. He would point out parts of the letter that that didn't flow or that did not make any sense at all. I would cry and say I couldn't do it. I knew it was important for us to stretch so that we could help our missionaries stretch, so the next day I would go back and try to make the letter more coherent.

Eventually, I felt like I was making progress so that by the time they left on their missions, I had a surprising large backlog of letters ready. In addition, I felt that I could write a letter, revise it myself, and not have to depend on Bob at all. In fact, the process helped me to learn to be a more coherent writer, which has helped me. I also came to recognize I could have my own voice and my letters didn't have to be like Bob's. The tears quit coming.

This letter project is still not easy for me. I often think, "How can I ever think of enough things to write about to fill 104 letters?" But because I was willing to change myself, I have been involved in an incredible experience with my husband and children. I have learned more about my children's feelings about things they have been through or are going through than I ever would have if we weren't writing those letters.

Even though we are miles apart, each week our family has profound spiritual experiences. In one of Ryan's recent letters, after making reference to an experience Kristin was struggling with and had written about, he wrote, "Whatever is painful is usually one of your weakness and needs the most work." That certainly rang true to me.

The letter writing is still painful at times, but it is not the weakness it was eight months ago. Getting rid of those weaknesses is what change is all about.

Note that when Delsa speaks of profound spiritual experiences, she is referring to home and not the mission field. Those experiences often came in the form of elevated conversations. When Ryan wrote the above sentence about weaknesses, Delsa could relate. At the dinner table, a mother and a son could suddenly talk about an issue of deep spiritual concern. Writing by the Spirit to our missionaries created conversations of the Spirit at the dinner table.

Delsa also saw impact in the mission field. Often the two missionaries expressed gratitude for the words of their inspired mother. The woman who feared she could not write wrote for 104 weeks now has an amazing volume of her own letters. In them, she has recorded the things of her soul. After the blood, sweat, and tears involved in writing these letters, imagine her reaction to reading messages like this from her children (this one from Travis):

> Mom, your letter helped me because my faith was lacking in my ability to teach the things I had memorized. I finished memorizing the first discussion so I began teaching it but I was nervous that I wouldn't be able to do it. After reading your letter I knew the Lord would guide me.

Honest Communication

Our goal was to create a dialogue of honesty and revelation. This meant that communication needed to be authentic both to and from the mission field, and the two missionaries would have an important role to play.

We asked Kristin and Travis to write as openly about their struggles as they did their successes. We simply wanted them to write the things of their souls so we could share their adversity as well as their joy. We knew how hard a mission could be, so there was no need to hide the difficulties of missionary life. We expected there to be struggles and failures, but we could only pray for them and write in response to their concerns if we knew their deepest concerns and feelings.

As a parent, I know that committing to not react when your child appears to be in trouble is no easy task, but I knew it was critical to the result we wanted to create. The following excerpt from one of Travis's letters while he was in the mission field helps to illustrate why it is so important that we put aside judgment and fear and not react to our child's honest letters.

> Anyhow, as I write this letter things are surfacing in my head that I need to do. I need to restructure my vision, check my spiritual bank account, and just remember and study on the Savior. The only thing that has kept me going is the idea of magnifying my calling. I think another thing that has got me down is that the success that came so easy last month just isn't there. I need to ground myself again in hard work. I also am struggling to more fully commit my companion to the notion of magnifying our calling. The problem is that we get along so well. I have a hard time praying each night about the zone because he is not used to it. Neither one of us really wants to push ourselves. Now, don't misunderstand, we still do everything, but I'm not being extraordinary. In my prayers, I'm feeling guilty because I'm not giving my all. I don't know how much sense that made, but it felt good to write it. I think it gave me some energy.

In writing an honest letter, some benefits accrued. First, Travis said that as he wrote this letter, he was getting ideas to change and grow. He was admitting and recognizing that he is human and there are changes he needs to make. At the end, he said he was gaining the energy to change. The simple process of writing in this honest way was creating real-time growth in my child.

When missionaries write honest letters and parents read deeply but do not judge or react, they change the relationship and they provide an important sounding board. The missionary and the parent both become adults in a relationship of equals. Writing opens the possibility for the missionaries and parents to learn to help themselves while redefining a pattern of authority that has existed for at least eighteen years.

Before his mission, Travis found any kind of writing to be a dreadful activity. As his mission progressed, he went from dreading his weekly letter home to cherishing the process. He often mentioned that writing was the highlight of his week because it was the time that he assessed the past week and reoriented himself for the coming week. As a mission president, I taught our missionaries to write in a similar fashion. They had the same experience as Travis, and some, because of their writing, referred to preparation day as revelation day.

As I think back on my own mission as a young man, I know that it was a period of intense growth. I allowed the Lord to teach me how to teach with power. Unlike Travis, I did not include what the Lord was teaching me in my letters home. Instead I wrote newsy letters and only occasionally included the deep things of my soul. I felt that my spiritual experiences and challenges were unique and I was used to hiding my real self from my parents. It was part of a nineteen-year pattern. I could not imagine sharing my inner soul with them, and it never occurred to me that they were my most important and interested investigators. The result is that I lost the opportunity to impact my parents and let them know who I was really becoming. I failed to bless their lives—and my own.

Here there is one final issue to note. When parents, siblings, and friends grow with a missionary, the missionary gains an additional benefit. The missionary returns home to an appreciative and supportive social network. Many missionaries find that the biggest barrier to their post-mission growth is a network of family members and friends who are uncomfortable with the missionary's spiritual development. To reduce their own discomfort, these well-meaning friends and family members put pressure on the missionary to return to the ways of the world as soon as possible. It is ironic and tragic. In contrast, people who have grown closer to Christ as the missionary grew closer to Christ will provide a very different kind of support system—one that will propel the missionary to further spiritual and professional progress.

Reflection

What benefits would be gained by a joint letter-writing project?

_____

_____

_____

Who could participate in a joint writing project? Consider siblings, extended family members, friends, neighbors, girlfriends or boyfriends, members with an interest in the missionary, members who need a meaningful experience, and non-members who would be elevated.

_____

_____

_____

Consider creating an action strategy based on whom you might involve and how you will share information and collaborate.

_____

_____

_____

Family Home Evening

Reread the account of the family home evening described in this chapter. How could you revise what was done to help your family?

Pick the story in this chapter with which you most resonate. Make a list of associated stories in your memory. Organize them into a family home evening agenda. Tell each story, ask questions, and listen. At the end, summarize what the family learned.

Chapter Four

EXPECT BLESSINGS

The family letter project had many positive results. Some were apparent right away. Some we saw years after Kristin and Travis returned from their missions.

Perhaps the most straightforward impact of the letter-writing project was instruction. Our two missionaries simply found many of the things in our letters to be helpful. In one letter, our son Ryan wrote to Travis and Kristin about being in a situation in which he was being unfairly criticized. He described how instead of reacting, he became like a "pillow" and allowed—even encouraged—the angry person to say all they had to say. He then shared a self-analysis with the person and suggested there were some ways he, Ryan, could improve his behavior. The encounter had a very positive turn and an almost miraculous outcome. A very short time after she read Ryan's letter, Kristin wrote the following account.

> I don't really know where to start so we'll go chronologically. As you know, the bishop has been very hard on the missionaries here. We had an interesting talk with the bishop this week. He started telling us all this stuff we needed to do differently with a family we are teaching. He was already upset about some other things and he wasn't being too tactful. Everything he was saying was true, but I had reasons for each thing I had done. I thought about Ryan's letter and just acted like a pillow and only responded to a very few things.
>
> It totally hurt, but I really didn't feel upset with him, more like a sad feeling. I don't really know how to explain it. In my head I had

31

resolved to do the things he was suggesting but I wanted to just get out of there. Yet trying to be diligent, I asked if I could share a scripture. I had no idea what to share and just opened up my scriptures. I don't even remember what it was—something in Nephi, but it talked about being humble.

I started to talk and tears just came pouring out. I thought about the humbling experience I had the week before and I told them—if we want to progress in anything, we have to humble ourselves. Sometimes we have to pray for experiences to be humbled and this is hard, because it means something painful is going to come, but if that is all it takes, I'm willing to do it, because all I want is to be as close to the Lord as I can be.

His poor wife didn't know what to do I was crying so hard. She just kept saying, "Oh, yes, yes, we know." The bishop didn't say anything at first and then he closed the door and we had this great talk about the difference between missionaries that come out. We talked about what we can do to get the ward more excited about missionary work. What a turnabout in the conversation; it was amazing.

Kristin's on-the-spot incorporation of what Ryan had sent her led to a small miracle. Ryan's letter impacted Kristin, and her letter back impacted all of us.

In another letter, my wife wrote about the notion of "pure testimony." She explained how when she was a young missionary, her mission president, Boyd K. Packer, taught her and others how to teach with pure testimony and she gave a number of examples. A short time later, Travis wrote:

Mom, your letter also had a tremendous effect on me. We were teaching a guy named Rich. He wasn't contentious, but I don't think he was very interested. I would give answers to his questions and he would pick the answers apart. We got on to the topic of judging people. He asked if I judge anyone. I told him that I loved all my friends to death and I would have done anything for them, even though they had different standards. I told him that anyone who really understood our church and believed in it feels the same way about judging. I then bore my testimony to him in tears. I was bold, plain, and simple. It was not drawn out. It was simply what I knew to be true and how I felt. That's when the miracle happened.

Rich had no more questions. He was quiet for the first time. I invited him to read and pray. His answer was, "I invited you guys over here today not to try to help me, but I wanted to change you. I wanted to open your eyes to other things. I wanted to see if you believed what you taught. That's why I questioned you so much. When you just told me that, I knew you weren't changing. I saw it in your eyes, that you know it's true." He would not read, but there was a dramatic change in his attitude and it was because I bore pure testimony.

A mother's letter elevated the power of her missionary. It was as if she too was in that room teaching Rich. Her lesson would be extended to every other person Travis taught on his mission. Remember, she started out believing she could not write. I believe every parent and sibling can do what she did, even if you are a new convert or not even a member. The fundamental starting point is that God wants to assist you in your righteous desire to bless your missionary. He will.

As time passed, there were many instances like the above two examples. Then Travis wrote something that we did not anticipate:

> Once again, your letters were each incredible. I am continually learn- ing from them. I have been taking notes on them so I can look back for stories and tips and know what letter to go to. I think I have such an advantage over other missionaries and even each of you when you started your missions because I get these lessons and answers every day through your letters. What it takes other missionaries a year to learn, I have gotten in two months through your letters.

The last sentence thrills me. Over the years, I have made many sug- gestions for family traditions, projects, and changes. While some ideas have been embraced, many have not. The letter project appeared to be a success. We were extending ourselves and writing letters of revelation for "the learning and the profit" (2 Nephi 4:15) of our loved ones.

By sending out multiple letters from various family members each week, we were providing a private tutorial for each of our two mis- sionaries. We were reading about their deepest concerns and prayer- fully responding as best we could. They were getting many different but heartfelt perspectives on their core issues. For instance, Kristin wrote of a time when a batch of letters all came on one day:

> On Monday night I got about ten letters from you and each one helped me realize something about my life. I'll touch on some of them. First of all, in Dad's letter when he talked about trying to

waste time on his mission and seeing that his companion secretly didn't mind, that was me on Monday. When my companion can't go out, the only way I can is with someone from the ward and that puts all the responsibility on me. That scares me. It scared me to death. The truth of the matter is that Saturday afternoon I didn't try very hard to get someone else to go out with me. In Dad's other letter he talked about rising above my environment—I need to stop feeling sorry for myself. I read Travis's letter and think, "If only I was speaking English, I would have no problem doing this." "If only I had an awesome companion that worked super hard and could teach me how to teach *charlas* (lessons) perfectly" the list goes on. Shawn's letter made me realize that I just have to get to work. Right now, I can't worry about all my ideals. I can't be the missionary I want to be eventually, right now. It takes time. Right now all I can do is work and try to learn Spanish and trust in the Lord.

We couldn't be with her physically, but we were surrounding her in love and counsel through our constant cycle of letters.

An increase in love is another wonderful impact of the letters. One of the most important messages of a family letter-writing project is not what is written in the letters but the simple fact that the family is committed to write. That commitment signals that the family loves the missionary enough to make sacrifices on his or her behalf.

Commitment

At this point, you may be thinking that you could never get your family to write regularly. I want to be clear about the fact that apart from the missionaries, there were only four people in the family who sent a weekly letter. The other four wrote on a more sporadic basis. Yet every time we were together, everyone had read all the letters and our conversations were focused on the missionaries and on Christ.

You do not need to have everyone committed to write every week. Don't feel discouraged if some people don't participate at all or even if you are the only one participating. While it is true that all of my children did not write every week, they did write regularly. Initially, four of us at home (plus the missionaries) were committed to the weekly process and sharing those letters with the entire family. Eventually, this drew the others back in to the process. Even if you are the only writer, you can make an impact. In the early years I was writing as an individual and I was often unsure if I was having an impact. You may not know what impact you are having until years later. Also, remember that you could create a letter-writing group from outside the immediate family. There may be a lonely member in your ward or an old friend from another ward or any other number of people who would jump at the opportunity.

The commitment to the process and what is written in the letters truly does matter. We were most touched by this observation from Travis:

> I want to express my love for each of you and your letters. I noticed something this week as I read letters. I love the doctrine and the lessons in each letter. I learn so much from them. One thing I really look forward to is the end of the letter when I can read "I love you Travis" or "Continue to be extraordinary" or whatever encouragement is there. When I read that part it brings me to tears. It gives me the strength to apply what I learn from the letters. My family is my strength. I love you for it. I feel so close to you as I read and write. I think it is important that I tell you that. I want so badly to be with each of you forever. I believe our family is, for the most part, what God had in mind when he created families. I pray I will be able to emulate our family in the future.

At a discouraging moment, a letter filled with loving statements is like a drink in the desert. Such letters not only result in the missionary feeling supported, they are often a source of testimony, and they provide the motivation to press on in the face of difficulties. Here is an example written by Kristin:

> You know we always talk about how you have to have Christ be your motive, but I have to be honest, I think a lot of the time you guys are my motive. It's just that you guys are something that I see, and I feel the influence of who you are in my life and I trust in your testimonies of the gospel as much as I trust in my own. I'm not saying Christ isn't a factor, but he became a factor in my life through your examples. Just so you know, Dad, I am going to stay committed and keep on acting on my courage and think of you while I do it. Thank you for everything you've taught me.

> The people at home were also elevated. If our missionaries write meaningful letters, we get to feel the spirit of their mission experiences. My mother was one of those people who benefitted. She had suffered a stroke and couldn't speak or move. Often she showed little

interest in anything. Here is a description I wrote of a simple but important moment with her:

Last Sunday we picked up Grandma and brought her home. As you might imagine she continues to slowly disintegrate. It is now very difficult to move her much. After I laid her on the couch, your mother indicated that she had read Travis's last letter to Grandma, but not the one from Kristin, and perhaps she would like to hear it. I found the letter and then knelt down and asked Grandma if she would like me to read. She nodded.

About a paragraph into the letter, Kristin wrote about how hard her mission was. Grandma got a very pained look on her face. After a page of agony, Kristin indicated that she was now going to write about the "good stuff." Grandma smiled.

The next two pages were about the wonderful families Kristin is teaching and how they are progressing. As I read, Grandma paid close attention. She kept nodding. I finished the letter and her face was glowing. She looked at me and nodded again. She had a look of deep pride on her face.

It was so striking. Despite her condition, Grandma was feeling Kristin's pain and her joy. She was being lifted by the fact that she had a family member with a divine commission and the courage to fulfill it. Kristin's attempts to bless the people in Argentina were also blessing a very fragile woman in Ann Arbor.

The courage shown by our missionaries often increases our own courage. The following account was written to Kristin and Travis from their brother Ryan.

I loved your letter this week, Travis. In fact, it caused me to repent. I shared a room in the hotel last weekend with a guy from my program at a professional meeting. I don't know why, but for some reason I felt shy and embarrassed about getting on my knees and praying in front of him at bedtime. I wanted to do it after the lights were out or while he was in the bathroom. But I thought about Travis bearing his testimony to every person in the line at the temple, and I felt ashamed for my embarrassment. I repented and said my prayers without worrying about what my colleague thought. He never asked about it, and it was silly of me to even feel that way, but thanks to Travis's inspiration, I did the right thing. So your mission and your letters influence more than just the people in Oakland.

On this same topic, our oldest daughter, Shauri, was wrestling with a number of difficult professional and social issues in her life. In one of her letters, she provided the following account:

Dad picked me up from the airport and on the way home he started to ask me questions about what and how I was feeling about my situation. At first the focus was just on the pain I was feeling and self-pity as I wondered what was wrong with me. I was just going over and over the problem. I wanted to wallow in the pain of the problem. I thought I was looking for a solution, but trying to find an answer to a problem I had no control over was only a more subtle way of staying in the pain. We discussed a few of the last letters that had been sent out by the family and some of the talk about purpose-finding inspired me.

As I thought about my situation, the realization came to me that purpose-finding and purification is not a process reserved for missionaries and maybe I should start looking to purify my life right now. In working to purify my life, I would be focusing on service and things of the Spirit rather than on my day-to-day problems. Doing this would allow the problem to resolve itself, while I turned my focus elsewhere. That turned out to be really helpful.

Thanks to the process of receiving and writing letters, our focus, our motives and our family conversations began to change.

Writing the stories of our discouragement and our joy is a very positive act. It helps us to see more clearly into ourselves. It also allows others to know our difficulties so they can pray for us and provide other forms of support. It gives them opportunities to come outside themselves and to grow in Christ.

As we "labor[ed] diligently to write, to persuade our children . . . to believe in Christ, and to be reconciled to God" (2 Nephi 25:23), we were made more alive in Christ. As this happened, we could say, "we talk of Christ, we rejoice in Christ, we preach of Christ, we prophesy of Christ" (verse 26). Our lives changed. We were blessed individually and as a family. We were elevated to a higher state of happiness.

The blessings also extended outside the family. Certain letters seemed to effectively address a common problem and we discovered later that they were passed about among the missionaries in our children's missions.

Shauri had a companion who was a convert and did not receive much support for her decision to serve a mission. She asked to be added as a recipient of our weekly letters. Decades passed. When she heard that we were working on this book, she told Shauri, "I still have most of the letters your parents sent me on my mission and have re-read some of them as I now write to my own daughter on her mission. So I know that writing like this can have a huge impact."

Some of the letters we wrote to our missionaries made their way across the planet. Years later, we were surprised to hear from a missionary or a parent who had been given one of the letters we had sent more than a decade before and the impact it had on them. Most were strangers but their comments lifted our souls.

Reflection

A dying grandmother listens to a letter from her missionary and is visibly altered. Why? What does this imply about letter writing?

_____

_____

_____

In this chapter are a number of examples of parents and siblings writing things that changed the perspective of a missionary and altered their behavior. Which example would you like to replicate?

_____

_____

_____

Why were strangers blessed by the writing project?

_____

_____

_____

Family Home Evening Ideas

Have family members read this chapter. Discuss the questions above. Ask family members to envision a letter project that would work in your family.

Chapter Five

ASK YOUR MISSIONARY TO CONVERT YOU

Kristin and Travis returned home from their missions in 2002. For reasons I could not explain at the time, I spent the next several years reviewing and refining the letters. Now think about this: my children were all home from their missions, and I was still working on the letters! I felt like I was fulfilling a calling from God but I had no idea why I was doing it.

In 2006, Delsa and I were called to preside over the Australia Adelaide Mission. The letters took on new importance. As we worked with and taught the missionaries, we drew upon the hundreds of core stories contained in the letters. When we taught from those stories, we did so with passion. As the missionaries listened, our stories resonated with their own daily challenges and they wanted to explore them further.

After a time, I began to use the letters more systematically. Each week after pondering the weekly letters from our missionaries, I determined a general need, consulted *Preach My Gospel*, selected an old letter, and rewrote it for the entire mission (a selection of these revised letters appears in Part II). These letters usually offered spiritual perspectives on solving practical, missionary problems. Many of the missionaries saved them. Sometimes a year later they would write that they used a letter to solve a pressing problem. Still later, they used them to teach their own younger siblings who were on missions.

A Two-Way Process

Missionaries are required to write a letter to their mission president every week. Often the process becomes a ritualized duty and the weekly letters serve limited functions. In the same way that I had invited my family to move to a new way of writing letters several years before, I now invited the missionaries in Adelaide to move to a new level of experience.

I first introduced the notion of change by asking the missionaries to identify their most interested investigator. They all gave me names. I told them that no one gave me the right answer. They looked shocked. I then told them,

> Your most interested investigators live back in Salt Lake or Malad or Hong Kong or Auckland. They live in your home. Each preparation day your mom or dad or someone else *runs* to the computer to read your letter. No matter how good or bad your letter is, they pore over every word. They share your letters or retell them to others.
>
> You have a prime responsibility to convert those people back home. Yes, your father may be a bishop or your mother may be a temple worker or your parent may be an angry apostate or a general authority. It does not matter. Your job is to invite them to come unto Christ.
>
> You do not do it by preaching to them. You do it by declaring your core stories, illustrating for them how God is operating in your life at this very moment. Even the apostate parent reads your letters and cares. When they read how God is nourishing someone they love, it opens a window through which the Holy Ghost can potentially work.
>
> You are in a position you have never been in before. You are now able to share the things of your soul in such a way that the lives of the people you love the most will change. You can prevent divorces, inspire courageous career decisions, and bring inactive family members back to church. These things will only happen if you learn to recognize your own core stories with God and write for the "learning and profit" of your parents.
>
> As you learn to effectively invite your family to Christ, you will also learn how to invite the people of Australia to Christ. Because you recognize, cherish, and teach from your core experiences with the living God, you will become an influential representative of God.

We spent a lot of time teaching missionaries to pay attention to even the smallest promptings. Every time they had a prompting or a spiritual experience of any kind, we encouraged them to record it. On preparation day, they could review their experiences and pick the one core story they felt most passionately about. They could then write in detail about the story. In their letter to me and in their letter home, this story could be the centerpiece. As they wrote the story, we taught them that the Spirit would open their minds to things they had not yet recognized. Preparation day would be revelation day.

Here I might insert a related note. Phil and Judy Howes recently presided over the Australia Sydney Mission. Phil is an advocate of teaching from core stories. He describes how he taught missionaries to do it.

> Each day, missionaries see several examples of the hand of the Lord in their life and labor. Simple little things, like following a prompting and a particular person was home in the middle of the day for some obscure reason, or any one of a dozen other little "miracles." I used to encourage them to write one or two words in their planner, so that at the end of the day they could remember the story. Otherwise, many of these core stories get forgotten. Then, after nightly planning, pull out a legal pad, and write a sentence or two about each of these core stories, so that they are not forgotten. By the end of the week, the missionary might have two or three or four pages of short stories. The instruction was to fold the pages, slip them into an envelope, and mail them home, with the instruction that after bragging about their missionary in High Priests, that the parent keep all these experiences secure until the missionary returns home. At the very least they have hundreds or thousands of great miraculous stories (many of which would otherwise be forgotten the same day), and by the time they return home, they have the material for their first book.

I love how Phil extended the concept. I smile when I read his words of parents taking pride in their missionary children. The observation further illustrates the open window: missionaries can make a difference at home where core stories can have a powerful, cumulative impact on readers—and on the missionary's posterity a hundred years in the future. Phil's input also raises a possibility for those of us at home. On a card or in our phone, we could record short reminders of our daily core stories and then review them and select the most powerful ones for our letter to our missionary.

Impacts

Our proposal to write to our family in a new way was one of the most immediately accepted changes in the mission. The missionaries desired to make a difference at home. Most could see how elevating the spiritual quality of their letters could make a difference, so there was rapid, widespread acceptance of the proposal. Many missionaries began to report that miracles were taking place at home. Parents, siblings, and more distant relatives and friends were changing their lives. These reports spread throughout the mission, reinforcing the message and inspiring more effort.

One sister described how the new perspective changed her daily practice. When she had any positive experience in the mission or even from a letter home, she would immediately note it in her daily planner. On preparation day, she would select the most meaningful story and begin to recount it. As she did, new impressions often came. She wrote:

> My father told me that he felt like my emails were scripture, and because the contents were so sacred, he decided to have them read during family home evening every Monday to set the tone he wanted in our home each week. My younger brother was not active at the time, and my brother told me how he would dread listening to my letter because he always felt called to repentance and towards the end of my time serving he said his heart became softer and when I came home from serving he was ready to change and I helped him. That brother of mine ended up serving his mission and is still active and faithful in the Church.

As a returned missionary, this woman continued to write letters to her siblings as they served missions. Like a caring parent, she continued to "look for miracles in [her] life, studying, praying and following the guidance of the Spirit as [she] wrote to them." She wrote weekly letters to her sister, who served in the Temple Square Mission. That sister reported that the letters of revelation were not only inspired, they were "exactly" what she needed each week. In the Temple Square Mission, she held positions of leadership. She sometimes used the letters to teach missionaries and saw great results. She claimed that because of the teachings of her older sister, she became a fully consecrated missionary.

She wrote,

> I loved the letters and felt like they were scriptures and would study
> them during my morning studies. For me they were a great spiritual
> feast and I would get so excited. . . . I am so grateful that my sister
> sent these to me EVERY WEEK.

Another missionary shares an example of his letters having impact.
He wrote letters of revelation to his sister, who was not attending church
and was experiencing some particularly difficult challenges. He was
careful to share his most Atonement-centered experiences. He wrote:

> One day she read one of my emails that talked about how the Savior
> not only took upon Himself our sins, but that He also felt every emo-
> tion we felt, that He experienced all the trials in life that we would
> go through so that He could personally help us in our times of need.
> She was a little skeptical about this. However I kept writing to her
> about the Atonement. One day she couldn't carry her heavy load by
> herself anymore and thought she would go and try to put what I had
> been sharing into practice. She applied those things that I had writ-
> ten in my email and this is what she wrote to me:
>
> "I had the most sacred and spiritual experience of my life. For
> the first time, I have gained my own personal testimony of the real-
> ity of our Savior. He is very real and I know He has a personal love
> for me."
>
> She went on to say, "Oh, by the way I thought you should know,
> because of you and your emails, I am now back at church and I am
> loving it!"
>
> Of all my converts that I had helped, my sister was the most
> important. This was one of the sweetest moments of my life.

Every time I read the words of this young man, my eyes fill with
tears. It strikes a deep chord in my heart.

There were many accounts like this. I particularly remember a large
Polynesian elder who approached me with deep feeling. He said, "My
father told me that he can see that I have become a man of God. When
I go home, he wants me to teach him the scriptures."

Our missionaries rejoiced in the fact that the letters they sent home
were changing the lives of the people they loved. They also found that
they could teach their regular investigators from the same core stories
they were sending home. When they bore witness of the things they

had seen and heard, the Holy Ghost confirmed what was said and the people listened, whether that message was spoken or written in a letter.

While there were many immediate impacts, some missionaries simply had to be patient. Some parents were in isolated villages where there was no computer. Some were illiterate and could not read the letters of their missionaries. Others, for reasons unknown to me, simply never communicated with their missionaries. Yet even in such cases, there was a benefit. The missionaries wrote core stories every week. If the 78 or 104 stories never touched parents and family, they remained to touch the missionary who wrote them and to touch the unborn generations who may yet read them.

What You Can Do

As a parent, there are several things you can do to invite your missionary to this perspective.

First, you can review, ponder, and pray about some of the above ideas. You can look for direction and form a personal vision of how you want to influence your missionary and your family.

Second, you can begin to model the process by elevating the spiritual content of your own letters. You can discern the needs of your missionary and then write the things of your soul. Your missionary will notice the difference and most will appreciate the message. In doing this, you signal that you now see your child as an adult you trust and admire. As you honor her or him with your core stories, they will consider sharing more deeply with you.

Third, without preaching, you can find ways to invite your missionary to move closer to Christ. Consider, for example, asking your missionary to write to you and teach you in the same way investigators should be taught, by revelation and divine voice.

Fourth, use scriptural examples. You can encourage your missionary to do what Nephi did by keeping a daily record of the things he or she has "seen and heard" (2 Nephi 4:16). Keep notes of each positive event, as did the sister above. Pick the most powerful event. Integrate it with scripture and *Preach My Gospel*. By so searching one's daily record, a missionary, like Nephi, can "abridge" the larger list into a smaller record—a carefully written letter that witnesses of divine contact. We (missionary and parent) can then send our inspired abridgements to our loved ones for all eternity (see 1 Nephi 6:3–6).

Again, the most influential way to invite your missionary to this kind of communication is to model it. Be what you want your missionary to be: an inspired extension of Jesus Christ.

Reflection

Why do missionaries tend to write superficial letters?

_____

_____

_____

_____

Why is it important for your child to send home meaningful letters?

_____

_____

_____

_____

How, without preaching, can you best invite your missionary to do so?

_____

_____

_____

_____

Family Home Evening

Review the key concepts from this chapter. Make a list and discuss what each family member can do to most positively influence a full-time missionary. Have each person write a letter to the missionary. Share your letters and discuss them.

Chapter Six

WRITE WITH INSPIRATION

A friend who is from another religious tradition sent me the following inspiring statement from Rev. Dr. Howard W. Thurman:

> It takes strength to affirm the high prerogative of your spirit. And you will find that if you do, a host of invisible angels will wing to your defense, and the glory of the living God will envelop your surroundings because in you He has come into His own.[5]

Prerogative means privilege, and it also means choice. The Spirit of Christ regularly invites me to a higher prerogative, privilege, or purpose. Pursuing such a purpose tests my faith, and I have a choice to make. I am often fearful, but when I do occasionally pursue the higher purpose, I begin to feel connected to something greater than myself. My faith begins to turn into hope. As I continue forward, my hope turns into charity. I feel enveloped by the glory or power of God because God has "come into His own." He is working through me and I delight in it.

This book is an invitation to affirm a high prerogative of the Spirit. It is an invitation to let God work through us in behalf of a missionary we love very much. For parents, it is a chance to teach children "to pray, and to walk uprightly before the Lord" (D&C 68:28) at a time when they are particularly ready to learn.

But there is a natural reaction to invitations to a higher prerogative. In the scriptures, we see it often. Here is one example.

> God said unto Moses, I AM THAT I AM: and he said, Thus shalt thou say unto the children of Israel, I AM hath sent me unto you. (Exodus 3:14)

47

When God called Moses to go into Egypt, he was inviting the man to a higher prerogative. The man's response was quite predictable and less than inspiring.

> And Moses said unto the Lord, O my Lord, I am not eloquent, neither heretofore, nor since thou hast spoken unto thy servant: but I am slow of speech, and of a slow tongue.

God listened to the response and then made a promise of importance.

> And the Lord said unto him, Who hath made man's mouth? or who maketh the dumb, or deaf, or the seeing, or the blind? have not I the Lord? Now therefore go, and I will be with thy mouth, and teach thee what thou shalt say. (Exodus 4:10–12)

I have a strong belief that the promise to Moses is also a promise to the readers of this book. Some parents will feel like they are just trying to get their child through a mission. You may not feel comfortable "raising the bar" by asking yourself or your missionary to do more. Others will feel like my son Travis, who said he once hated to write. Still others will feel like my wife, Delsa, who was sure she had nothing to write. Such concerns are real and overwhelming. Yet the promise holds: "Now therefore go, and I will be with thy mouth, and teach thee what thou shalt say."

Two Issues

In this chapter are some hints on how to write an inspiring letter. Hopefully they will help you choose to move forward and test the promise that the Lord made to Moses. Before we turn to the how, we will spend some time on the why. Being clear on your purpose and the purpose of a missionary is important.

Without thinking about it, most people have an unstated purpose when they write to a missionary. Some write to keep the missionary up on recent news. Some write with the intention of reducing stress by entertaining the missionary. Some write to correct. Some write to convey their love or ease the pain of separation that they feel. These are all understandable intentions. Yet I think we can elevate our effectiveness if we clarify (and possibly change) the result we want to create.

Before determining our own purpose, it might be helpful to look at what our leaders have stated is the missionary purpose.

Preach My Gospel is very clear about the purpose of a missionary. It is to invite people to Christ and the restored gospel. When they arrive in the mission field, most missionaries have not internalized this purpose. Some are deeply prepared, confident, and full of testimony. They are ready to try, but as they encounter the realities of missionary life, they can become discouraged. Others are less prepared. They are fearful and unsure of their testimonies. They are not at all ready to try. Becoming a missionary is hard work for everyone. (Challenge 1 in Part II of this book clarifies how hard the work is and helps you see the process from the point of view of the missionary.)

On page two of *Preach My Gospel*, missionaries learn that "redemption cometh in and through the Holy Messiah" (2 Nephi 2:6). They are to teach that no one "can dwell in the presence of God, save it be through the merits, and mercy, and grace of the Holy Messiah" (2 Nephi 2:8). The next paragraph makes an important prediction about the motivation of missionaries. It states that as our understanding of the Atonement grows, our desire to teach the gospel will increase, and we will feel the great "importance to make these things known unto the inhabitants of the earth" (2 Nephi 2:8).

These words are precious to me. As a mission president, my task was to ever more effectively invite every missionary to Christ. Trying to do that taught me something of great significance. When the Atonement ceases to be a concept and instead becomes an emotional reality, we become "alive in Christ" (2 Nephi 25:25). When we are more alive in Christ, something happens. We begin to naturally do an unnatural thing: we begin to "talk of Christ, we rejoice in Christ, we preach of Christ, we prophesy of Christ" (2 Nephi 25:26).

As a mission president, my every act was designed to simultaneously challenge and love the missionaries so as to ignite their desire to be alive in Christ and to internalize the purpose of their calling. I tried to help every missionary become an Atonement-centered missionary. To do this, I had to be alive in Christ. I had to teach them by revelation. I did my best, and I often watched as some insecure young man or woman suddenly found the faith to give more than they had ever before given. It was then that the great transformation would occur. From that moment, the missionary would do missionary work because they loved to do missionary work. Because of their love of Christ, missionary work became their highest prerogative and they were filled with the power and the glory of God.

Please, please consider the above words carefully. If your purpose in writing is to help your missionary internalize his or her purpose, you will become a missionary to your missionary. It is also likely that your missionary will become a missionary to you. Your love for each other will climb to new heights.

Your highest objective is not to entertain, inform, or correct. Your highest purpose is to ever more effectively invite your missionary to the Atonement of Jesus Christ. The single most important thing you can do for your missionary is to help them become more alive in Christ. A way to do this is to constantly move yourself closer to Jesus Christ. As you do, you will become increasingly sure that, like He was with Moses, God is with your mouth and is teaching you what to say. The things you say will help your missionary to become increasingly sure that God is with his or her mouth and is teaching them what to say. When you help a missionary internalize their purpose, you change all of eternity.

Nevertheless, you, like Moses, are unlikely to know how to accomplish this high prerogative when you first start. God expects us to learn by faith. In the mission field, I relentlessly told missionaries that their purpose was to ever more effectively invite people to Christ. The challenge was not only to demonstrate the faith to go out every day and try to do what they did not know how to do; it was also to demonstrate the faith to get better every day. It was to evaluate, listen to the Spirit, try something new, and then repeat the cycle. For us as letter writers, the challenge is the same. It is to let God be with us and teach us what to say and do as we pursue the purpose He has given us.

This chapter is designed to help you go to Egypt and stumble through the learning process just as Moses did. You do not need to do all the things you read here. You do not need to write according to any special formula. You do not have to live up to some imagined standard. Just consider these questions:

- Do I love my missionary?
- Do I want my missionary to be alive in Christ and internalize the missionary purpose?

- In reading the letters of my missionary, do I believe God will give me impressions from the Spirit?
- Do I have experiences that cause me to love Christ and feel the power of the Atonement?
- Am I willing to write to the needs of my missionary by recognizing, examining, and declaring my experiences with Christ?
- As I move forward in faith, do I believe God will teach me as he taught Moses?

If you answer yes to these questions, you have all you need. The content found in the rest of this chapter is simply ideas, processes, and tools that may serve as additional aids. They are not meant to be followed with exactness, only to inspire and help. I begin with an account of my own evolution as a letter writer, and then I share some guidelines that may be helpful.

Personal Evolution

As each progressive child served a mission, my letter writing evolved. For instance, I moved from a weekly to a daily practice of letter writing and included it as part of my daily scripture study. On Sunday, I would write a very rough and short draft of my thoughts. On Monday, I would rewrite what I wrote on Sunday and extend it a bit. On each following day, I would repeat the process. By Saturday, I would have a letter I could not have dreamed of writing the previous Sunday. This evolutionary process seemed to have a life of its own.

In the beginning, I was concerned about the time the letters would take to write and the level of work and effort they would require. By the time my second and third children were missionaries, my letter writing time was taking longer, but I did not resent the increasing time demand. On the contrary, I was rejoicing in it. The process of letter writing that was intended to impact my children was also impacting me. I was changing. I was in a greater relationship with my children, my God, and myself. I began to see my letter writing was a very rewarding form of study and prayer.

The process had a great influence on my life. In the Church, we are often instructed to keep journals, take notes in meetings, and otherwise record the manifestation of the Spirit in our lives. I believe that we are expected to recognize, cherish, and record the whisperings of the Holy Ghost so that we might have it as a more constant companion. If we do this, our witness of Jesus Christ will be constantly refreshed and our testimony will flourish.

Yet I often find it hard to refresh my testimony. In fact, I continually fail. I let go of faith and slip into the state of fear. I hold onto my pride and lose humility. Doing the work of genuine gospel study takes discipline and effort. Over time, I found the letter-writing process became an asset in this struggle. Writing to my missionaries became a discipline that helped me refresh my testimony of Jesus Christ and focus my efforts on more meaningful study and prayer. I tuned in more to lessons and talks and took better notes, hoping for content for these precious letters. Writing them often took me into the presence of God.

Guidelines

From my experiences described above, I derived the following guidelines. You can approach this as an exercise, if you like, by grabbing a pen and some paper. As you read, record the impressions that come to you from the Spirit.

1. Read with Love

Your missionary will send messages home. The messages may be long or short, mature or immature, clear or fuzzy, authentic or forced, sacred or secular. It does not matter. Treat each letter as if it were a love letter. Examine it deeply, trying to understand the deepest feelings and thoughts of the author.

2. Listen for New Impressions

I usually begin with prayer. After my first, normal reading, I do a second reading. During this reading you can lay the foundation for a "mind map." The purpose of mind mapping is to unfreeze the mind. You can use one as you read the letter of your missionary. I always begin my mind map with the foundation "bubbles" found in Mind Map 1.

3. Identify the Theme of Your Letter

As I read each sentence of my missionary's letter, I ask, "In writing this sentence, what is my missionary feeling?" I record the impressions that come in the top left corner connected to the "Missionary's Letter" bubble. When I finish, I review my mind map, which might have a lot or a little. I read them again and think about the impression(s) that I feel most strongly about and then I try to select the single most important

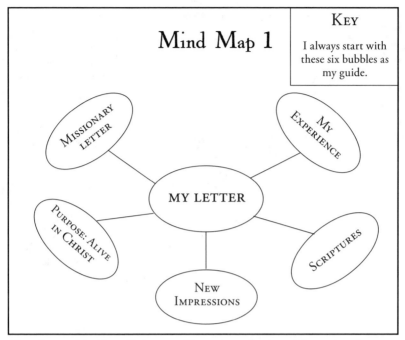

idea. I star this idea. Doing so allows me to write with passion because I feel the topic was given to me by the Spirit.

Let's imagine, for example, that it is your missionary's first week in the mission. At the Missionary Training Center, your missionary wrote very upbeat letters. This one is different. The apartment is very small and it's in a rough neighborhood. Her or his companion comes from another country and is hard to understand. The food is different. She or he is also feeling physically ill.

It will be hard to put aside your feelings of worry and the desire to pick up the phone and call the mission president—or to get on a plane and pick your child up. Try to put your own concerns aside and to listen to the feelings of your missionary.

If it were my child, I might list impressions about newness, living conditions, safety, getting along with companions, learning to eat, coping with discouragement, faith, prayer, or any number of other things. Let's suppose that when you evaluate your list, only one of these stands out. Perhaps it is coping with discouragement.

In the upper left area are some sample impressions I might have gathered from my missionary's letter. After recording them, I put a star next to discouragement because I felt so strongly that this was what I should focus on.

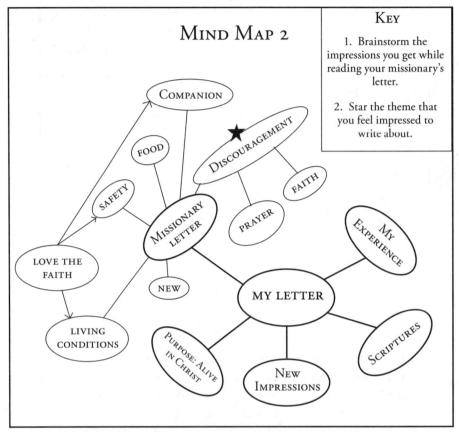

MIND MAP 2

KEY

1. Brainstorm the impressions you get while reading your missionary's letter.

2. Star the theme that you feel impressed to write about.

COMPANION

FOOD

DISCOURAGEMENT

SAFETY

FAITH

MISSIONARY LETTER

PRAYER

MY EXPERIENCE

LOVE THE FAITH

NEW

MY LETTER

LIVING CONDITIONS

PURPOSE: ALIVE IN CHRIST

NEW IMPRESSIONS

SCRIPTURES

4. Let the Ideas Flow

Once you've identified the subject you want to map (discouragement, in this case), the purpose of the map is to just let ideas come. Write quickly and don't try to be linear or organized. Record anything that comes to mind and feel free to jump around.

You might, for example, think of a time in high school when you were very discouraged. Next to the experience bubble, you might record, "Day I failed the first test." This may bring to mind another experience, such as losing a loved one. As you connect this one to the bubble, you may suddenly think of a scriptural story, such as Lehi traveling through the darkness for many hours (see 1 Nephi 8). As you write, "Lehi in the darkness," you may have a brand new idea. You could record it next to new impressions. Suddenly you may recall that the Lord helped you with your discouragement in high school. You can go back and record this next to the high school entry. You may then receive an impression about Lehi, the Tree of Life, the love of God, the Atonement, and the purpose of your letter. The idea is not to edit yourself but to just keep filling your paper as quickly as possible.

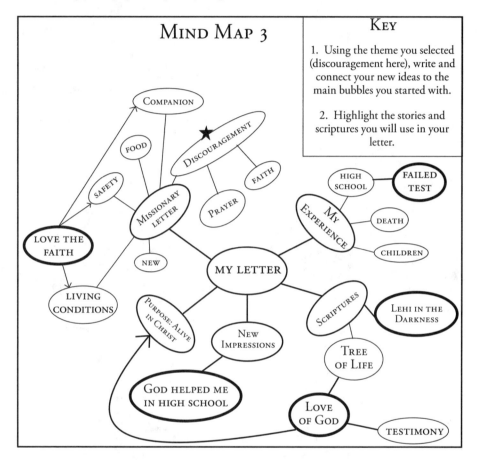

MIND MAP 3

KEY

1. Using the theme you selected (discouragement here), write and connect your new ideas to the main bubbles you started with.

2. Highlight the stories and scriptures you will use in your letter.

5. Evaluating

Once your mind map is filled, you can do another evaluation. Highlight the phrases you feel most strongly about. In this case, I highlighted failed test, Lehi in the darkness, love of God, and God helped me in high school.

From the ideas you just highlighted, you can create a list of ideas you want to use in a rough outline in the lower left corner, or on the other side of your document. You might pick any combination of ideas, but I usually ended up with a couple of personal experiences, a scripture story, one or two new impressions, and a strategy. Whatever ideas you have the most feeling for are the best seeds of a new letter.

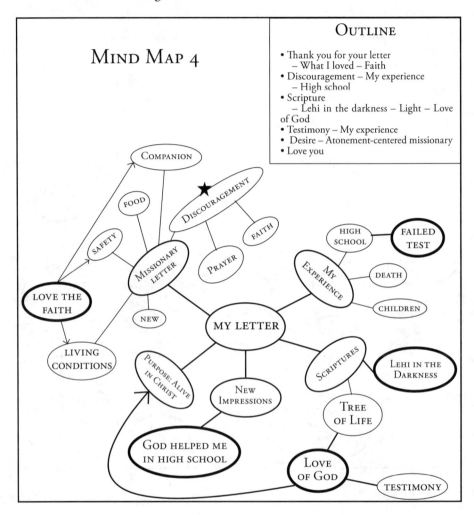

6. Initial Rough Draft

Now you can take the rough outline and formalize it. If you already created an outline on the mind map, you are ready to move right to the rough draft. If you just wrote your final list of ideas, take a couple of minutes now to create your outline. Here is an example:

Dear Missionary,

- News from home
- Last letter

- Thank you for writing
- Impressed by how hard you are working
- Loved the faith you are showing
- Discouragement
  - Working hard often brings discouragement
  - My experience in high school – failed - wanted to quit
  - Finally prayed – impact on me and on others
- Scripture
  - My experience reminds me of Lehi
  - Traveled in darkness
  - Revelation of Tree of Life
  - Love of God
- Testimony
  - When working hard, discouragement is likely
    - Atonement is real
    - God will respond
    - Pure love of Christ changes everything
- Love you
  - An example of what I feel when I read your letters

In writing the rough draft, you can refer to the last letter and tell the missionary the things that impressed you most. You can then turn the focus to discouragement. You can write of your own experiences with discouragement and recognizing the hand of God. You can then connect your experience to similar experiences in the scriptures—like the experience of Lehi. You can then bear testimony from your soul and express you love to your missionary. In expressing that love, you might want to ground it in a statement based on something he or she has written that greatly lifts your soul.

7. Inspiration and Rewriting

When I first started writing to my children, I think my letters were a bit sterile. As I evolved, I tried to find more authenticity. I found that mind mapping was helpful. I could dump out all my thoughts and then evaluate to find the things I really cared about. I could then do an outline and write a first draft with genuine feeling. The key was to have authentic feeling throughout my letter.

If you choose to do the same, you will be sending a letter that will be meaningful to your missionary. You will be blessing the life of your missionary and your family. As you get more comfortable with the process, however, you may begin to access a great weekly asset, on-going revelation that illuminates your mind and your letter. Consider the following possibility.

I suggest you write your draft on the first day of the week. Then allow God to spend the week helping you rewrite. Think of Oliver and Joseph and the process of translation. God told Oliver, "Behold, you have not understood; you have supposed that I would give it unto you, when you took no thought save it was to ask me" (D&C 9:7). Adding this step is not just to make a better letter for your missionary; it is a way to open your life to personal revelation.

On day two, your scripture study is very likely to take you to new impressions that connect to the letter you are drafting. You might weave these in. Day three might be Sunday. In sacrament meeting, a member may give a talk that relates to what you are writing. You may pick up several powerful new ideas that you can weave in.

On day four, you might have a very discouraging moment and then receive revelation that fills you with hope. This new experience might be inserted into your draft after you tell your story about high school. It may turn out to be the most powerful story in your letter. If you proceed in this fashion each day, the letter you produce at the end of the week will likely be very different from the letter you drafted on the first day.

Writing the first draft prepares you for a week of revelation. The final version will be a true love letter. The missionary will feel your love and be taught by the Spirit. You will feel the love of your Savior. Your letter writing will purify and bless you as well as your missionary. You will be led to declare, "God has been with my mouth and has taught me what I should say." Your letters from home will do more than just remind your child of home. They will lift your missionary and unify your family as you draw closer to the Lord.

24 Challenges

In this part of the book, I have included 24 of the letters I sent out to our missionaries while serving as a mission president. These were based on the letters I originally wrote to my children. Each one was rewritten for our missionaries in the Australia Adelaide Mission (2006–2009) and was organized around a common missionary challenge, such as adapting to new circumstances, facing discouragement, deciding to stay, becoming a missionary, and so on.

Because the letters were rewritten for an entire mission, they are more formal than the original letters. I begin each one by clarifying the challenge they might face. I then refer to existing guidance in *Preach My Gospel*. I then draw on missionary stories, primarily from family members, with a particular leaning towards our last two missionaries, Kristin and Travis, because that was when our letter project was up and fully running, and their letters tend to give a very full and intimate picture of missionary life.

The letters, or 24 challenges, are included in this book for several reasons. First, by reading the letters you can get in touch with the challenges faced by your missionary. The letters address real issues. As you read, you can see the experience of your missionary from the point of view of a missionary and a mission president. You are likely to have increased empathy for what the work is really like, what makes it difficult, and how a missionary can move closer to Christ and internalize his or her purpose.

Second, when your missionary writes home, he or she will be coping with many of these same challenges. If your missionary, for example, is having difficulties with a companion, you might go to the letter on becoming unified. There you may read something that brings new impressions from the Spirit. From your impressions and further study and prayer, you may be able to formulate what your missionary needs to hear.

Third, the letters are full of stories. These narratives were intended to help our missionaries to see their challenges more deeply and imagine how they could confront them more effectively. I hope these stories help you to remember some of the challenges and solutions from your own life. While you are welcome to share the stories and statements you read, your own core stories will have particular influence on your missionaries.

Fourth, and most importantly, as you read these 24 letters carefully, you will see the unique evolution of Travis and Kristin. In early letters, they were full of insecurities and fears. As they moved forward, they encountered the problems that every missionary encounters. They wrote frankly about each experience and offered an intimate view of the struggles of missionary life. By the end of their missions, they were doing things that the natural mind would not expect of two young people. They became confident disciples of Christ filled with power. How they obtained that power, and how they used it, is an inspiration.

Please also notice something else of great import. As you read Kristin and Travis's stories, notice that I am a student of my two missionaries. As I pored over their letters, they taught me as powerfully as do the prophets in the scriptures. I then took the lessons they taught me and fed them back. They could see that they were teaching me. They saw their own power.

I also carried their lessons to others. In this case, I carried Travis and Kristin's lessons to an entire mission, and to each reader of this book. When your missionary can see that he or she is teaching you at the deepest level, they will become open as never before and you can teach them by revelation. This communication will have eternal consequences. Someday your missionary will say, "I came to best know my (mother, father, sister, friend) when I was away for two years on my mission."

Again, please remember that these letters to the Adelaide Mission are more formal than the ones you are likely to write. The original letters to my children were more intimate. Typically, each one began with a heartfelt exploration of what was in the last letter from the missionary, my feelings for my missionary, and sometimes even a little news from home.

Remember to start where you are. Use the 24 challenges if they are helpful; ignore them if they are not. The objective here is not for you to follow some method. Instead, the goal is to do what Moses did: accept the call to a higher prerogative, travel in faith, and be filled with the glory and power of God. If you do, your missionary is more likely to accept his or her highest prerogative, travel in faith, and be filled with the glory and power of God. If you join with your family or others in celebrating and recording their story and your stories, you will establish a sacred record with the potential to unite your family across eternity.

Challenge 1

ADAPTING TO NEW CIRCUMSTANCES

My Dear Fellow Servants,

Entering the mission field is a challenge. It requires that we adapt to a very new set of circumstances. I will begin this letter with the story of two missionaries fearfully entering the field. I will end this letter with the story of two fearful people trying to adapt. Each one has a dream and each makes remarkable progress. In these stories are some principles necessary for adapting to new circumstances.

In chapter four of *Preach My Gospel*, we read of how to recognize and understand the Spirit. The first sentence on page 89 is from Joseph Smith:

Salvation cannot come without revelation; it is in vain for anyone to minister without it." All through *Preach My Gospel*, we are reminded that if we treasure up in our minds "the words of life, it shall be given in the very hour that portion that shall be meted unto every man" (D&C 84:85). On page 89, it goes on to explain: "This is the principle on which the government of heaven is conducted—by revelation adapted to the circumstances in which the children of the kingdom are placed.[6]

I love that last line. A mission is not meant to be easy. Often we find ourselves in circumstances that challenge us. The temptation is to give up, but the key is to keep moving forward, adapting, and receiving revelation. We read, "How long can rolling waters remain impure? What power shall stay the heavens? As well might man put forth his puny arm to stop the Missouri river in its decreed course, or to turn it up stream, as to hinder the Almighty from pouring down knowledge upon the heads of the Latter-day Saints" (D&C 121:33). As we move forward in faith, we are purified and we draw down revelation from heaven.

New missionaries may have a hard time believing they can draw down revelation from heaven, but they can. In their first letters from the mission field, Kristin and Travis wrote very similar accounts. They both described their mission presidents, they both worried about their first companions, they both were concerned about their ability to teach investigators, and they both expressed painful self-doubt as they attempted to adapt to the circumstances in which they were placed.

Kristin wrote:

In fact, right now I am scared out of my mind. My companion came and got me; her name is Hermana Gomez. She is from Uruguay. She is extremely cool; I like her a lot. But we got here and I started unpacking and I had this horrible feeling in my stomach and I spent a half hour trying not to cry, and my companion asked if I was feeling okay and I said no and started crying. I felt so stupid but she was really cool and was like, "I was a new missionary once too, I remember." You guys, I can't stop crying. It's not even that I really feel scared, it's more because I am frustrated that I can't fully communicate and what the heck am I doing? I know what I'm doing here, but . . . I don't know. I think I'm just really tired.

Travis wrote:

I'll start with my area. There are very few nice parts. Part of our area is basically the worst part of Oakland. It is weird. It is just like you see on TV and I'm living in it. We walk down streets and we are the only white people anywhere. People look at us like we're crazy. You see everything down here.

I have had a lot of struggles and a lot of high points. I'll start with the struggles. First I have found it very hard to tract. I think it is because I hate to be bothered so I hate to bother others. When people say, "I'm not interested," I just want to be like "okay thanks" instead of keeping them talking. I feel like I will offend them. I also feel like sometimes we pressure them into listening. When this happens, it seems we teach them for no reason because they aren't listening because they were pressured.

I guess I thought I would baptize every person I talked to, but I was wrong. I am trying to get over this by always telling myself how important the message is and that they need it in their lives. . . . I also get very tired in the middle of the day. I lose my focus and then I start to have thoughts of home or other things that make me lonely. It is a lot more lonely when you are around just one person all day, even though Elder Tanner is great. I'm working on that also.

The process of adjustment continued. When Kristin had been out for two weeks she wrote:

Okay, I've been here for one full week and you said you wanted me to be honest, right? Okay, if I had *ANY* idea how hard this would be I wouldn't be here right now. Sorry, I know that's a sad commentary, and it kills me to write it, but you don't know how bad I want to zap myself back and change my mind sometimes. Every morning I wake up with a *sick, sick* feeling in my stomach thinking about another day. But, it's not as bad anymore. The first five days were, but now by the time I hit lunch I'm feeling good and even really happy sometimes.

I've been thinking about why this is so hard. First of all, I've never had to deal with anything that *really* stretched me emotionally. I've felt it physically from basketball—I know I can do it and how to handle that feeling of not being able to do anything more, but then doing it because it's handed to you and you just have to. But I don't know how you do it emotionally. I've never had to feel anything like this.

Right now it's from not having any real relationship with anyone here, and from frustration of not communicating, and accepting my role as a junior companion, and finding the balance between learning from those who know what they're doing and implementing what I learned in the MTC and from you guys.

But I got a glimpse last night of more emotional pain that is yet to come. We had a first *charla* (lesson) with a couple in their 40s, Raul and Estela. They have four kids and a lot of their relatives are Mormon. So we had this AWESOME *charla* and I was *so* happy inside and they were telling us, please, please come back. It was like I had this enormous love for them and I had only known them for an hour. While we were walking home I realized how much you could grow to love someone, and if they don't accept what you've taught them, it would kill me. I can only imagine how painful it would be.

The transition was difficult. Kristin saw her writing as a sad commentary and she said, "it kills me to write it." Kristin shared an analysis of why she was discouraged. She indicated she was being stretched emotionally. Kristin had been a star basketball player and she had learned what it meant to be at her limit physically and then have to dig down deeper and give more.

Yet being a missionary is different than being a basketball player. As a new missionary, she was lonely. She couldn't communicate well. She was a junior companion and she saw a difference between what she learned in the MTC and what her senior companion was actually doing.

That week I wrote to Kristin and Travis about the need to face their fears and move forward. If they did, revelatory answers would come to them in the "very hour" of their need. Their mother wrote about exercising faith and trusting in the Lord for guidance. In response, Travis wrote:

> Dad, your letter about facing my fears really helped me. I was a little bit nervous about tracting because I hate getting yelled at so I usually laid back and let Elder Tanner talk. I decided I would start talking more.
>
> The effects have been enormous. First, I really enjoy tracting because I am now part of the conversation. I always felt like I did nothing the whole time. This also paid off when I went on team-ups with the zone leader. We were tracting and in the five hours we were together we taught three standard discussions, two introductories (teach them a little about the Church and get a return appointment), and gave away two Book of Mormons.
>
> This is amazing because it takes an hour just to give a standard. Many companionships have these numbers for a week. Mom, your letter also helped me because my faith was lacking in my ability to teach the things I had memorized. I finished memorizing the first discussion so I began teaching it but I was nervous that I wouldn't be able to do it. After reading Mom's letter I knew the Lord would guide me.

When we enter the mission field, it is natural to feel overwhelmed. I can think of a specific case. In March of 1999, a couple returned from the Florida Fort Lauderdale Mission and gave a report to our stake leaders. With great feeling, the wife, Mary, told about the defining moment in her mission.

When Mary entered the field, she was called to be the mission secretary. Like Kristin, she was overwhelmed by her new role. The technology and software were totally new to her. The number of tasks seemed impossible. Everything was urgent and she could not do it all. She became very discouraged and felt that she could never measure up. After a number of frustrating days, she was on the verge of giving up.

Instead of giving up, she turned to prayer. She pleaded for help. In her hour of discouragement and pleading, revelation came in the form of a dream. In her dream, she saw a little girl who was trying to climb a steep set of stairs. The little girl was struggling and failing. She became frustrated and was ready to quit when she noticed that there was a man at the top of the stairs. She looked up at him. He told her in a loving voice, "Just take one step at a time." She did and she began to move slowly but steadily up the stairs. Mary said that she woke up knowing that she was the little girl and the man was Jesus.

From that morning, everything changed. She took her challenges one step at a time. Every day she learned something new but she did not become discouraged by the things she could not yet do. She was climbing the stairs one step at a time and thus moved continually closer to Jesus Christ. She proceeded to have a wonderful mission. She loved what she accomplished.

Mary's story reminds me of an experience of my own. As a new missionary, I was feeling much like she was feeling. I began to plead for help. That day I was talking to a man about how overwhelmed I felt. He opened the Book of Mormon and pointed to the following verse: "And see that all these things are done in wisdom and order; *for it is not requisite that a man should run faster than he has strength.* And again, it is expedient that he should be diligent, that thereby he might win the prize; therefore, all things must be done in order" (Mosiah 4:27; emphasis added).

A short time later I was talking to another man. I told him of my frustration and how the verse makes an important difference. He shared a story of a personal revelation. As he did, it became my revelation.

He described his conversion and baptism and the immediate development of a very intense commitment to build the kingdom. He was determined to become perfect. He tried to live every commandment. He soon learned that the single biggest barrier to his own spiritual growth was the imperfection of the other saints. They were not fulfilling their callings. So he concluded that he could not fulfill his. Over time, he became increasingly angry and intolerant of the members. As he became so angry, he felt deserted by the Spirit.

The man began to fast and pray about his problem. One night he had a dream. There was a steep mountain that took the shape of a chocolate kiss. He would try to run up the mountain as fast and as far as he could. He would start out by making rapid progress, but each time he reached a certain height, he would start to slip and then he would fall to the bottom. This process was repeated over and over, until he became exhausted.

Lying at the bottom of the mountain, he heard a noise, and looked to the side. He then noticed that other people were engaged in exactly the same activity and were obtaining the same frustrating result. After a time, a man came down the mountain and gave everyone instructions. Following the instructions, everyone joined hands. Instead of running up, now one person took a step up, and then they held the next person, as they took a step up. Gradually everyone moved up the mountain. Their progress was much slower, but it was constant and no one fell to the bottom. Eventually everyone made it to the top.

The dream had great impact on the man. He realized that the man at the top of the mountain was Jesus Christ. To move closer to Christ, he had to repent of his negative feelings about others, and he had to learn to work with imperfect people. He said that after that dream, all of his anger went away. He was no longer frustrated with those saints who did not magnify their callings. He continued to magnify his own calling but stopped judging others and simply tried to serve them with love.

This last story illustrates another important principle. Because the man defined himself as being alone, he was alone. By judging others, he isolated himself and was left to live in anger and blame.

When we focus only on ourselves, we see only the mountain to be climbed. Many missionaries become committed and begin to climb alone. They may come to define the other missionaries as the problem: "The other missionaries are not committed and only pull me down."

The other missionaries may not be committed. Occasionally, some may stand in the spacious building and mock our attempts to live more righteously (1 Nephi 8:26–27). And yet, as hard as they may try, they cannot pull us down if we hold to the iron rod. When we move closer to Christ, we tend to become less tolerant of our own weaknesses while becoming much more tolerant of the weaknesses in others. We learn to recognize the Spirit, move towards Christ, hold ourselves accountable, and leave the judgment of others to the Savior of the World.

As a missionary, we are to become expert in revelation. We can learn to trust that in the hour of our need, we will receive revelation. In the face of adversity, we can learn to turn to revelation. Filled with the love of Christ, we can feel and think things we could not previously feel and think. Filled with the love of Christ, we have the power of God. We can then invest great love into small things, the everyday tasks of missionary life. We can learn to adjust to the circumstances of our lives.

I love each one of you.

Be extraordinary in Christ,

President Quinn

Challenge 2

Facing Discouragement

My Dear Fellow Servants,

In this letter, we will consider a challenge that can come to each of us each day: the feeling of discouragement. We will consider three stories of missionaries facing failure and discouragement. The first is about me when I was a brand new missionary. The second is about the father of David O. McKay when he was in the middle of his mission. The third is about an elder who was at the end of his mission. With these three stories in mind, we will review an insight from Elder Richard G. Scott and I will make you an unusual promise.

On page three of *Preach My Gospel*, we learn that the gospel is "the power of God unto salvation to every one that believeth."[7] (Romans 1:16) We are to teach the gospel by the power of the Holy Ghost. If we do, we are promised that the Holy Ghost will:

- Teach you new truths and bring the doctrines you have studied to your remembrance (see John 14:26).
- Give you words to speak in the very moment you need them (see D&C 84:85).
- Carry your message to the hearts of the people you teach (see 2 Nephi 33:1).
- Testify of the truthfulness of your message and confirm your words (see D&C 100:5–8).
- Help you discern the needs of the people you are teaching (see Alma 12:7).

These are wonderful promises. But what if we are not experiencing the fulfillment of these promises? What if we are not teaching with power and not having success? Many missionaries find themselves in this situation and they become very discouraged.

In 1965, I was a new missionary. I was surprised at how difficult it was to engage my new role. I arrived in the mission field with a testimony. I wanted to do the work. As a convert, I had some sensitivity for investigators. I was also reasonably aware of what missionary work was like. I knew it was going to be hard and I thought I was prepared to face it. I was not.

The first day we went out to knock on doors. There were several things about the process that made it difficult. First, there was the sense that we were intruding. People saw us as strangers with an agenda for them. It made them uncomfortable and they had predictable, rejecting responses.

Second, we were very ineffective. They would say things like, "I am a Catholic and I am not interested." We would say something equally routine, thank them, and leave. If we visited a member, they would eventually tell us something routine like "all our friends are members." We would nod our heads and we would leave. In either case, we had low impact.

Third, our days were generally void of promising tasks. Since we were relatively ineffective, there was little to do but knock on doors and there we experienced continued rejection. There was a sense of meaninglessness and impossibility. It was so much harder than I anticipated.

All of this was compounded by the problem of a transition in my identity. Just a few days before, I was Robert Quinn. I had people around me who knew me. They knew my strengths and weaknesses. They had expectations for me and I for them. Now I felt I was without an identity and I had little to offer. My first week in the actual mission field, I only knew two of the discussions and I was not experienced in teaching them. I did not know the area. I could not even find my way back to my apartment. Everyone was a stranger. No one knew my strengths. My invisibility made me yearn for the comforts of home; like Laman and Lemuel, I longed to return to my Jerusalem.

Given all these negative feelings, I found I had little appetite for going out to knock on doors. I got creative in generating alternatives. I would say something like, "I need sheets for my bed; we better go down to the mall and buy some." Or I would say, "Let's stop at the drug store and look at the magazines." The list went on and on. I noticed that each time I made such a suggestion, my companion would complain and then reluctantly agree. Off we would go. We were doing a natural and normal thing. We were avoiding the pain of doing the work.

The next two weeks were very dark. Each day I felt increased guilt because I was not doing what I was supposed to be doing. This intensified until I could not stand it. In darkness of agony, I prayed with real intent and I came to an important insight: I realized that doing the work was extraordinarily painful and not doing the work was extraordinarily painful. There was, however, a difference between these two forms of pain. Not doing the work resulted in pain and guilt. Doing the work was painful, but at the end of the day there was no guilt, and I felt the comfort of the Holy Ghost confirming that I was doing the right thing.

This discovery about the two kinds of discomfort led to a decision to engage the pain of missionary work. I began to work hard every day. In the weeks that followed this commitment, contrary to my expectations, the work did not result in immediate success. Yet it did result in a series of changes in me. I was very slowly learning.

The unnatural choice to move forward into the pain of missionary work proved to be profoundly important not only in my mission but for the rest of my life. Because I chose to fully embrace my purpose, I was eventually transformed. I became more alive in Christ. I became more extraordinary in Christ. The rest of my life, I was blessed because of that transformation.

We can make the decision to engage the work, but then we may go for long periods without external success. During such periods, we may make unfortunate decisions that lead us into further darkness and discouragement.

President David O. McKay tells a wonderful story about his father when his father was on a mission:

> I know that the Lord communicates with his servants. I have not doubted this as a fact since I was a boy and heard the testimony of my father regarding the revelation that came to him of the divinity of the mission of the Prophet Joseph. I feel impressed to relate that

circumstance and add his testimony to the one that I am now giving. He accepted a call to a mission about 1880. When he began preaching in his native land and bore testimony of the restoration of the gospel of Jesus Christ, he noticed that the people turned away from him. They were bitter in their hearts against anything Mormon, and the name of Joseph Smith seemed to arouse antagonism in their hearts. One day he concluded that the best way to get these people would be to preach just the simple principles, the Atonement of the Lord Jesus Christ, the first principles of the gospel, and not bear testimony of the restoration of the gospel. It first came simply, as a passing thought, but yet it influenced his future work. In a month or so he became oppressed with a gloomy, downcast feeling, and he could not enter into the spirit of his work. He did not really know what was the matter, but his mind became obstructed; his spirit became clogged; he was oppressed and hampered; and that feeling of depression continued until it weighed him down with such heaviness that he went to the Lord and said: "Unless I can get this feeling removed, I shall have to go home. I cannot continue my work with this feeling."

It continued for some time after that, when, one morning, before daylight, following a sleepless night, he decided to retire to a cave, near the ocean, where he knew he would be shut off from the world entirely, and there pour out his soul to God and ask why he was oppressed with this feeling, what he had done and what he could do to throw it off and continue his work. He started out in the dark towards the cave, and he became so eager to get to it that he started to run and was hailed by an officer who wanted to know what was the matter, as he was leaving the town. He gave some non-committal but satisfying reply and was permitted to go on. Something seemed to drive him; he had to get relief.

He entered that place and said: "Oh, Father, what can I do to have this feeling removed? I must have it lifted or I cannot continue in this work;" and he heard a voice, as distinct as the tone I am now uttering, say: "Testify that Joseph Smith is a Prophet of God."

Remembering, then, what he tacitly had decided six weeks or more before and becoming overwhelmed with the thought, the whole thing came to him in a realization that he was there for a special mission, and that he had not given that special mission the attention which it deserved. Then he cried in his heart, "Lord, it is enough," and went out from the cave. You who know him know the mission he performed.

As a boy, I sat and heard that testimony from one whom I

treasured and honored as you know I treasured no other man in the world, and that assurance was instilled in my youthful soul. The inspiration and testimony of God has come since, and today I testify to you that God lives, and that he is guiding this Church, that he has inspired those at the head, and that he will continue to inspire them and lead them through this turmoil and unrest in the world, caused by unrighteousness, wickedness and lack of faith in God."[8]

When I think of this story of discouragement and change, I think of another story that was told a few years ago in stake conference by our full-time mission president. It was about a boy whose family moved from Japan to New York City. He was called on a mission to South America. He was stunned because he was sure he would be called to Japan. He called Salt Lake to see if a mistake had been made. He was assured that the call was correct. In the MTC, he found he could not learn Spanish and again inquired of Salt Lake and again was assured of his call. For 22 months, he remained a junior companion who could not speak well. During this time he was very disillusioned and discouraged. He saw himself as a failed missionary.

One day at a train station, a Japanese man approached him and the discussion led to an appointment. At the appointment, there were 62 people! The missionary was invited to teach in Japanese, and these people were all baptized. They had been reading an old Book of Mormon they brought from Japan. When they showed the book to the young man, he opened it and found the testimony of his own father, who had recorded the testimony and then given it to the old man many years before. This missionary became the Lord's instrument for completing the work that was started by his father. He was indeed called by a prophet. There was indeed a larger plan in place that he did not understand.

In these stories there are some lessons that emerge. From the first case, we again learn that missionary work is hard and discouragement is a natural consequence. We also learn that succumbing to our discouragement leads to guilt and darkness. To engage the pain is a better decision than to try and flee from the pain. To commit to the work and move forward in faith will lead to experiences that will transform us, bring the blessings of heaven, and bless others for all eternity.

From the second case, we learn that we can make mistakes that will take us into darkness; we will feel "obstructed, clogged, hampered, and depressed." The key is to not allow these feelings to drive us down to stagnation but to channel these feelings so that they drive us to prayers of real intent. Yearning prayer will be answered.

When we, like President McKay's father, receive answers to our yearning prayers, the experience becomes a "core story." A core story is one of the defining moments in one's life. Whenever we have direct contact with God, it is a core story. For the rest of his life, this man would tell this story. What was the impact? One impact was years later when the missionary's son listened to that core story. That missionary's son then claims, "As a boy, I sat and heard that testimony from one whom I treasured and honored as you know I treasured no other man in the world, and that assurance was instilled in my youthful soul." In other words, by moving closer to Christ in the mission, that man was also choosing to convert his own unborn son. That son became a prophet and touched millions of lives. When we make our lonely decisions as missionaries to engage the work and move closer to Christ, we have no idea how much influence we are wielding forward and backward into eternity. In sacrificing to engage the pain of missionary work and serve others, we serve our own posterity in profound ways.

From the third case, we learn the profoundly important lesson that God has a plan. The Japanese elder came to the logical conclusion that he should have been called to Japan. In doing so, he demonstrated a lack of faith in the fact that his mission call was inspired. As a junior companion for 22 months, he lived a discouraged life. Only at the end did he discover that God had a plan for him. It was a miracle. He learned that his assignment was truly inspired. He ended up baptizing many. He ended up knowing that God lived. In the process, he had a core experience with God. His story will become an inspiration and a witness that God lives and that it is important to trust the prophet, mission president, district leader, or senior companion that we are inclined not to trust.

When I think of stories such as these, I think of a wonderful statement and promise made by Elder Richard G. Scott. He said,

> I have seen valiant missionaries brave icy wind, resist torrential rains, slosh through slippery, muddy streets, and conquer fear. Often they bear a powerful testimony, only to be rejected and roundly criticized. I have seen them struggle to communicate truth in a new language.

Sometimes the listener stares in puzzled silence. Then there dawns the shattering realization that the message is not understood. But I wouldn't change any of it, even if I could, because there are those golden moments of success that make all of the hardships worthwhile. Such rewards come when the Spirit touches a heart for eternal good because someone like you was there. To share truth in difficult circumstances is to treasure it more. When you push against the boundaries of experience into the twilight of the unknown, the Lord will strengthen you. The beauty of your eternal soul will begin to unfold."[9]

I love those last three sentences. I would like to translate these beautiful sentences into an unusual promise.

If you choose to fully engage the work and to stay engaged no matter what, you will begin to see and define the word *mission* in a new way. There are two very different ways to define that word. From one perspective, a mission is an assignment, duty, or job. In the army, for example, one is always told one's mission or job. By this definition, a mission is a task we do because we are expected to do it. We do our job because it is our duty.

An alternative way to define the word mission is a grand purpose or objective, an end that defines one's life. Here a mission is not work that we have to perform. Rather, it is a calling to greatness. It is the journey we take because it is the primary way to experience our own divinity. When we are more fully converted, more fully alive in Christ, we are filled with God's love. We stop working out of duty and we start working because we always want to be filled with God's love. As this happens, our desire is to invite people to Christ. "Any time we experience the blessings of the Atonement in our lives, we cannot help but have a concern for the welfare of others. . . . A great indicator of one's personal conversion is the desire to share the gospel with others."[10]

If you choose to move forward, teaching the "truth in difficult circumstances," if you "push against the boundaries of your own experience into the twilight of the unknown," you will experience discouragement. How you respond to that discouragement is crucial. If you respond by dropping to your knees in prayers of real intent, I promise you will experience a sense of "victory over self."[11] Your soul will begin to "unfold." You will have core experiences with the living God.

You will gain a greater sense of your part in God's great plan. You will rejoice in the Atonement, and your discouragement will turn to joy. Your motivation will be internal instead of external. You will work for the glory of God.

As this happens, you will begin to find success where you concluded that success was impossible. In the process, you will realize that your mission is your purpose and that it is no longer a duty but a calling to greatness for which you may be eternally grateful. As you pursue this call to greatness, you will have core experiences with the living God and you will recount your core experiences for decades to come. Your children's children will rejoice in a testimony of the living God.

I love each one of you.

Be extraordinary in Christ,

President Quinn

Challenge 3

DECIDING TO STAY

My Dear Fellow Servants,

In this letter, we will consider a challenge faced by most new missionaries: the desire to go home. We will examine three important stories and the notion of faith and courage as it applies to one of the first big challenges of missionary life.

On page 4 of *Preach My Gospel*, we learn we have authority and that we are to teach with power. We are told not to "be afraid or shy about fulfilling this commission." This invitation to courage and engagement and power may sometimes be a challenge. Some missionaries have been shy all their lives. All missionaries tend to experience fear when they first encounter the difficulties of missionary work. Some feel the need to escape and they develop the desire to go home.

Her first week in the MTC, my daughter Kristin wrote of a great struggle:

> One of the first things that struck me after being here was at a meeting when the speaker told us one of our reasons for being here is to learn to communicate with God, to pray fervently. Let me tell you, last night I remembered that and I needed it. I was so discouraged. We were in class and I was getting horribly frustrated. The more frustrated I got the more I thought about home and vice versa. I was holding back tears with everything I had. When I got back to my room I prayed fervently. I begged Heavenly Father to make Satan leave me, to help me learn, to feel connected to my district and so on. The Spirit comforted me; I fell asleep and today was a breakthrough

day. I can't believe the roller coaster the MTC is. The strength and presence of the Spirit is AMAZING.

I think many missionaries have experiences like this in the MTC. Kristin was taking on a new role; she traveled far away from her family and friends; she entered a new, demanding environment; and she tried to learn a new language. This was a very painful process. She got discouraged and was tempted to disengage from the pain. She began to think about home. At home, she had not had to face the kind of pain she has to face as a missionary. To think about home is to mentally return to a place of psychological comfort. It is natural and normal for all of us to seek this type of comfort.

Missionaries have a problem when they begin to disengage. The Spirit of Christ keeps inviting missionaries to reengage, to move forward "with an eye single to the glory of God" (D&C 4:5). It invites us to move forward into the challenge of missionary work. As Kristin wrestled with this issue, she felt agony, and the agony drove her to pray with real intent. Prayers of real intent tend to bring the comfort of the Holy Ghost.

The comfort of the Holy Ghost is different than the comfort of psychological disengagement. Often the comfort of the Holy Ghost includes a sense of "breakthrough" or progress. After the Holy Ghost comforts us, we are often able to do something we could not do before. At such moments, we have increased access to the love of God and the power of the Atonement and we become more capable, more able to do what we could not previously do. We become more alive in Christ.

In the above story, Kristin was doing hard work while in the MTC. Many of us have such experiences and hence express love for the MTC. Yet when we arrive in the mission field, we discover that the actual grind of daily work is even more challenging.

A friend of mine who was a mission president told me of a call he received from one of his new missionaries. After one week in the mission, the elder said, "I want to go home. I am not cut out to do missionary work." The mission president started laughing. This confused the missionary who thought he was addressing a most serious issue. The mission president said, "Of course you are not cut out for missionary work. None of us is cut out for missionary work. Missionary work is so hard no one wants to do it. It is only by doing what you do not want to do that you learn to do it and then you learn to love it."

What an inspired statement! Missionary work is hard. It is an invitation to row against the current. It is natural and normal to not want to do it. To overcome that inner resistance and engage in missionary work is an unnatural act. When we find a person who loves doing missionary work, we find a person who is no longer normal. We find a person who has experienced the miraculous transformation promised in the first pages of *Preach My Gospel*.

The miraculous transformation promised sometimes happens all at once as in the case of Paul or Alma. But usually, it does not occur all at once; it happens over time. A missionary experiences one difficult challenge after another and each time chooses to pursue the purpose of the Lord and engages in the unnatural act of moving forward into the pain of doing the work he or she does not want to do.

I once listened to the biography of President Gordon B. Hinckley, *Go Forward with Faith* by Sheri Dew. In the introduction, Sister Dew tells a story about her encounter with President Hinckley after he read part of the first draft. He told her there was too much Gordon Hinckley in the book and that adulation had been the ruin of many a good man and woman. He said,

> I do not want this book to portray me as something I am not." She thought about this and replied, "You want me to write a book that says you are a common, ordinary man?" He responded, "Well, I am. . . . I was just a normal little boy who played marbles, and got in fist-fights and dipped the pigtails of the girl who sat in front of me in the inkwell on my desk. I have done nothing more than try to do what has been asked of me and I have tried to do it the best I could. Now I do not want you to make more out of my life than is there.

Sheri Dew then makes the following observation:

> So herein lay the challenge. My subject did not want to be depicted as larger than life. Yet it was clear from the outset that I was dealing with a man who was anything but ordinary. This is a man that the Lord has had in his care and keeping all his life, a man whose work transcends his resume, a man who was foreordained to great responsibility, and a man who has been refined, prepared, and made ready for the position he now holds by a divine schoolmaster whose

79

curriculum has been complete and all-encompassing. Very simply, President Gordon B. Hinckley is a prophet of God.

As I reflect on the words of Sister Dew, my question is this: was President Hinckley an ordinary man? He was a man; and so, in many ways, he was no different than any other man. He was also a man of God; and so, in many ways, he was very different from other men. He learned how to serve God with real intent. Where did he learn that crucial lesson?

As a new missionary, young Elder Hinckley had the same ordinary reaction to missionary work that everyone else does: he tended to withdraw from the pain. Consider the situation. The people in his area appeared unrefined and uninterested. Anti-Mormon forces made the work particularly difficult. The physical climate made him ill.

Discouraged about the painful demands and his own ineffectiveness, he wrote home telling his father that he was wasting his time and his father's money. His father wrote back, "Dear Gordon, I have your recent letter. I have only one suggestion: forget yourself and go to work."

This story is often told and many of us know of this line—but Sister Dew adds to the story. She writes:

> Earlier that day he and his companion had studied the promise recorded in the Gospels: "For whosoever will save his life shall lose it; but whosoever shall lose his life for my sake and the gospel's, the same shall save it" (Mark 8:35). That scripture, combined with his father's counsel, seared his soul. With the letter in hand, he went into his upstairs bedroom at 15 Wadham Road and got on his knees. As he poured out his heart to the Lord, he promised that he would try to forget himself and lose himself in the Lord's service.

Many years later, Elder Hinckley indicated the significance of that series of events. Sister Dew quotes him,

> That July day in 1933 was my day of decision. A new light came into my life and a new joy into my heart. The fog of England seemed to lift, and I saw the sunlight. Everything good that has happened to me since then I can trace back to the decision I made that day in Preston."[12]

For me, that paragraph reads like scripture. I believe every missionary should have it where it can be seen regularly.

Notice that after Elder Hinckley made a promise to the Lord, something happened. He says, "A new light came into my life and a new joy came into my heart." That day, an ordinary boy chose to become an extraordinary missionary. That day, Gordon B. Hinckley became more alive in Christ, and an ordinary boy became an extraordinary man of God.

When we embrace the Atonement, when we commit to the work because we want to do it, we see with new eyes. Everything changes. Notice another important sentence from President Hinckley: "Everything good that has happened to me since then I can trace back to the decision I made that day in Preston." Until that day, Elder Hinckley was enduring the challenge of missionary work because it was his duty. After that day, he embraced the challenge of missionary work. His mission became a call to greatness. In accepting that call, Gordon B. Hinckley moved closer to Jesus Christ and would continue to do so all his life.

Although you may not realize it, you—like President Hinckley—have been "in the care and keeping of the Lord" all of your life. You were foreordained to be a missionary. You have been "refined, prepared, and made ready by a divine schoolmaster." The curriculum has been "complete and all encompassing"; every good and bad experience you have ever had has prepared you. Because of those experiences, you are unique in your potential.

You now determine if you are going to be extraordinary in your current role. You do this by controlling your mind and allocating your attention to the love of God. When Kristin was at the MTC, she descended into darkness and the desire to go home. Instead of remaining there, she "prayed fervently," "begged" for help, and help came. Your hunger to go home is natural. How you respond can be natural or unnatural. Making the choice Kristin made—the unnatural choice of turning to God with real intent—is crucial. It is crucial for now and for all eternity.

I love each one of you.

Be extraordinary in Christ,

President Quinn

Challenge 4

My Dear Fellow Servants,

In this letter, we will consider a challenge faced by everyone who serves a mission: how do we turn from who we were the day before we arrived into a powerful missionary of Jesus Christ? We will examine the doctrine of the Atonement and how it relates to acquiring the love of missionary work. We will consider three stories of transformation and the actual process by which we repent and come to love Christ.

The first chapter of *Preach My Gospel* is about purpose. A missionary's purpose is to invite people to Christ and the restored gospel. Our motivation and effectiveness in attracting people to Christ is a function of a spiritual condition, the degree to which we are alive in Christ.

On page two, we are taught that "redemption cometh in and through the Holy Messiah" (2 Nephi 2:6). We are to teach that no one "can dwell in the presence of God, save it be through the merits, and mercy, and grace of the Holy Messiah" (2 Nephi 2:8). The next paragraph makes an important prediction about the motivation of missionaries. It states that as our understanding of the Atonement grows, our desire to teach the gospel will increase, and we will feel the great "importance to make these things known unto the inhabitants of the earth" (2 Nephi 2:8).

This is a very important claim. It suggests that as missionaries we can move closer to Christ. As we do, we will come to more fully understand the Atonement and that change in us will result in new feelings, including a strong desire to invite others to Christ. In other words, a change can take place in us in which the Atonement ceases to be a concept and instead becomes an emotional reality. The scriptures refer to this as becoming more "alive in Christ" (2 Nephi 25:25). When we are more alive in Christ, we naturally begin to do an unnatural thing: "we talk of Christ, we rejoice in Christ, we preach of Christ, we prophesy of Christ" (2 Nephi 25:26).

When I was a brand new missionary, I did not understand this notion. Only after much long effort did I begin to feel fully alive in Christ. In hopes that you might learn faster, I share three stories that might help you.

When my daughter Kristin was in the MTC, she wrote home and she told about a discussion she was having with one of her teachers. Kristin was very committed to serve with her full heart, might, mind, and strength (see D&C 4:2), yet she worried that she might run out of energy or that she might make a mistake and cost someone their eternal opportunities. To her, these fears of failure were very real. When she expressed them, her teacher responded as follows:

"But don't you understand that is just what the Atonement is for? Part of our imperfection is that we can't do our very best and drop exhausted into bed every day. You just have to offer what you have done, recognize what you could do better, and work on it. That is what the Atonement is for." This statement suggests that we should not become immobilized by negative feelings such as fear, guilt, shame, or depression. To understand the Atonement is to be able to live in a state of positive feelings, like self-respect, confidence, peace, love, and joy.

Together Kristin and her teacher read D&C 46:8–9. It indicates that gifts are given to those who keep the commandments and also to "him that seeketh so to do." In other words, our positive desires and efforts count even if we do not always succeed. Then they read D&C 45:4–5 in which the Savior asks the Father to spare us not because of what we have done, but because of what He (Christ) has done. In other words, we are not saved by our righteousness but by His (see 2 Nephi 2:3). Kristin wrote the following about that exchange of ideas:

> I just realized that this talk was an answer to my prayers. I told you how I was praying to have a re-affirmation of my testimony of God, and when I first bore testimony of him in Spanish, I did. Well, now I've been praying to know Christ is my Savior and Redeemer, and when Hermana Hansen was explaining this, the Spirit testified to

me that it was true. My Savior has done so much for me. He is my advocate, He wants me to live with him, and I know He'll stand by me, accepting my sacrifices and paying for what I can't. Wow, I'm so blessed. I'm glad I realized what my answer is.

In the above situation, Kristin learned something about the Atonement and the love of God. As she does so, the Atonement stops being a concept and becomes an emotional reality. She has new feelings for Christ, and those new feelings are elevating her desire to serve. She is becoming more alive in Christ.

At about the same time as the above event, my son Travis was also in the MTC. I had just written him a letter based on the last fourteen verses of Section 121 of the Doctrine and Covenants. Travis said that when he read the letter, it "hit him hard." He read about the necessity to have the power of God and how we cut ourselves off from that power if we "cover" our sins. He said he suddenly became aware of sins he had been hiding. He writes the following:

I knew I had to repent. I could not keep my mind off my guilt. I decided to go talk to the branch president after a lot of struggle. I was so scared I could be sent home because I did not come out completely clean. By the time I went in to see him I felt like I would rather be dead than deal with this pain I felt. I went in and talked to him and I felt better for getting it off my chest. He was so awesome. He must have sensed that I wasn't over it and told me he would talk to the district president, who is over him. He told me that I had done the right thing and some people just go through their whole mission and life with the burden of not repenting because they were scared. I went home that night and still felt guilty. I prayed and received no answer. The next day I was called in by the district president. When I was walking to his office all I could think of was I was going to be sent home. My face was pale and that feeling was back. I walked in the office and we prayed. He told me the branch president had called him and told him to talk to me to make sure I was all right.

In the office, the district president counseled with Travis. In the process, he felt inspired to tell Travis he had been forgiven. Travis felt it was true. Travis wrote:

The pain was gone. I felt reborn. I walked out uplifted. I truly felt like I might be sent home because I came out unclean, but Heavenly

Father allowed me to stay. He answered my prayers. He always does. That night I promised in prayer that my life was His for the next two years. I need His help and there is nothing I want more. As President Hinckley told us, "I want to lose myself in the work." I love the Church and I love the Atonement. I've learned so much from the MTC and have grown so much. If I do any little thing wrong I feel guilty and that is how it should be. I love Jesus Christ and am thankful. The Church is true and I'm going to tell all of Oakland that Gordon B. Hinckley is a prophet of God. I know this as a fact.

This is a marvelous story. As Travis grew closer to the Spirit, he took a new view of himself. He began to see flaws where he did not before see. Behavior that he could previously rationalize, he could no longer rationalize. At one point he says, "I would rather be dead than deal with this pain I felt." After going through the process, he writes from a very different perspective. He indicates that he wants to lose himself in the work and that he loves the Church. He loves the Atonement and Jesus Christ. He is anxious to tell everyone in his mission that there is a living prophet.

This story reflects the same pattern we see in the life of Alma at the time of his conversion (see Alma 36). Through repentance, Travis became more alive in Christ, the Atonement becomes an emotional reality, and Travis had a natural desire to invite others to Christ. He, like Alma, desired to do missionary work and to invite everyone to the love of Jesus Christ (see Alma 29:1–2, 7).

In the General Conference of October 2004, Elder John H. Groberg talked about the love of Christ. He began with the claim that God's love fills the universe and that we can feel God's love. He then tells a story of being a young missionary on a remote island in the Pacific. He describes how much he disliked his living conditions. The heat was overwhelming, and the mosquitoes and the mud were constantly present. The language was most difficult and the food was unappealing. In short, like all natural men and women, he found missionary work to be very hard.

The island was struck by a devastating hurricane. Homes were destroyed and crops were wiped out. The telegraph—the only connection to the outside world—was rendered useless. The people decided to ration their food and wait for the government boat that visited every month or so. Weeks passed and no boat arrived. Elder Groberg found himself in a state of increasing hunger. Over time, he lost strength, and by the eighth week, he was hardly able to move. He simply sat under a tree, read scriptures, prayed, and pondered the things of eternity.

In the ninth week, the external condition remained the same. Yet something happened to his internal condition. A transformation occurred. Elder Groberg indicates that he felt the love of God "more deeply than ever before." The experience altered his perception, his way of seeing, feeling, and thinking. He gives the following report:

> I was pretty much skin and bones by now. I remember watching, with deep reverence, my heart beating, my lungs breathing, and thinking what a marvelous body God had created to house our equally marvelous spirit! The thought of a permanent union of these two elements, made possible through the Savior's love, atoning sacrifice, and Resurrection, was so inspiring and satisfying that any physical discomfort faded into oblivion.

Here there is a notable change. Elder Groberg's natural or normal mind had been previously occupied with his unpleasant physical situation. Then his attention shifted to prayer and scripture study. In the process, he said he was filled with the love of God. This experience altered how he felt; the Atonement became an emotional reality. When we feel the reality of the Atonement, we think and we behave differently. We repent, and repentance brings a new view of God, of self, and of the world (see Bible Dictionary, "Repentance"). We become more alive in Christ.

Based on his experienced alteration, Elder Groberg tells us that when we become enveloped in the love of God, fear evaporates. Our concern for worldly things vanishes. The importance we place on power, fame, and wealth decays dramatically.

Fear is the opposite of faith, and Satan encourages us to live a fear-based life. Of all the ordinary fears, the fear of death tends to be the greatest. Yet Elder Groberg makes an unusual claim—especially for a nineteen-year-old. Even though his mortal life was on the verge of termination, he was virtually certain that his life would continue, and it did not matter to him if it continued here or in the spirit world. His fear of death was gone. The only thing that mattered was how much love he had in his heart. Elder Groberg claims he was freed from all fear, including the fear of death.

Elder Groberg goes on to make further claims about the impact of God's love. Please read the following very carefully. It contains a message of great import for every missionary:

> God's love had changed everything. The heat, the mud, the mosquitoes, the people, the language, the food were no longer challenges. Those who tried to harm me were no longer my enemies. Everyone was my brother and my sister. Being filled with God's love is the most joyous of all things and is worth every cost. . . .
>
> When filled with God's love, we can do and see and understand things that we could not otherwise do or see or understand. Filled with His love, we can endure pain, quell fear, forgive freely, avoid contention, renew strength, and bless and help others in ways surprising to even us.[13]

This is an extraordinary claim. It reflects a deep understanding of the power of the Atonement. When we fully bathe in God's love, we are magnified and transformed. When the Atonement is an emotional reality, we hunger for the gifts of the Spirit because we hunger to effectively invite others to live in the love and power of God.

God's love is always available. The Light of Christ is given to every person, and it continually invites us to move closer to Christ. The invitation is to do something good that is often difficult. If we do it, we are filled with light and we feel the power of God.

Unfortunately, much of the time we avoid the difficult invitations that come from the conscience. So we do not move closer to Christ. When we are not moving closer to Christ, we lose the light we already have (2 Nephi 28:30). When we are losing light, we tend to live a life of fear and self-deception. In a General Conference address, Elder F. Enzio Busche tells us how we can move closer to Christ. Please read this inspired description with great care; understanding it will make you a more effective missionary forever:

> Enlightened by the Spirit of truth, we will then be able to pray for the increased ability to endure truth and not to be made angry by it (see 2 Nephi 28:28). In the depth of such a prayer, we may finally be led to that lonesome place where we suddenly see ourselves naked in all soberness. Gone are all the little lies of self-defense. We see ourselves in our vanities and false hopes for carnal security. We are shocked

to see our many deficiencies, our lack of gratitude for the smallest things. We are now at that sacred place that seemingly only a few have courage to enter, because this is that horrible place of unquenchable pain in fire and burning. This is that place where true repentance is born. This is that place where the conversion and the rebirth of the soul are happening. This is the place where the prophets were before they were called to serve. This is the place where converts find themselves before they can have the desire to be baptized for the remission of their sins. This is the place where sanctifications and rededications and renewal of covenants are happening. This is the place where suddenly the atonement of Christ is understood and embraced. This is the place where suddenly, when commitments have solemnly been established, the soul begins to "sing the song of redeeming love" and indestructible faith in Christ is born (Alma 5:26). This is the place where we suddenly see the heavens open as we feel the full impact of the love of our Heavenly Father, which fills us with indescribable joy. With this fulfillment of love in our hearts, we will never be happy anymore just by being ourselves or living our own lives. We will not be satisfied until we have surrendered our lives into the arms of the loving Christ, and until He has become the doer of all our deeds and He has become the speaker of all our words. As He has said,

"I am the vine, ye are the branches: He that abideth in me, and I in him, the same bringeth forth much fruit: for without me ye can do nothing" (John 15:5).[14]

The message of this letter is that as we come to understand the Atonement, our desires change and we gain an internalized need to teach of Christ. The above statement explains how the process works. We can go on and on covering ourselves with the robes of self-deception. We can live from our fears and from our feelings of pride, guilt, shame, and unworthiness. Yet eventually there will come a moment of desperation, a time when we finally recognize our need for the enlightenment of God. Enough light will come to motivate us to pray with real intent. At that moment, it is likely that we, like Travis in the above account, will be "led to that lonesome place where we suddenly see ourselves naked in all soberness." It is at first a "horrible place of unquenchable pain in fire and burning," but it is also a place where "repentance is born." It is a place where "conversion and rebirth" happen. It is a "place where suddenly the Atonement of Christ is understood and embraced." It then becomes a place of joy, a place where people "sing the song of redeeming love."

As our minds become enlightened, we feel the "full impact of the love of our Heavenly Father." The Atonement becomes an emotional reality. Then, "we will not be satisfied until we have surrendered our lives into the arms of the living Christ, and until He has become the doer of all our deeds and He has become the speaker of all our words." At that point we become more alive in Christ. We desire to have the gifts of the Sprit so we can do the one thing that makes us happy: invite others to Jesus Christ.

Please note that this place of transformation is a place where prophets often have to go. It is a place where converts often have to go. It is also a place where missionaries often have to go.

The process doesn't have to be so painful if we are willing to regularly ask and respond to the question, "What can I do right now to move closer to Jesus Christ?" Return to our earlier illustrations. In the first illustration, Kristin desired to do the work perfectly and she learned that the Atonement is available so that she did not need to have feelings of shame and guilt. Since her intent was right, she could turn herself over to the Lord and move on in peace and love. Learning this excited her, and the Atonement became an emotional reality. Travis dreaded repenting, did it, and then rejoiced in the Atonement. Elder Groberg learned that an intense focus on God over many weeks might lead to a personal transformation in which the Atonement became an emotional reality. He gained an astounding new view of what it means to be a missionary. If we make the effort every hour of every day to take off our robes of self-deception and move closer to Christ, if we are ever in the process of moving, we can bask in his love and we do not need to endure the pain that Alma, Travis, and others had to endure when they entered the lonely place.

With continuous movement towards Christ we become alive in Christ and we obtain the gifts of Spirit. With the gifts of the Spirit, we are better able to bring others to Christ. When we are filled with the gifts of the Spirit, we talk, rejoice, preach, and prophesy of Christ (see 2 Nephi 25:25). The testimony of Jesus Christ is the "spirit of prophecy" (Revelation 19:10).

I love each one of you.

Be extraordinary in Christ,

President Quinn

Challenge 5

Becoming Unified

My Dear Fellow Servants,

In this letter, we will consider a challenge faced by most new missionaries: the difficulty of living in unity with a companion. We will examine some stories of companionship difficulties and of transformations. In them you may come to understand the notion of unity in a new way. If you do, you will acquire the power to do things you currently cannot do.

In *Preach My Gospel*, we are told, "Your teaching will be more powerful and interesting if you and your companion work together in unity" (178). This is a fascinating promise. Why would unity produce interest and power? Please remain focused on these two words. We will return to them.

During his mission, my son, Travis, wrote:

> I've been spoiled by having great companions. When we went on team-ups this week I was with this kid who wouldn't leave his apartment. I felt helpless. We ended up sitting around for three hours and working for two. I know getting a tough companion will be hard on me. It is a shame people come out here and break rules and do nothing. It made me realize how important it is to be extraordinary. I have to always do my best. This elder taught zero discussions in the last two weeks. I would go crazy. I recommitted myself to always work hard after that day.

Over the years I have listened to many missionaries report on their missions. There are at least three common themes. First, they usually indicate that they have grown tremendously. Second, they usually speak of some important teaching and conversion episode. Third, they often describe going through at least one struggle while living with a difficult companion.

Being a missionary means living continuously with another human being. At no other time will you face such a challenge. Even when you are married, you will not be required to be with your spouse twenty-four hours a day. Living with another human being is a skill of immense importance. The world is devastated by the inability of people to live effectively with others. This fact is demonstrated by the high divorce rate in many countries. In professional life, it is illustrated by the endless conflicts in organizations that result in the loss of billions of dollars. One of the amazing truths of human experience is that people do not know how to effectively live with other people. I do not mean some people. I mean me. I mean you. I mean everyone. One of the greatest opportunities you will have on your mission is learning how to transform a problem relationship into a relationship of love. People who learn how to do this tend to live successful lives because they can do something few people can do.

When I arrived in the mission field, the zone leaders met with us and gave us an orientation. Then we had a small testimony meeting. That afternoon I met my first companion, a missionary from Hong Kong. We lived with two other missionaries, one from the United States and one from Japan.

My first impression of my companion was positive. He was very friendly. As the days went by, however, I found the relationship increasingly challenging. As we experienced the rigors of the work, points of tension emerged. I started to identify his faults. It was not an overtly contentious relationship, but it was often strained. At that time of transition into the role of missionary, I was unsure of many things, but I was certain about one thing. I was sure where the problem was in the relationship. I could list the many imperfections of my companion.

After two months, I received a new companion. He was wonderful. During the first couple of weeks, I felt the same positive feelings that I felt during the first couple of weeks with my first companion. As more time passed, however, again tensions began to arise. I was very troubled because I began to suspect the unthinkable: perhaps the problems were not just with my two companions. Perhaps I played a role in these problems.

This was a shocking thought. All my life, when there were interpersonal problems, I was always sure it was the other person who was at fault. For the first time, I was beginning to suspect that I might be the carrier of the disease I was condemning. Perhaps I was bringing out the negative behaviors in others. As I examined things more objectively, I began to see that when there were interpersonal problems, the problems were almost always a signal that I needed to change.

This discovery is a mark of maturity. Most people do not learn it until much later. I was once, for example, talking to an executive in one of my classes at the University of Michigan. He described an interesting sequence. His job situation turned sour. He quit and went to a new job in a new company. Everything was fantastic. Then he began to notice that he was surrounded by the very same problem patterns that he experienced in the former job. He said that it was then that he began to suspect the unthinkable: perhaps he was in some way the source of the problems. Until then, he had always had a rational explanation for each problem and it always concerned someone else. In fact, he had been sure he was the only one who was not contributing to the problem patterns. Now he had to rethink his position. He had to begin to explore his own role in the problems. The insight changed his life.

As a mission president, I had leaders advise me to be slow to transfer companions who are in conflict. Why would they say this? President Kimball had an answer. He once labored fruitlessly to help a young married couple that wanted a divorce. As you read what he wrote, apply his words to a pair of missionaries in conflict:

> The escapist never escapes. If two people, selfish and self centered, and without the spirit of forgiveness, escape from each other, they cannot escape from themselves. The disease is not cured by the separation or the divorce, and it will most assuredly follow along in the wake of future marriages. The cause must be removed. Being young, both of you are likely to marry again. Each of you is likely to carry into the next marriage all the weaknesses and sins and errors you have now, unless you repent and transform. And if you will change your life for a new spouse, why not for the present one?

This statement has perfect application to missionary work. If we do not repent of our current weaknesses, we will carry them into our next companionship. If we want to create a better companionship next time, *why not start right now?* President Kimball is asking us to repent. Many of us will respond, "But what can I do?" Consider three illustrations of relational change. They may give you some ideas.

When a companionship, like a marriage, becomes full of conflict, we tend to deny that we have a role in the problem. We see ourselves as the victim, even though we are actually part of the cause. The bad news is that we all do this all the time. The good news is that we have the power to change how we feel and think to turn bad relationships into good relationships. If we bridle our passions, we can be filled with love (see Alma 38:12). If we recognize our negative feelings and channel our attention to God, we will find the capacity to change what we thought could not be changed.

Once I was invited to consult with a woman who was seeking to transform a major medical system. We were in a workshop and she was addressing the people who worked for her. A discussion emerged about why it was difficult to bring change in the organization. The name of a particularly difficult senior administrator entered the conversation. While I did not know the man, I knew, from the reactions to the name, that this was a very difficult person.

The reaction of this woman was not to argue but to tell a story. She told her people a story about a time when she and her husband were driving across town. He was doing something that he always did, and she was getting angry as she always did. As she was about to express her anger, she decided to choose a new response. "I told myself, *This man is driving me crazy.* I was about to tell him a thing or two when another thought crossed my mind: *He is not driving you crazy; you are driving yourself crazy. The issue is not what he is doing; the issue is how you are reacting to him.* I thought about this and decided to change my reaction. Pretty soon he started to change his behavior."

Note that her natural reaction was anger, and if she had gone with her natural reaction, her problem would have increased. Yet she monitored her feelings, recognized that they were negative and that she had a choice to behave in an unnatural way. She could bridle her passions and thus choose a new response. She did this counter-normal work and it transformed her and the relationship. This is an example of a person practicing repentance.

The woman had more to say: "Now you all know what that doctor (the difficult senior administrator) is like. Well, two months ago he was behaving as he always does and I said to myself: *This man is making me crazy.* The phrase led me to recall the episode with my husband. I then decided that I would change how I reacted to him. That was two months ago. Let me tell you how he is treating me now." She went on to describe a series of incidents with the good doctor. People sat in disbelief. They could not imagine the man behaving as this woman was now describing. I was most impressed. Here was a woman who understood that she played a role in her own problems. She could monitor her feelings, bridle her passions, and choose a more effective response. She was a leader.

My son Shawn has a strong belief that if two companions do not love one another, they cannot teach by the Spirit. He was once given a companion who had a history of being hard to work with. One particularly annoying habit was that the missionary took an hour and a half to get ready in the morning and then it took him another half hour before he was able to leave the apartment. This meant that Shawn could not have any companion scripture time with this young man. It bothered Shawn because he wanted to have a good relationship with his companion.

Rather than criticize his companion, Shawn started getting up at 5:30. When his companion asked why, Shawn explained that he wanted to get done in the bathroom before this missionary was awake. That way there would be an extra half hour and they could have study time together. A few days later, Shawn's companion approached him and said, "If you can get up at 5:30, then I can get up at 5:30 and that will give us an hour to study." This single act was the beginning of a much larger growth process for Shawn's companion.

The interesting thing is that many other missionaries had tried to work with this elder. They encountered his morning patterns and tried to force change. This never worked. Shawn encountered those same problems and instead of reacting in the normal way, he decided to bridle his passions. He decided to change himself. In doing so, he modeled love. Instead of using force, he attracted this young man into a new life pattern. Soon Shawn's companion was radiating love and the companionship was more effective than it had ever been.

My daughter Shauri had a companion that she tried to change by using force. When it failed, Shauri learned an important lesson:

1 John 4:18 says, "There is no fear in love; but perfect love casteth out fear; because fear hath torment. He that feareth is not made perfect in love." I had a companion on my mission that was terrified of knocking on doors and terrified of talking to people that she didn't know. I tried to be patient with her and give her time, but finally I became frustrated, and when we would go to the doors I would tell her it was her turn, but she wouldn't knock, so finally I would knock on the door (and there is an unwritten rule in missionary work that whoever knocks is going to do the talking) and to her surprise when the person would answer the door I would just stare at them and then look at my companion as if we had planned all along that she would be the one to speak. She would become very flustered and one time she simply burst in to tears. This wasn't the outcome I was looking for and I felt very bad about my attempt to force her out of her fears.

I learned very clearly that we can't force people to let go of their fears, or to do anything for that matter. What is interesting is that when I realized this, I had to do all of the talking for a while, but there came a point when we were out teaching and all of a sudden she just started talking. I didn't understand why at the time but I think I do now. "There is no fear in love. Perfect love casteth out fear." She knew that I loved her because I accepted her limitations and showed her love anyway. She had started to really love the people that we were teaching and the work. Love cast out her fear.

The perfect love that Shauri is talking about is charity. When we are full of charity, we have no negative feelings. We feel and think as God feels and thinks. This means we have repented. We take a new view of God, of self, and of the world (see Bible Dictionary, "Repentance"). If we are in a problem relationship, the way to change it is to refresh ourselves through repentance. If we move closer to Jesus Christ, we will see in a new way, we will engage in new patterns, and the relationship will be more likely to turn positive. Effective missionaries do counter-normal work: they engage in self-change. Because they insist on being full of love, they live in relationships of love. They live in unity and, because they do, they are more interesting and more powerful.

I love each one of you.

Be extraordinary in Christ,

President Quinn

Challenge 6

BECOMING POWERFUL

My Dear Fellow Servants,

There is a tendency for new missionaries to undervalue themselves. There is a tendency for senior companions and other missionaries to undervalue new missionaries. This is a mistake. It is possible for every missionary to bring the transformational power of the Holy Ghost into a relationship in such a way that it results in conversion. In this letter, I share a story that every missionary should read. It is from Travis, and it demonstrates that the impossible is possible for new missionaries.

Chapter 11 of *Preach My Gospel* is about keeping commitments. On page 198, there is a section that informs us that we should bear testimony frequently. The section tells us that a testimony is spiritual witness given by the Holy Ghost. It is a simple and direct declaration of belief. It then says, "Bearing your testimony often is one of the most powerful ways of inviting the Spirit and helping others feel the Spirit."[15]

In my letters I have shared stories about the missionary experiences of my children. The stories have included expressions of frustration about their inadequacies, particularly as new missionaries. Yet in the early weeks of their missions, they often discovered that they were actually having impact.

In reflecting on this notion, Kristin shared a story from her teacher in the MTC. Her teacher was worried about being a new junior companion and not being able to contribute. Then a man who was baptized told Kristin's teacher that although she never said much during the discussions, she nevertheless taught him. Despite her inability to speak the language, she still communicated. Kristin found this story inspiring. Later, as she entered the mission with the same feelings of limitation, she described having a similar experience. Even if we only communicate from our hearts, we can help to change people.

When Travis was out for about two and a half months, he told a story that is one of the most important missionary stories I have ever heard. It is very much about exercising faith and making divine contact with investigators and members:

> I want to share a story about bearing testimony and the power of doing so. I was working at the Temple Pageant. My job was to go through the line and talk to as many people as possible. We were to try to get them to give referrals. I did it the last two nights. Two things made these good nights. There were a lot of people in line and there were enough missionaries there to allow us to actually talk to people for a while. The first night was good but it was nothing special.

I have attended pageants and watched missionaries such as Travis visit with people in line. The comfortable thing for them to do is to greet a person, start a nice conversation, and try to gently move the conversation to the gospel. If the conversation does not go there, they move on to the next person. Because it is comfortable, it is the normal or ordinary thing to do. It is what most missionaries do most of the time. Travis continued his story.

> The second night, I decided I would bear my testimony to every person I talked to, whether they were members or non-members. I started off by talking to a non-member. A sister grabbed me to talk to this girl who had questions. She was kind of against the Church because her parents didn't like it but she came to support a friend. As I talked to her I bore my testimony many times and it didn't seem to go anywhere. I felt the Spirit strong but she acted the same. This was hard for me because I had never really shared my testimony with someone, felt the Spirit, and not had them feel it.

Travis made the bold commitment to bear testimony to every person. He tried it with the very first one. While he feels the Spirit of his testimony, she shows no response. He is surprised at this. In this situation we might expect Travis to become discouraged. We would expect him to let go of the commitment to bear testimony to every person. Travis described what actually happened.

I decided not to let this get to me and I began going down the line talking and bearing testimony. As I did this, I began to feel the Spirit stronger and stronger. At first I wasn't getting the reaction from people I was hoping for. They would take a referral card and say thanks. But I felt the Spirit more and more. I felt as if I was being purified by bearing my testimony.

Travis made the important decision to not react to his negative emotions but to return himself to his purpose. He chose to keep his commitment. While he felt the Spirit even stronger, he still failed to get anything other than a normal reaction. People just took the cards. Yet as Travis continued to pursue his purpose in the face of this disappointment, he stated, "I was being purified by bearing my testimony." This is an interesting claim. What does it mean to be "purified" by the bearing of testimony? Travis continued:

I had no more fear. I approached everyone, even those who were in a hurry. They would stop and listen. Bearing bold testimony to people I didn't know started to seem natural. I didn't know what I was saying anymore. The words were coming from somewhere else. In fact, I don't remember many conversations; I just remember the feeling and the result. I felt as if I was in another sphere. I was filled with the Spirit and completely confident.

Travis continued forward, even when it was uncomfortable. Suddenly he is transformed. He no longer has fear. He enters an extraordinary state. People begin to respond, not in an ordinary, but an extraordinary way. The words begin to come from heaven. He is given the words "in the very hour" (see D&C 84:85; 100:6; 124:97). Travis became the mouthpiece of God. He moved forward with complete confidence.

This event was sacred to me. It was the first time I exercised faith and acted upon it. As a result I saw a miracle. Later in the week, I was studying in D&C 84:61, which says, "For I will forgive you of your sins with this commandment—that you remain steadfast in your minds in solemnity and the spirit of prayer, in bearing testimony to all the world of those things which are communicated unto you." This is what literally happened to me. As I bore testimony, I was purified. My sins were pushed out and the Spirit filled me. The Lord then began to speak through me. As a result, people felt the Spirit and were interested.

Please reread the above scripture. Then examine the scripture in the light of this story. Note the claim of purification, of being filled with the Spirit, of having the Lord speak through him. Travis then makes a claim about the people. With that claim in mind, consider the following: "Soon I began to notice a difference. Every person I talked to seemed to feel the same Spirit I did and would ask for a couple referral cards. They were excited to give names. Non-members were filling their names out on the cards. They felt something."

Here he made a claim that is truly out of the ordinary. Members and non-members suddenly filled out the cards. They did this because they could feel something that was extraordinary. Travis told us what he thinks happened:

> As I bore my testimony I felt like Heavenly Father purified me to the point where people began to see a little of Him in me. I don't say this conceitedly because I know it had nothing to do with me. I know it was Him, but it felt good that He felt that he could use me. Testimony is powerful and can change people's lives. I know that. I've seen it change people. Please be open to always telling people what you know. It is an incredible blessing to know what we know and to have what we have. You owe it to share it with everyone. It is the greatest gift you can give.

In process of bearing testimony, Travis is purified and transformed. He becomes a conduit of God's power. He becomes evidence of the claim, "Bearing your testimony often is one of the most powerful ways of inviting the Spirit and helping others feel the Spirit."

The story did not end there. Ten months later, Travis wrote home telling of something remarkable:

> We were asked to shake hands with the crowd at a stake baptism. As I walked through the crowd introducing myself a lady stopped me. She said, "Elder, do you remember me?" I had no idea who she was so I put my head down and answered, "No, should I?" She told me I shouldn't and then explained, "Last summer at temple pageant we brought a friend. She had taken the discussions many times before and had no interest anymore. She was simply at the event to support a friend. As you approached us you were glowing. She told you she was uninterested. You asked if you could simply share your testimony with her and she agreed. The Spirit was overpowering. You

then asked her if she would take the discussions again. She agreed and in November she was baptized." This moment is possibly the most sacred of my mission. I don't know how much of her conversion had to do with me. I'm sure the missionaries who taught her played the bigger role. I do know that God was able to speak through me that night because of my choice to act upon the promptings I had been given.

There is a way for you to have an experience like the one Travis describes. Here are some potential guidelines:

- "To bear testimony is to give a simple, direct declaration of belief—a feeling, an assurance, a conviction of gospel truth" (*Preach My Gospel*, 198).
- "For your testimony to have convincing power, you must be sincere. Powerful testimony is dependent . . . on the conviction of your heart" (*Preach My Gospel*, 198).
- Start with members. Set the objective to make divine contact with every member of the ward. Let them know you rejoice in Christ. Try to say something that will bless their lives. Make sure what you say fits the situation in terms of time and appropriateness.
- To get yourself prepared, make a list of fifteen to twenty brief statements that you can make with conviction. Write these down. Try them on your companion. Come to agreement that the statements are appropriate and sincere. Review the list before you go into the church and then put then put the list away. Here are some examples of ten-second testimonies:
  - Welcome to the Church of Jesus Christ. I love the Savior. I know you will be blessed today by renewing your covenants.
  - What a beautiful Sunday! I know that keeping the Sabbath holy is a commandment of God and it is a pleasure to welcome you to His holy house.
  - Hello Sister Jones, it thrills me to see you at church. I want you to know that Jesus is the Christ and the gospel has been restored. I hope you have a great Sabbath.
  - Welcome to the house of God. I know the scriptures are the word of God and I am glad we can come here and hear God's word.

- Welcome. I know that God has a plan for our lives. I am pleased that we can come together and learn about His plan. Have a wonderful Sunday.

Start greeting people with some of the statements you remember and then surrender to the Lord. Let him take over and speak through you just as he spoke through Travis.

As the morning goes on, continue to make appropriate and enthusiastic contact with the members. Continually pour light into the lives of the members.

If you can think of another setting in which you can do what Travis did, then use that setting to radiate the light of Christ.

I love each one of you.

Be extraordinary in Christ,

President Quinn

Challenge 7

BECOMING PEACEABLE

My Dear Fellow Servants,

In this letter, we will consider the challenge of becoming a "peaceable follower" of Jesus Christ (see Moroni 7:3). Chapter six of *Preach My Gospel* is about the development of Christlike attributes. The very first question in that chapter is "How can I develop attributes that will make me a more powerful and effective minister of the gospel of Jesus Christ?"

In chapter 7 of Moroni, Mormon gives us some advice on how to do this. To understand his advice, I will begin with a story from Kristin, in which she teaches a very simple but important lesson about focus. I will then share two stories from Travis, one about fire and one about potato chips. Each is important. With the stories in mind, we will consider how to acquire Christ-like attributes.

Kristin wrote:

> On Monday night I got about ten letters from you and each one helped me realize something about my life. I'll touch on some of them. First of all, in Dad's letter when he talked about trying to waste time on his mission and seeing that his companion secretly didn't mind, that was me on Monday. When my companion can't go out, the only way I can is with someone from the ward and that puts all the responsibility on me. That scares me. It scared me to death. The truth of the matter is that Saturday afternoon I didn't try very hard to get someone else to go out with me.
>
> In Dad's other letter he talked about rising above my environment—I need to stop feeling sorry for myself. I read Travis's letter

and think, "If only I was speaking English, I would have no problem doing this. If only I had an awesome companion that worked super hard and could teach me how to teach *charlas* (lessons) perfectly." The list goes on.

Shawn's letter made me realize that I just have to get to work. Right now, I can't worry about all my ideals. I can't be the missionary I want to be eventually, right now. It takes time. Right now all I can do is work and try to learn Spanish and trust in the Lord.

Kristin was fully challenged. Yet she recognized that she coud not focus on what she thought was wrong. She had to be patient and keep moving forward. This is a key notion. There are always things that are wrong. We can focus on them. We can then wish that we were like other missionaries who all seem to have it "easier."

If we do this natural and ordinary thing, we will live in a reactive state. We will become "acted upon" (2 Nephi 2:13–14, 26–27). We will live as helpless victims. We will stagnate and live lives of increasing darkness. Instead, we would do well to clarify our purpose and move forward. We have to embrace the pain of the work. As we move forward into the work, we will move closer to Jesus Christ and something miraculous will happen to us. We will become like Jesus Christ.

Travis wrote about his first companion leaving to go home. While Travis remains a junior companion, the transfer changes his role. He must take on new levels of responsibility. Because of this simple change, Travis finds himself more engaged in the work:

This week has been the fastest week of my mission. I think it is because Elder Tanner went home and a lot of responsibility shifted to me. I was the one the investigators knew now and it was my job to get my senior companion acquainted as quickly as possible. Also, I was the one who knew the area so I had to actually pay attention when I was in the car. I also took a greater part in scheduling because I knew where people lived. I found that I am more comfortable teaching now that I know the first two discussions. . . . I feel like I need to be an example for the first time. I feel I always need to work hard because my new companion might need a little help sometimes. I have found this has helped me not get tired anymore. I am always focused. I am comfortable. All these things help the Spirit to be with me more often. I really, truly feel I have caught fire. I love it.

A seemingly small change in responsibility resulted in a new outlook and a large change in the quality of experience. Because he was more engaged and paying more attention, a number of things happened. The time began to fly by. He was more focused and less tired. He was more comfortable and felt the Spirit more often. The truth is Travis really had "caught fire," and that fire was purifying his soul. Travis was spending more time and energy on the things of Christ, and the Light of Christ was burning more brightly in his heart and mind.

If a missionary gets more engaged in the work and keeps striving to move closer to Jesus Christ, he or she evolves to a higher level of awareness and capacity. This process of development tends to follow a process of personal discipline and is accompanied by a change in motives. As we learn to follow the Spirit of Christ and do things with "real intent," we do them because we have a purpose (see Moroni 7:6–9; 10:4). That purpose is to invite people to Christ because we love Christ. We become more charitable, and we relate to others in a more positive and peaceable way.

A great illustration of this change comes from something else Travis wrote. When Travis was growing up, he had an idiosyncrasy that was troublesome. He often brought home some kind of food—like a pizza, a burger, or a bag of potato chips. If anyone touched "his" food he would get uncontrollably angry. This pattern was so deeply ingrained that we as parents gave up trying to change it. He had been on his mission for nearly three months when he was made a new senior companion. He was working very hard. He then wrote home and told a story that most readers would see as insignificant, but family members found the story to be an astounding indicator of change.

In the story, Travis describes living with several missionaries. One of them has a number of problems and Travis makes an extra effort to support him. Yet the elder tends to wear people down. He has extreme outbursts that make him hard to get along with. He will not work or study. He sleeps in until 10:00 or 11:00 AM. Everyone, including Travis, is losing patience with him. Travis wrote:

> Basically, he has problems and it is hard not to wring his neck. Now the other day I noticed all of my chips were gone. I mean, I had this huge bag. So I'm not too mad until I ask his companion about it and he tells me that he told him not to eat the chips and he said, "I don't

care what Quinn thinks." Now this and all of the times he makes comments made me really want to kill him. I was about to go smack him on the head, wake him up, and yell at him, and if he hit me, kill him. I told myself to wait a few minutes and chill and finally I decided I'd just ask him nicely to stop eating my chips and he said, "Okay." This was real hard for me.

Again, to the reader is may seem like a silly story. But when we read of this incident, we could hardly believe the words. Something was happening to Travis Quinn. He was drawing closer to Jesus Christ and in the process his most basic characteristics were being transformed. Travis was learning to transcend his natural tendencies. The light of Christ was burning in Travis, and Travis was becoming a more "peaceable follower of Jesus Christ."

A few months later I wrote to Kristin and Travis, "You have been transformed. You have faith in Christ. You practice disciplined obedience. This pattern has changed how you feel, how you think, and how you relate. You report that missionary work is a constant struggle, yet you seem to rejoice in the struggle. You both point out that you love the work and the people you teach. You recount the difficult challenges of working with companions in a tightly yoked relationship but your accounts show empathy and loving effort. You have become what Mormon calls 'peaceable followers of Christ.'"

According to Mormon (in Moroni 7), peaceable followers of Christ are people filled with hope of one day living in the presence of God. This hope allows them to exercise faith in the face of uncertainty and move ahead without knowledge. In doing so, the faith that comes from hope becomes knowledge. Their hope and faith cause them to behave in unnatural ways, in extraordinary ways, in the ways of the saint.

Peaceable followers of Christ are people who experience "victory over self and . . . communion with the Infinite."[16] They are filled with love because they are obedient. When we observe them, we notice that their behaviors are different than the behaviors of the "natural man" (Mosiah 3:19). They are "anxiously engaged" in good works "of their own free will" (D&C 58:26–28). They are doing what they do because they love to do it. They are people of real intent.

In writing about the Spirit of Christ, Mormon gives us a model of development. It is difficult for an evil or divided person to give a good or whole gift. Mormon tells us that "a bitter fountain cannot bring forth good water; neither can a good fountain bring forth bitter water; wherefore, a man being a servant of the devil cannot follow Christ; and if he follow Christ he cannot be a servant of the devil" (Moroni 7:11).

We experience the Light of Christ as the conscience. It directs us in differentiating good and evil. If we follow it closely, we can overcome ourselves. This is what Kristin taught us in the above passage. She indicated that she had to ignore the negatives, stop making excuses, and move forward in the work. When we do this, we feel greater and greater integrity or oneness of heart, mind, and purpose. If we ignore the Light of Christ and rationalize our behaviors, we deaden the signals until the Spirit of Christ is almost undetectable. The light grows dim.

It is critical that we search diligently "in the light of Christ" so that we can differentiate good from evil (Moroni 7:19). If we do this and "lay hold on every good thing" (Moroni 7:21), we will become children of Christ. Christ himself said, "Whatsoever thing ye shall ask the Father in my name, which is good, in faith believing that ye shall receive, behold, it shall be done unto you" (Moroni 7:26; 3 Nephi 18:20). So it is through faith in Jesus Christ that we "lay hold on every good thing."

When a missionary prays for the Holy Ghost in teaching investigators and has those prayers answered, the missionary is exercising faith in the promise of Jesus and is laying hold on a good thing. When the missionary reads a scripture to an uncooperative investigator and the entire situation is suddenly transformed, the missionary is using faith in Jesus Christ to bring forth a miracle. The missionary has created a "good thing."

Miracles such as the transformation of a conversation continue even though Jesus Christ has ascended to heaven. There Jesus Christ has taken his place with God and he claims his rights. Because he fulfilled the law of justice, he can extend his mercy to all people who have faith in him. He can do this because people who have faith in him tend to hunger and thirst after righteousness and tend to strive for "every good thing." Notice that the faith leads to righteous desires and to choosing and internalizing goodness. In the midst of her pain, Kristin chooses to move forward. This is an exercise of her faith. Travis becomes more engaged and is filled with light. He reports that he is on fire.

Mormon tells us that miracles continue. Angels continue to minister unto humans. It is their responsibility to "call people unto repentance" and to "do the work of the covenants" (Moroni 7:31) which the

Father has made to his children. The angels are subject to Christ and they minister according to His directives. They show themselves "in every form of godliness" to "people of strong faith and a firm mind," and they declare "the word of Christ" to the "chosen vessels of the Lord" (Moroni 7:29–30). These chosen vessels or servants of God can then bear testimony of Christ. By this means, humans can have faith in Christ and the Holy Ghost can find a place in them. It is in this way that the Father brings to pass the covenants he has made (see Moroni 7:32).

Here is an important point. Go back and reread the above paragraph but substitute the word *missionaries* for the word *angels*. As a missionary engages the work and surrenders to Christ, they become the angels of Christ. You are the angels of Christ. You are the workers of miracles. As you feel the feelings of Christ, think the thoughts of Christ, and speak the words of Christ, you do the very same thing that angels do (see 2 Nephi 32:3).

Salvation follows faith. If angelic manifestations were to stop, it would be because of unbelief. All would be vain. It would be as though no redemption had been made. The lack of faith may be in the people, but the lack of faith may also be in the person called to play the angelic role. If we do not fulfill our stewardship, if we withdraw from the work, we cease to be Christ's angels. Christ then has less of an army with which he can do his righteous work. The decision that Kristin made to focus on the work, and the decision that Travis made to become more fully engaged, were decisions of eternal consequence.

Faith comes through hope. We gain faith as we begin to hope—through the Atonement and resurrection of Christ—to be raised up to eternal life or life with God. Hope and faith are inseparable. One brings the other but neither can exist unless we are "meek, and lowly of heart" (Moroni 7:43). When meekness and lowliness of heart lead us to confess, by the power of the Holy Ghost, that Jesus is the Christ, then we are filled with charity.

We learn from both Mormon and Paul that if we have not charity, the pure love of Christ, we are nothing (Moroni 7:45; 1 Corinthians 13:4–7). Charity leads us to long suffering and kindness in relating to people. When we are filled with the pure love of Jesus Christ, we do not feel envy, pride, selfishness, or anger. We are more peaceable. We have no evil thoughts. We find our joy in truth instead of iniquity. We rejoice in the truth, we bear all things, believe all things, hope all things, and endure all things (see Article of Faith 13). When we lack charity, we are nothing (1 Corinthians 13:1–3). Charity never fails (1 Corinthians 13:8). Charity is the greatest of all (1 Corinthians 13:13). If we are possessed of it on the last day, all will be well with us (Moroni 7:47). We should pray intensely for charity (Moroni 7:48). It is given to all who are true followers of Christ and it allows us to become His sons and daughters because when He appears we shall be like Him (1 John 3:1–3). At that point we shall see Him as He really is. Our hope must be that we will be purified even as He is pure. At that point our extraordinary decisions will have had truly extraordinary results.

One of the surest measures of our progress on moving ever closer to Christ is found in how we relate to others. Like Travis, we learn new behaviors. Followers of Christ learn to "bridle their passions" so they are "filled with love." As this happens, contention occurs ever less frequently. We no longer want to kill someone for eating our potato chips. Over time we become ever more peaceable. We have a "peaceable walk with the children of men" because we have moved ever closer to Jesus Christ.

As we engage the painful work, we are transformed. As we move closer to Christ, we learn to bridle our natural passions (see Alma 38:12). As we do this we are filled with love. Then, when someone eats our potato chips, we respond with love because that is what we genuinely feel. As we become peaceable followers of Christ, we can endure all the offenses of men—without losing our temper—because we are more fully alive in Christ.

I love each one of you.
Be extraordinary in Christ,
President Quinn

Challenge 8

My Dear Fellow Servants,

When we first arrive in a mission, we go through a role transition. We shift from following the expectations that people have for older teenagers to the expectations people have for missionaries. In doing this, we are externally determined. We are doing what others expect. In this letter, we consider the need to not only make a shift but to actually internalize a new identity and to become a constant follower of Christ. To understand the process, we will consider a number of stories and ponder how we can become constant disciples of Jesus Christ.

On page four of *Preach My Gospel*, we are told that we are to live worthy of our calling. We are to be examples of obedience and Christlike characteristics. In fact, at the end of the chapter, we are told by President Hinckley, "Your obligation is as serious in your sphere of responsibility as is my obligation in my sphere."[17] My perception is that the person who occupies the role of President of the Church has a pretty serious responsibility. That person fully invests in doing the things a Church President must do. Because they internalize and magnify their calling, they bless others and experience the pure love of Christ. To internalize and magnify the role of missionary requires the same level of commitment. Yet it is natural to do the outward duties of a missionary while actually trying to minimize our efforts.

A similar thing happens to movie stars. When a movie actor is making a movie, the actor plays a role. During the day, they emulate a given character. They do what the character is supposed to do and they

111

say the words the character is supposed to say. Some actors make a minimal effort and play their role rather poorly. Others play their role so well that they begin to internalize the identity of the person they play.

This can happen to a missionary. If person moves closer and closer to Jesus Christ, they begin to feel the feelings, think the thoughts, say the words, and do the deeds of Christ. They hunger to serve Christ and they become *constant* in Christ because they have the *constant* companionship of the Holy Ghost. They are always missionaries.

They internalize the role. There is no "onstage" and "offstage" difference. They take their role as seriously as a Church President takes his role, and they hunger to "improve their knowledge and abilities." The hunger exists because they want to be effective in the work of Christ.

Years ago, I listened to a talk about missionary work. The speaker was teaching a version of this concept. To communicate it, he used the phrase "24-hour missionary." A 24-hour missionary is a person who has internalized the role. The missionary never leaves the role because it is no longer a role. It is an identity. The missionary is no longer conforming to a set of external expectations coming from prophets, mission presidents, missionary leaders, members, or parents. The person is no longer performing out of duty but out of love. It is now natural, normal, or ordinary for the person to be extraordinary in Christ. The person naturally talks of Christ, rejoices in Christ, preaches of Christ, and prophecies of Christ. For such a person, leaving the presence of Christ, leaving the work of Christ, and leaving the role of a missionary is painful. (Notice the inversion. When a person becomes a new missionary they may find it painful to engage in missionary work. When they become more fully converted to Christ, they find it painful to not engage in the work.)

The process of becoming *constant* in Christ may begin in the MTC. While still in the MTC, Travis, for example, began to notice that when he was not progressing, he was miserable, and this created a desire to recommit. He wants to be more *constant in Christ:* "I have really come to realize that the point of life is progression. In the last few weeks I have not progressed and in so doing I have regressed. I do not feel like working. I make excuses. I decided to set serious personal goals each week to help me progress. We also set companionship goals to help us progress. I really found I needed to change myself. I hated feeling guilty. . . . I figure as I take small steps by accomplishing each goal each week I will better myself as a person and as a missionary."

As Kristin gets near the end of her MTC experience, she is also very much focused on her role as missionary and she is *constantly* thinking about how to teach more effectively. She wrote:

> I am focused here. I am learning about the gospel and how to help others learn it. I have been told a million times that the Spirit is the most important asset I have. I am called to preach the gospel and let the Spirit teach the gospel. D&C 50:13–14 reads, "unto what were ye ordained? To preach my gospel by the Spirit, even the Comforter which was sent forth to teach the truth." I am trying my hardest to master that skill and I was thinking that the perfect example of that was Mom at our farewell. Mom, you preached the doctrine and as you told the Joseph Smith story I could feel the Holy Ghost take over and teach everyone in that chapel. No one can deny the power of the Spirit.

In these statements, Travis and Kristin were beginning to internalize the role of missionary. They both had a hunger to become more effective. They read scriptures and listened to instructors and then began to act on these external ideas and expectations. As they did, they began to make progress. Their minds became focused on making still more progress. When they did, they were joyful. When they did not make progress, they were miserable because they felt guilt. So they kept recommitting to move forward. They wanted to become more *constant in Christ*.

Once a person leaves the MTC, they tend to experience the shock of trying to play the role of missionary in the real world. Then, like young Elder Hinckley or young Elder Groberg in our previous discussions, they have to decide if they are going to feel the pain or engage the pain. If they have faith in God, the pain drives them to God and they become more alive in Christ. Here is a report from Kristin when she first arrived in her mission:

> I don't even know where to begin. You guys, it is so hard. . . . But here's the thing, never, never, in my life have I had to depend so much on God, for everything. He is the only one who understands

me and what I'm feeling. I pray constantly for His help and comfort. He's become so real to me. It's hard for me not to cry every time I say a prayer out loud because it means so much more now. I know He is listening to us. I mean, I really know it and I know He does everything He can to help us.

The pain of loneliness and ineffectiveness drives Kristin closer to Jesus Christ, and by moving closer, she becomes alive in Christ and Christ becomes more alive in her. If, as a missionary, a person continues on this same path, they will eventually internalize the role of missionary, and they will become *constant in Christ*. Being a missionary will become their identity. They will have the heart and mind of Christ and it will be painful to not be engaged in the work.

The notion of being *constant*, of being a 24-hour missionary, is very, very important to me as a mission president. People often indicate that a mission president's first responsibility is the body of missionaries. I agree. But what is it his responsibility to do? Some say it is to teach them obedience. Others say that it is to increase baptisms. Some say it is to love the missionaries. I think that all three of these are very important. Yet they are simply supports to my real goal. My purpose is to ever more effectively invite every missionary to move closer to Jesus Christ. My responsibility is to more fully convert every missionary. My objective is to help every missionary become more *constant in Christ and to internalize the role of a missionary.*

When I became a mission president I wrote the vision I wanted to pursue. Here is part of that vision: "Because they accept this difficult invitation to faith and repentance, they become more alive and more constant in Christ. They talk of Christ, rejoice in Christ, and preach of Christ. In everything the missionaries write, in every conversation, in every lesson, in every meeting, they communicate the spirit of prophecy, which is the testimony of Jesus Christ. Their family members and mission president are more fully converted by weekly letters that witness firsthand experiences with the living God. Their companions are more fully converted because the love of Christ permeates the companionship. Church members are more fully converted because every conversation is a meaningful dialogue in Christ. Strangers are converted because they are approached with the boldness of Christ and taught from the heart and mind of Christ. Because they are constant in Christ, leaders at all levels design all meetings as if they were temple dedications where Christ will visit. Because they are alive in Christ, the missionaries are extraordinary in finding, teaching, and baptizing."

So how would I know if I were a successful mission president? It would be clear to me; letters I would get from missionaries would change. When I read them, I would cry because I would feel the power of God in them. Family members would write me letters telling me that missionary letters had changed. When they read the letters from their missionaries, the family member would feel more alive in Christ. In interviews, missionaries would tell me how much they love their companions and I would feel the power of God. Members would tell me how missionaries changed their behavior in members' homes and at church. They would tell me how the missionaries had become more powerful than the members could ever remember. The missionaries would show more love while seriously inviting members to move closer to Christ. Referrals would naturally increase and baptisms would reach new heights.

These new behaviors would tell me that I have succeeded as a mission president. Here I would like to elaborate on one of the above statements and use it as an illustration of how things might change: "Church members are more fully converted because every conversation is a meaningful dialogue in Christ." I aspired to lead a mission in which every missionary was *constant* in Christ. At church this means they would spend every hour being absolutely focused on helping every member increase their testimony of Christ. Every missionary would hold extraordinary conversations in the halls, in class, in the parking lot, everywhere, all the time. In members' homes the missionaries would teach to convert, not to fill time. How would a missionary do such a thing?

Before I answer this, let me describe what usually happened in our house, over many years, when missionaries came to visit. The missionaries would come to our home for dinner. They were always nice people. We would have a nice, casual conversation. They would eat and then share a routine thought and leave. It was pleasant for all concerned, but I never remembered their names because they added limited value to my life. They did not think to come with the purpose to make my life better, to more fully convert me to Christ, because they were not

24-hour missionaries. They instead acted as they thought I expect them to act, as young men or women in the presence of an older Church leader. They were thus externally directed.

How might things change? A missionary might become a 24-hour missionary, a missionary who is *constant* in Christ. The missionary would not respond to external expectations. The missionary would be driven from within. The missionary would go to church or to a home with the intent of helping members improve their lives by moving closer to Jesus Christ. The missionary would never be obnoxious or offensive because the missionary would be Christ-centered and filled with love.

In the hallways of the church, the missionaries would do and say extraordinary things. The missionary would testify of Christ and ask the member if the missionary could meet to rejoice with them in Christ. Sitting in meetings, the members would notice that the missionaries took notes on every talk. They would give positive feedback to every speaker on what specific thing the speaker said that touched the heart of the missionary.

At a dinner, the missionary would guide the conversation to Christ. After dinner, the missionary might hand out the Book of Mormon questions from page 107 of *Preach My Gospel* and ask the member which of the questions is most important in their life. The missionary would say, "Great, should we read that chapter right now, and see how we can all move closer to Christ? I cannot wait to share my testimony with you." The missionary would teach, testify, invite, and commit. The missionary would follow up. The missionary would treat each member as the missionary would treat a golden contact.

The members would feel honestly engaged by the missionaries. They would marvel at how the missionaries intended to truly bring everyone to Christ. They would marvel at how extraordinary the missionaries had become. Trust would go up. Relationships would improve. Referrals would increase.

When I was a missionary, I sensed this lack of meaningful connection with the members and blamed the members. It is not the fault of the members. They respond in ordinary ways to ordinary stimuli. They would respond in extraordinary ways if they were exposed to extraordinary stimuli. A missionary who is constant in Christ is an extraordinary stimulus.

Now here I use members as an example. Please apply the same vision to how a constant missionary would treat companions, other missionaries, family members, and investigators. We would see similar kinds of change.

I love each one of you.
Be extraordinary in Christ,
President Quinn

Challenge 9

BECOMING PATIENT

My Dear Fellow Servants,

Many people assume that our personality characteristics are fixed. Yet as we become constant in Christ, we begin to change and we acquire Christlike characteristics. One of these is patience. Here we will consider several stories about acquiring patience and we will discover the blessings that come from doing so.

Chapter six of *Preach My Gospel* is about acquiring the attribute of patience, and it turns out that patience is particularly important in the development of an effective missionary. The book states, "Patience is the capacity to endure delay, trouble, opposition, or suffering without becoming angry, frustrated, or anxious. It is the ability to do God's will and accept His timing. When you are patient, you hold up under pressure and are able to face adversity calmly and hopefully."[18] On a mission, we most certainly face delay, trouble, opposition, and suffering.

As we draw closer to Christ, we may discover a new kind of suffering. We learned about this new kind of suffering from both Travis and Kristin. One week Travis wrote that doing hard things brings joy.

> I started thinking I didn't really have a mission scripture. So I started searching this week. I just happened to be reading about the sons of Mosiah. I found my scriptures. There are a few of them but they all tie in together. The first is in Alma 27:8. It is talking about what happened as they served. I'll write the scripture with some words changed to fit me more.
>
> "And this is an account of (Elder Quinn) and his brethren, their journeyings in the land of (Oakland), *their sufferings* in the land,

their sorrows, and *their afflictions,* and *their incomprehensible joy,* and the reception and safety of the brethren in (the Kingdom of God). And now may the Lord, the Redeemer of all men, bless their souls forever."

I love that scripture. The reason I do is because of the italicized words. The first three are pretty similar. They are understood to be negative things. However, the fourth emphasized part is what I like, "incomprehensible joy." That wouldn't normally follow the first three phrases. The sons of Mosiah understood that hard things brought joy. I am coming to understand this also. I could go on a lot longer about this scripture, but I don't have time. I just feel this is the perfect scripture for my mission.

Travis suggested that a mission involves doing hard things. One may experience suffering, sorrow, and affliction—but such feelings are related to experiencing incomprehensible joy. How can this be? Kristin gave us a clue. She wrote that as we move closer to God, we learn to live in faith, hope, and charity. Living in the love of God then stimulates the desire to continue in the love of God. In this elevated state, we become more sensitive. Kristin wrote the following accounts:

- "Later that night we started talking about our differences and my companion pointed this out to me and started to cry. Man, I felt so bad. Just like the most horrible companion ever."
- "Ruben (an investigator) gave me some rough feedback. He's like, 'I love that you love everything you share and you've got so much faith that it is just oozing out of you, but sometimes I feel like all the enthusiasm is smothering me.' Ouch. That hurt pretty bad."
- "By the time I started *charla* (lesson) 2, it was too late. We had been there too long. We had to rush through the principles. We didn't even finish it. I felt horrible. I mean horrible. Why is it so hard for me to just do what the Spirit says? Ah!"
- "We got home after the *charla* and I started to pray. As I prayed I just cried and cried. I love these people so much, you guys. I'm serious, I love them and it physically hurts when I leave *charlas* like these and they don't chose to do something to progress in the gospel. I felt so inadequate. As I prayed I just realized my nothingness, which is fine if we can trust in the Lord to make

us powerful, but I feel like I'm nothing and I have no idea how to let the Lord make me something."

- "All I know is I love the people here and I love the gospel. It kills me every time one of them doesn't choose to follow it, in whatever action they take. I really don't know how I can take this emotionally for another 10 months."

- "The other night I couldn't even sleep thinking about all my investigators and their problems. We had this doctor guy come talk to us and he told us that as missionaries we have as much stress as any high-powered executive has. Yikes. I'm feeling it."

Like Travis, Kristin had grown a great deal. She was more confident and capable. Yet in these statements we see a young woman who is often in agony and greatly stressed. There is a reason that she was experiencing these feelings.

King Benjamin taught his people that they had to make a change: "For the natural man is an enemy to God, and has been from the fall of Adam, and will be, forever and ever, unless he yields to the enticings of the Holy Spirit, and putteth off the natural man and becometh a saint through the Atonement of Christ the Lord, and becometh as a child, submissive, meek, humble, patient, full of love, willing to submit to all things which the Lord seeth fit to inflict upon him, even as a child doth submit to his father" (Mosiah 3:19). As Kristin diligently served her mission, she grew closer and closer to God. In the process, her desires and behaviors became less "natural." She worked very hard to "yield to the enticings of the Holy Spirit." As she did the work, she became a saint and she became a child of God who was acquiring more and more Christlike characteristics. The great evidence of this change was captured in statements like this: "I'm serious, I love them and it physically hurts when I leave *charlas* like these and they don't choose to do something to progress in the gospel. . . . All I know is I love the people here and I love the gospel. It kills me every time one of them doesn't choose to follow it, in whatever action they take. I really don't know how I can take this emotionally for another 10 months."

In her missionary efforts Kristin had been "spiritually begotten" of Christ; her heart had been "changed through faith on his name" (see Mosiah 5:7–8). Because she had been born of Christ, Kristin was filled with charity or the pure love of Christ. She loved the children of God as

God loves his children. People who love are people who live with open hearts and people who live with open hearts become vulnerable. Kristin was vulnerable to godly sorrow. What does this mean?

Enoch had a vision. In it, God was crying. Enoch was surprised and asked why God was weeping: "The Lord said unto Enoch: Behold these thy brethren; they are the workmanship of mine own hands, and I gave unto them their knowledge, in the day I created them; and in the Garden of Eden, gave I unto man his agency; and unto thy brethren have I said, and also given commandment, that they should love one another, and that they should choose me, their Father; but behold, they are without affection, and they hate their own blood" (Moses 7:32–33). The people of the earth are children of God. They have divine potential. They have been given knowledge and agency. They are commanded to love one another. Instead of loving one another they are filled with hatred and live in conflict. Because they are not using their knowledge and agency to live in love they are not experiencing the joy of eternal progression. They are wasting their divine potential and God weeps over their condition.

To love like God is to honor the agency of others while becoming vulnerable to the agency of others. When we acquire godly love we are likely to experience godly sorrow. As a person is born again in Christ, patience becomes a crucial attribute. To lose our patience is to expect others to give up their agency to meet our expectations. That loss of patience leads us away from humility and charity. As we learn to open our hearts and live in love, we must also learn to experience godly sorrow with patience.

When we become filled with the love of God and committed to the conversion of his children, we may become like Alma, who desired to be an angel. He wanted the power to shake the earth so that every person would repent and sorrow would be taken from the earth. But as soon as he had this thought, he recognized it to be a sin and says, "I ought to be content with the things which the Lord hath allotted unto me" (Alma 29:3). After some reflection, Alma concludes, "this is my glory, that perhaps I may be an instrument in the hands of God to bring some soul to repentance; and this is my joy" (Alma 29:9).

Filled with love and the desire to succeed in her work, Kristin said, "I really don't know how I can take this emotionally for another 10 months." Many missionaries come to feel this kind of stress. What is to be done?

The introduction to this letter included the following statement from *Preach My Gospel*. As you read it this time, you may find it to be an extraordinary statement: "Patience is the capacity to endure delay, trouble, opposition, or suffering *without becoming angry, frustrated, or anxious. It is the ability to do God's will and accept His timing. When you are patient, you hold up under pressure and are able to face adversity calmly and hopefully.*" The claim would make little sense to the natural man or woman. These words suggest an ability to walk through adversity while staying centered in Christ. When we do, we can function and even grow in the face of stressful stimuli.

King Benjamin stated, "And see that all these things are done in wisdom and order; for it is not requisite that a man should run faster than he has strength. And again, it is expedient that he should be diligent, that thereby he might win the prize; therefore, all things must be done in order" (Mosiah 4:27). This scripture suggests a healthy tension between patience and diligence. A person should not run faster than they have strength, but they should be diligent in gaining strength.

This diligence in the pursuit of personal effectiveness suggests that patience may be connected to two other concepts: accountability and feedback. As Travis grew as a missionary, his faith grew. He eventually made a surprising claim and observation (which I have emphasized in italics):

> I had another insight this week. I realized that I have learned a very valuable lesson on my mission. I have learned that everything is possible with the help of the Lord. This has become the theme of my mission. *I now expect that every person I talk to will get baptized. I expect every missionary I work with to be converted. I expect members to want to give referrals.* The reason I expect it is because the Lord expects it. If He expects it, it will happen. I just have to be the instrument.
>
> Now this is where I've really changed. *If something doesn't happen the way I expect it to, I immediately look at myself. I have found that I very rarely make an excuse anymore.* Instead I leave a situation and say: "She didn't commit to baptism. What am I doing wrong?" I realized this with a family the other night. I don't blame them for not getting baptized. Once they do, I will know that I was the pure instrument that I needed to be. I think this may be the best trait I've picked up.

Wow!

In this condition, Travis expected success, but when it did not occur, he did not seek to take away the agency of the children of God. Instead he exercised his own agency. He became more diligent in his own pursuit of personal strength and capacity. He turned his focus on becoming a more effective "instrument in the hands of God to bring some soul to repentance" (Alma 29:9).

This kind of diligence requires openness. As a mission president, one of the things I regularly teach the missionaries is that "feedback is the breakfast of champions." If we desire to learn and progress, we must have enough desire and patience to accept feedback. If we cannot stand feedback, people will stop giving it to us. But randomly getting feedback is not enough. We have to search for it—even create it—by constantly examining our every effort. Great performers in any area tend to be people who have evolved to the point that they can objectively assess and criticize their own performance. They give themselves feedback. They learn to do so because they love what they do and they are driven by the desire to genuinely improve.

One reason feedback is the breakfast of champions is that the natural man avoids feedback. It is too painful. As Kristin diligently pursued her work, she got negative feedback from her companion and her investigator. This suggests that she was not being as effective as she would have liked to be. She had strong emotional reactions to her weaknesses because the outcome matters so much. She continually struggled and the struggles drained her of her energy. She got very discouraged.

This discouragement is natural. I once had a stake president who was a very strong and confident leader. One night we were coming to the close of a high council meeting. What he told us surprised us. He said that leading the stake was very difficult; he greatly loved the people but often felt inadequate. He said he tried to lead with authenticity, intimacy, vulnerability, and pure motive. Yet every now and then someone criticized or rejected him. When this happened, he said it sometimes immobilized him for a long period. He said he would go inside himself and hide. It was very painful. He said that at such times he was unable to lead.

Given the age and experience of the stake president, it is not surprising that Kristin or any other missionary would feel devastated by negative feedback. Yet as we move closer to Christ, we can develop the attribute of patience. We can acquire the Christlike "capacity to endure delay, trouble, opposition, or suffering *without becoming angry, frustrated, or anxious.* It is the ability to do God's will and accept His timing. When you are patient, *you hold up under pressure and are able to face adversity calmly and hopefully.*" Acquiring this attribute changes us forever. We can do things the natural man or woman will never be able to do. What a blessing it is to acquire patience.

I love each one of you.

Be extraordinary in Christ,

President Quinn

Challenge 10

Becoming Enthusiastic

My Dear Fellow Servants,

In this letter, I write of one of the most interesting of all challenges: becoming an enthusiastic disciple of Christ. Many people believe they are, by nature, not enthusiastic, and that they never could be. What if this is a false assumption? What if moving towards Christ naturally breeds enthusiasm? What difference would the enthusiasm make? In this letter, I want to tell you of a most unusual dog and the missionary lessons we can learn from the dog. In the story, we will find some surprising answers to this question.

On page four of *Preach My Gospel*, we are told that our authority and power should be "evident" as we "work and teach." Our "power may be manifest in many things" we do. It then lists many ways in which we might do inspired work.

On page eleven is a study box with scriptures describing the feelings of many faithful missionaries. Most of the scriptures indicate that as missionaries become fully engaged, they become concerned about other people. In the process of doing the work, missionaries sometimes become "weighed down" because of the wickedness of the world, yet they are often instructed by God to "fear not," to be of "good cheer," and to lift their heads and "rejoice" because of their faith and their blessings. So, while it is natural for missionaries to get "weighed down with sorrow" and to go through "much tribulation and anguish of soul," the message from heaven is "lift up thy head and rejoice." It is to be of "good cheer."

Another way to say this is that we should be enthusiastic in our work. The word enthusiasm comes from the Greek and combines two ideas: *en* (inside) and *theos* (god). Enthusiasm means being full of passion, having a sense of zeal and fervor, conveying strong excitement, and having revelations from God. An enthusiastic missionary is inspired by God and full of positive feelings that he or she radiates to others. A key point is that enthusiasm is a message more powerful than words. When you are enthusiastic, you change people before you even speak to them.

When I was a boy, my stepfather once came home with a puppy that we named Candy. When she was very little, Candy became sick. While it seemed for a long time she would die, Candy miraculously survived. Perhaps that brush with death had something to do with the personality she developed.

Candy was not very attractive physically. In fact, if you just looked at her, you would say she was ugly. But Candy loved to see people. In fact, when she encountered someone she knew, she would become a bundle of joy. Instead of wagging her tail, she would enthusiastically shake her entire body. She never jumped on anyone or did anything irritating. She just circled people with her whole body communicating that she was happy to see them. Her enthusiasm was infectious. Candy made people feel like they mattered.

Everyone reacted positively to Candy. My friend used to say that he had been scared of dogs until he met Candy. Candy changed his outlook. The mailman used to look forward to coming to our house. It was the high point of his day. The insurance man used to come by once a month to collect his money. When he came and Candy was not around, he wanted to know where she was. Walking down the street, Candy would approach complete strangers with that same expression of joy and they would melt in the in the face of her warmth.

Candy was not much to look at, but I think everyone saw her as attractive. What came from the inside altered how people made sense of her external image. Candy did not behave in an ordinary way, so people had to stop and make sense of her. Because she was so excited about seeing them, they concluded that they were attractive to this unusual dog and they became filled with positive emotions.

Now if an enthusiastic dog can have the capacity to change people, certainly an enthusiastic missionary should have the capacity to change people. I think Candy has something to teach us about missionary work because missionaries who are enthusiastic have a greater likelihood of finding and teaching effectively.

Consider some examples. Kristin once wrote about her first experience in the referral center at the MTC. She indicated that it is the "most dreaded place in the MTC." She indicated that in making phone calls, missionaries encounter many "rude people" and that is why "they hate to go there." Despite these comments, she shared a surprising story of success.

> My district *LOVES* the referral center. We have this teacher, Brother Hazzenbueller, and our first day he got us so pumped up we were ready to convert the world. He bore his testimony and his excitement was infectious. Whenever one of us would have a cool call we would tell everyone about it, and if people were on the phone Brother H would make us tell him all about it. We were on fire!
>
> One night we had 30 referrals in one hour. I've heard of districts getting 10 in two hours. I know the people we talk to can hear the excitement in our voices. When I'm waiting for a call, I'll listen to people around me and they testify so sincerely I know the people they are talking to have to feel the Spirit. I have had some of the greatest experiences ever in there.

Why did her district have so much success in the place of "dread"? There was one person, their teacher, who prepared not only their heads but also prepared their hearts. He used feelings to elevate feelings. Through genuine testimony, he created infectious excitement. He then had them share every success, and the shared enthusiasm grew. This had an impact not only on the missionaries but also on the contacts. Kristin stated, "I know the people we talk to can hear the excitement in our voices."

The enthusiastic missionaries were conveying their positive energy and the contacts on the phone were responding positively. This positive response then returned to the missionaries and had an elevating effect on the positive emotions they were already feeling. What was the result? Please read what I call the Psalm of Kristin:

> I am ecstatic! The referral center was *AWESOME*! I am seriously bursting with happiness. I had tons of people ask for the missionaries. There are tons of people looking for the gospel. The field is ready

to *HARVEST*. I believe that with my entire soul. The Church is true! Jesus Christ is the Savior of the world and I am doing his work. I am overwhelmed by that idea. I am his servant. I lay at his feet and am ready to do *ANYTHING* for him. I love him. I love the gospel and want all the people in the world to have it.

A psalm is a song of the heart. Kristin did not know she was writing a psalm, but she was. Because Kristin entered the place of "dread" and experienced the power of success, she was filled with the love of God.

When we are filled with the love and power of God, we become inspired, we take on more Christlike characteristics and we radiate more positive energy. Teaching from the head carries information. Teaching from the head and heart carries information and energy. This kind of communication is infrequent, and when people encounter it, they tend to become open to it.

One day my son Ryan told me that he wanted me to read a passage that he had just read. I am not sure where he found it. The passage was about two missionaries teaching a student at Harvard. After they taught the essentials of the Restoration, the student said, "That is the most incredible story I have ever heard. If I really believed all of that, I wouldn't be able to sleep. I would run down the streets screaming it to everyone. Why aren't you more excited about it?"

We talked about this interesting question. Then Ryan told me a story. One day he and his companion were out contacting. His companion said, "If we really had testimonies, we would be running from house to house telling people about it." Ryan said, "You are right" and took off running. He said he and his companion ran to every house for an hour. He said the funny thing is that they had more callbacks in that hour than any other of his mission.

This claim reminds me of an experience that took place when I was a new senior companion. I wanted to be successful, so we worked very hard. Over a three-week period, we knocked on every door in a large neighborhood and had no success. I started to get discouraged. Each day it grew harder. I had to drag myself. Increased work only brought increased frustration. One morning we were out knocking on doors and the discouragement peaked. I took my companion and went back to the apartment. I sat down and stared at the wall. The Spirit prompted me to pray. I did not want to pray. A war raged inside me. Finally I fell to my knees and said, "Father." As soon as I did, a mural opened up in my mind.

On the left side of the picture were my parents and sister before they joined the Church and on the right side were the same three people after they joined the Church. Before they joined the Church, they were very ordinary. They were leading the normal blue-collar life. My stepfather would come home from work, get out a six-pack of beer, and sit in front of the television. My mother would work all day and then collapse in exhaustion. After they joined the Church, there was a dramatic shift in their lives. They started to function at a higher level. Soon my stepfather was the branch president. My mother was the primary president. Fulfilling those callings required efforts that they would never have dreamed of in their previous lives. I looked at this dramatic contrast and then the Spirit said to me, "Could anything but the truth have done this?" For me, the answer was clear. This incident was an electric experience. I felt filled with the power of God. My sense of testimony intensified.

Now, how do I know this story is true? I know because of what happened next. While a short time earlier I was ineffective, discouraged, and unable to go on, now I stood up, took my companion, and went back to the houses we had already visited. Nearly everyone we talked to expressed interest. In two days, we made enough commitments to fill our appointment book for two weeks. This dramatic shift in effectiveness was a tangible indicator that a transformation had taken place, I had moved closer to Jesus Christ, and I was filled with love and enthusiasm. The same people who had previously rejected us could feel our enthusiasm, and they wanted to invite us into their lives.

Why did Kristin have success in the referral center? Why did Ryan get more commitments in the one hour they ran to every house than in any other hour of his mission? Why did the same people who a short time before rejected my companion and me now accept us? What was different? It was the condition of the missionaries that had changed.

If the condition of the missionaries determines the reaction of the people, missionaries can be in control. We usually assume the very opposite. We assume the people are in control. We invite them, and they then choose to slam the door or not.

Now there is a paradox. Both views are correct. *Where the control lies depends on the state of the missionary.* Under normal circumstances, an ordinary missionary knocks on a door and gets an ordinary reaction. When a missionary is filled with love and enthusiasm, that missionary is no longer ordinary. That missionary is extraordinary in Christ and His power is evident.[19] When an extraordinary person knocks on a door, the situation is no longer normal. The person at the door must react to the extraordinary stimulus and there will be greater tendency for the person to become mindful. They have to figure out what is going on. When they have to be mindful, they are more likely to open up to the situation. When they open up and feel the enthusiasm, they are more likely to be drawn instead of repelled. The chances of their reacting positively go up.

This concept of being in control is hard for people to understand. Few people experience it because few people are willing to exert the effort necessary to alter the routines in which they live. I once casually told the story of Ryan running from house to house to two missionaries in my home mission. The next month, they came back to tell me a story. They said they experimented with the notion of running from house to house and they were shocked by how much their rate of success climbed. They were zone leaders and could not wait to tell the missionaries in their zone. To their surprise, the missionaries in the zone were uninterested. When the asked why, one of the elders said, "We do not want to look like fools."

The reaction of the missionaries who did not want to look like fools was understandable. They were having a natural reaction. They were more concerned about how they looked—the "honors of men" (see D&C 121:35)—than accomplishing their purpose. Ordinary people get ordinary results because they fear looking foolish.

I think of a small illustration. Just before I left home to become a mission president, I passed two missionaries at church. I said hello and they both grunted at me. They looked like two very unhappy people. I worried about those two. Was it a temporary condition? Was this a typical condition? My first thought was, "I would not want them to teach any of my friends." Notice that if others have this reaction in the hallway, the missionaries are less likely to get referrals and are less likely to have success and are less likely to be enthusiastic. They are trapped in a downward cycle.

People who are extraordinary in Christ eventually get extraordinary results. The idea that we can choose to be enthusiastic is a hard concept. Some young people arrive in the mission field with an identity that excludes enthusiasm. Some have had little experience with positive passions. Others have never learned to express positive passions. Since these things are outside of their identity, they believe that expressing enthusiasm would be an inauthentic act. They believe, given their identity, that they could never express enthusiasm.

I believe we can choose to be enthusiastic. There are two things to remember. First, it is not normal to do so. For most of us, it is outside our ordinary role. Many of us feel that we should not express our feelings. We fear we would look like a fool. This suggests that we might want to experiment. As companions, we might talk about enthusiasm and try out what it would be like to express it. We might even try running from door to door.

Personally, I tend to be an introvert. I do not feel that I am a naturally enthusiastic person. To become enthusiastic, I often have to make a choice to become enthusiastic. This raises a question about authenticity. It is normal to say, "I cannot fake positive feelings." I agree. Yet when I was a missionary, I learned an amazing thing. I learned that when I was not feeling enthusiastic, I could actually shift myself into a state of enthusiasm and the enthusiasm immediately became real. As soon as I make the shift, I actually *was* enthusiastic.

As a missionary I learned that enthusiasm changed my rate of success in finding. Then I read about a simple technique for shifting myself into an enthusiastic state. I would hold a smile on my face, stand on my toes, close my eyes, squeeze my fists, and bounce up and down until I could feel the energy flowing. Then I would walk rapidly up to a door and knock. When the person came to the door, I would greet them with enthusiasm. It was amazing how much this one technique changed things. It was so powerful that I used it the rest of my life. Even today, if I feel low and I am going to an important meeting or presentation, I sneak off somewhere and I do this simple technique. Whenever I share it, people laugh. They think it is silly. I think it is a powerful tool available to people who care more about effectiveness than being cool.

Why does it work? If I change my attitude and my behaviors, I change myself. This is called repentance. When I repent, I move closer to God and I take a fresh view of God, of self, and of the world (see Bible Dictionary, "Repentance"). Repentance fills me with joy. The fire of the Spirit burns within and radiates to others.

As I indicated at the outset, enthusiasm means "God within us." When I have enthusiasm, the people are touched because they feel what I radiate. They feel God. When you change yourself, your power becomes evident and begins to lift others.

I love each one of you.

Be extraordinary in Christ,

President Quinn

Challenge 11

My Dear Fellow Servants,

There is something that underlies the meeting of all missionary challenges. It is learning to learn by faith. In this letter, I would like to illustrate how learning by faith actually works. The process is illustrated in a potent story told by my son Shawn. I present it at the end of this letter. I hope you will ponder it and never forget it. The story could make you successful for the rest of your life.

Chapter two of *Preach My Gospel* is about effective study. It tends to emphasize the examination and internalization of the scriptures. Yet it also suggests a second kind of study that builds on the first. On the first page of chapter two, it states, "While learning from a good teacher is important, it is more important that you have meaningful learning experiences on your own."[20]

At the outset of chapter six, we read about faith: "When you have faith in Christ, you believe in Him as the Son of God, the Only Begotten of the Father in the flesh. You accept Him as your Savior and Redeemer and follow His teachings. You believe that your sins can be forgiven through His Atonement. Faith in Him means that you trust Him and are confident that He loves you. Faith leads to action, including repentance, obedience, and dedicated service."

These two quotations are related. When we live by faith, we trust Christ and are confident He loves us, so we are willing to do good things that we have not yet learned to do. This leads us to new actions and "meaningful learning experiences."

In one of the first stories in the Book of Mormon, Lehi asks Nephi and his brothers to go back to Jerusalem to get the brass plates (1 Nephi 3–4). While this was a very difficult challenge, Nephi responded, "I will go and do the things which the Lord hath commanded" (1 Nephi 3:7). While his faith was strong, the mission proved difficult. The first strategy was to ask for the plates. When this failed, his brothers wanted to go home. Nephi indicated that they would not go home until they accomplished what the Lord sent them to do. This led to a second strategy, which also failed.

No logical strategy was left. They did not know what to do. So Nephi sets the goal to obtain the plates. Then he says he "crept into the city and went forth" (1 Nephi 4:5). What was his plan? "And I was led by the Spirit, not knowing beforehand the things which I should do" (1 Nephi 4:6). In other words, he had no plan. After trying all the logical strategies he could come up with, he turned himself completely over to God.

I believe this is one of the most important lines in all of scripture. It says that Nephi was so committed to accomplish his purpose that he was willing to work by the Spirit and learn how to do what he needed to do in real time. As he moved forward, Nephi was fully engaged in the process of asking, seeking, and knocking. Nephi was then asked to do things that violated all he had previously learned. Like Abraham before him, he was engaged in an extreme test of faith and learning. Please keep this process in mind as you read the next two stories.

My daughter Kristin described an incident in the MTC:

> The other night I was in class with Hermano (Brother) Hazzenbueller. He wanted to have a "one-on-one" with me. He asked me to bear my testimony in Spanish and a couple of cool things happened. First, I've been praying to Heavenly Father to reinforce my testimony of Him and who He is and what He means to me. When I said in very simple Spanish that He is my Father, He lives and He loves me, He has to or He wouldn't have sent the Savior, I felt the power of the words as I said them and I got an answer to my prayer.
>
> The second thing is that when I was done, my teacher was just looking at me funny and he goes, "Do you realize that you only made one mistake?" We just looked at each other in semi-shock because this was not a few lines I memorized in Spanish. I was talking. The next day we were waiting for this guy to come and Hermana (Sister)

Hansen says, "And while we wait, Hermana Quinn is going to bear her testimony to us." So I did, and while it wasn't perfect, the words just flowed like they did the night before. That just doesn't happen with my Spanish! I can't believe all of the little miracles around me. But I guess I probably just have my eyes open now.

Like Nephi, Kristin had a purpose. She wanted to be an effective servant. She therefore had two short-term goals. She wanted to increase her testimony (obtain truth) and she wanted to learn her language (obtain capacity). She was seeking to know how to do these two things. This meant she was in a state of inquiry. She was seeking as she struggled forward. This included trying new things, taking risks, expressing her testimony, and speaking in front of people when she did not know how to speak. As she did these things, she continually had new experiences—and she learned from those experiences.

This image is not an image of simply kneeling in a corner asking for help. It is an image of being in a very special condition. It is a young missionary trying to become more than she is by trying to do things she does not know how to do. *When we try to do things we do not know how to do, we become very hungry for help, we pray with real intent. Prayers of real intent often bring a manifestation of power.* As Kristin entered this state, she was lifted to a new level of testimony and of language. She saw this lifting as a miracle. She then noted that her life was full of miracles.

Kristin also wrote something very important, "I guess I probably just have my eyes open now." I love that last sentence. When we move forward in a righteous purpose, trying to do what we do not know how to do, when we ask, seek, and knock, we get revelation and it makes us aware of things we could not see before (see Matthew 7:7; Luke 11:9; 3 Nephi 14:7; D&C 88:63). We feel as if our eyes have been miraculously opened.

Here is a second illustration of the process. My son Shawn had only been a missionary for only a few weeks in Toronto when he was made a senior companion. His junior companion was brand new and neither one knew anything about the area. The previous missionaries had left no one in the teaching pool. There was no help from members. These two people were committed to be good missionaries, but they felt lost. They had no idea what to do.

Before I share what Shawn actually did, consider a question. What would be the normal reaction to this situation?

I suspect many people would respond as did Laman and Lemuel when the first strategy failed. They would be ready to quit. In doing so, they would be "acted upon" by the situation (see 2 Nephi 2:13–14, 26–27). The situation would be in control of them. They would be floating downstream in the river of life. Most people spend most of their lives being "acted upon." Lehi understood this and explained that we are to "act" and not be "acted upon." In every situation, we should be actors and not reactors. We do this by continually clarifying our purpose. We continually ask, seek, and knock as we move forward trying to do what we do not know how to do.

Some of Lehi's sons were actors who moved forward, doing what they did not know how to do. Some were reactors who continually expressed a desire to return to their zone of comfort. The difference in the two orientations impacted many generations of people. Our orientation in the mission field today will also impact many generations of people, including endless people who are dead and endless people who are not yet born. What we do, or what we do not do, matters. Our decisions today will partially shape the lives of our grandchildren and their grandchildren.

Pause for a moment and try to envision a grandchild. The child is sitting on your lap, talking with you. Ask yourself how you will feel about this child? What do you want for this child? Then ask, "How do my decisions today shape what this child will experience many decades from now?" The linkage is real. You currently influence your future posterity and also the current state of your ancestors. You currently touch the grandchildren of your grandchildren and you touch the grandchildren of grandchildren of your investigators. You are an influence for all eternity.

It is one thing to study the concepts of eternity. It is quite another to apply the concepts when we feel we are in an impossible missionary situation. To get help, we will return to Shawn. Remember, he was out only a few weeks, his companion was brand new, there was no one to teach and he had no idea what to do. It was hopeless. Earlier I asked you what the typical reaction would be, and I suggested most people would do what Laman and Lemuel would do. Here is what happened:

> Instead of finding something to eat at lunch, I fell on my knees and began to pray. Actually, I fell on my knees and began to cry. I did not

know what to do and I told the Lord all about it. I do not remember much of what happened during that prayer. I just remember getting up from the prayer and looking at the clock. I had been on my knees for two hours. I felt relieved and was given the thought that I just needed to begin to work.

I got my companion and we took off to one of the closest buildings to where we lived in our area. I told my companion we were not going to leave that building until we had taught a discussion. The building was thirty stories tall and we started at the top and went right down to the bottom. We had a few good talks with people in which we set up some appointments but did not teach any discussions. Finally while between floors my companion was sitting on the stairs and asked if we could please go get something to eat. It had been about six hours since entering the building and so I decided we could go down to the little pizza place at the bottom of the building but then we would come right back in.

We had dinner and then started back at the top of the building. We knocked on the doors of the people who were not home earlier in the day. We never ended up teaching a discussion that day but we had worked very hard. I felt the Spirit with me a lot more and had a much better perspective and came up with many ideas of how we could go about working in the area. I had learned one of the most important lessons in this life. When you do not know what to do or how to start a certain job or project, you just need to put you head down and start to work. Once you have started the work you will begin to see it is not impossible and that you will be all right as you take one step at a time.

Shawn went on to describe his first three weeks in that area. He worked very hard but was able to put no one into the teaching pool. He kept seeking, asking, and knocking. One night he received a referral for two men. As he went to visit them and stumbled through the process of teaching them, he was filled with love. As he continued to teach them, he was filled with power. The men were baptized. Shawn claimed that from this process, his confidence in God began to increase dramatically. He went on to serve a very successful mission. He was successful because he was ever willing to set about learning to do what he did not know how to do. He refused to be acted upon; he insisted on acting and learning.

While this was happening, I met two missionaries in another part of the world. They were facing a very similar situation. I asked the senior companion how he was handling it. He said he was spending a lot of time riding around his area getting to know the geography. He was practicing work avoidance and I could understand why he was doing this. It was an ordinary or normal human response.

Yet in situations like this one, the Spirit of Christ usually invites us to do what Shawn did. It invites us to become a person of purpose. It invites us to enter the active state. It invites us to go to work, to begin to row against the current. It invites us to become fully engaged and to move forward doing what we do not know how to do. It invites us to get into a situation where we have to ask, seek, and knock.

Through his actions, Shawn provides a model for us to consider. Please note each step in the process.

- He continually clarified his purpose as a person and as a missionary.
- He started the journey and began seeking.
- He got down on his knees and prayed with real intent and listened for direction.
- He received revelation ("Go to work").
- He went to work in the state of asking.
- As he moved forward in doing what he did not know how to do, he asked himself what he needed to do next. He was "study[ing] it out in [his] mind" (D&C 9:7–9).
- He failed to find anyone yet gained knowledge about how to do what he did not know how to do. As the insights came, he developed a vision for how to work the area.
- By moving forward, he was growing in faith, hope, and charity. He was purifying himself so revelation could come.
- When the door of revelation opened, there was a miracle. Christ provided people to teach. Shawn did not find them; Christ provided them.
- While teaching the two men, Shawn received an endowment of revelatory power and as he taught with the love of God, his investigators changed and he grew in capacity.

The model is a model of acting and not reacting. In the process of acting, we find purification. It is not stagnant but "rolling waters" that tend to purify themselves (D&C 121:33). The Lord pours down "knowledge from heaven" on people when they engage this action process. Blessings follow faithful action. We get heat after we put the log on the fire, not before.

I believe that when we fully extend ourselves in the work, it is often then that God miraculously provides someone who is ready. Over the years, I have heard so many missionaries report home and tell some version of the same story. I call it the "story of the last door" or the "story of one more door." It is a story in which the missionaries reach exhaustion but then go the extra mile. Often it takes the form of knocking on one more door, a door that they do not want to knock on. It is then that they are often miraculously provided with an investigator who is later baptized.

The story is so frequently told that I often wonder if we have the logic of missionary work right. It seems that when baptizing seems impossible, baptisms tend to come by the exercise of extraordinary faith. In the end, Shawn did not find the two men to baptize in the building where he was working so hard. They came from another source. Yet if he was not working so hard, I wonder if the story would have had the same ending. I doubt it. The miracles come "after the trial of your faith" (Ether 12:6; see also 1 Peter 1:7). I think the Lord often provides people after we have demonstrated to ourselves that we are trustworthy, because in the process we are purified.

Let me emphasize one other point. The lessons that we learn from the process of seeking, asking, and knocking stay with us the rest of our life. In the same letter, Shawn wrote about an experience he had as a new elders quorum president. In the process, he again describes moving forward doing what he does not know how to do. Again the outcomes are dramatic. Nephi was willing to "go and do" the things the Lord commanded (1 Nephi 3:7). That eventually led to the crucial statement, "And I was led by the Spirit, not knowing beforehand the things which I should do" (1 Nephi 4:6). When we begin to do this, we have experiences like Shawn had. When we learn by faith, we are transformed and empowered.

I love each one of you.
Be extraordinary in Christ,
President Quinn

Challenge 12

Turning Your Field White

My Dear Fellow Servants,

Across the world on a daily basis, missionaries recite Section 4 of the Doctrine and Covenants. In that section is the following line: "The field is white already to harvest" (4). It suggests that there are people just waiting to get baptized. As a young missionary, this scriptural line began to trouble me. In my assigned areas, it was not obvious that the field was white and all ready to harvest. I began to think that either there was something wrong with me or with the scripture. You may have similar feelings.

In this letter, I will offer an entirely new interpretation of this scripture. I will begin with a story about Travis in the later stages of his mission. He evolved and became so confident that he expected to baptize everyone. I will also include a story of Kristin teaching with similar confidence and power. Then I will turn to Jesus teaching the woman at the well. From their two stories and the experience of Jesus, we will learn something that will entirely change our perspective on the above line of scripture. It has the potential to greatly alter your mission and your life.

The purpose of chapter nine of *Preach My Gospel* is to "strengthen your faith that the Lord is preparing people to receive you and the restored gospel." Among other things, the introduction states:

- "He will lead you to them or He will lead them to you."
- "You are to build up the Church by finding 'them that will receive you' (D&C 42:8)."

- "Such people will recognize that you are the Lord's servants.
  They will be willing to act on your message. Many of these
  people have been 'kept from the truth [only] because they
  know not where to find it' (D&C 123:12)."

Is it wise to believe such promises?

In a previous letter, I quoted Travis, who wrote of a new orientation. He was beginning to grow confident in God, and he was starting to hold himself to new levels of accountability. In the weeks that
followed, this theme intensified. One week he wrote something that
particularly caught my attention. Please read his words very carefully:

> I had another insight this week. I realized that I have learned a very
> valuable lesson on my mission. I have learned that everything is pos-
> sible with the help of the Lord. This has become the theme of my
> mission. I now expect that every person I talk to will get baptized. I
> expect every missionary I work with to be converted. I expect mem-
> bers to want to give referrals. The reason I expect it is because the
> Lord expects it. If he expects it, it will happen. I just have to be the
> instrument.
>
> Now this is where I've really changed. If something doesn't
> happen the way I expect it to, I immediately look at myself. I have
> found that I very rarely make an excuse anymore. Instead I leave a
> situation and say: "She didn't commit to baptism; what am I doing
> wrong?" I realized this with a family the other night. I don't blame
> them for not getting baptized. Once they do I will know that I was
> the pure instrument that I needed to be. I think this may be the best
> trait I've picked up.

His words are so important that we need to examine each point
that he made:

- Travis believed that everything was possible with the help of
  the Lord.
- This belief became a central theme in his mind.
- He held the unusual expectation that everyone would be
  baptized.
- He expected that every missionary would be converted.
- He expected members to want to give referrals.
- Because the Lord expected these things, they would happen, if
  Travis was an effective instrument.

- If one of his expectations was not met, he did not make excuses; he looked at himself, and sought to identify what he did wrong.
- This new orientation was the best trait he picked up on his mission.

When we read that the "field is white already to harvest" (D&C 4:4), we interpret it to mean that the Lord is doing the work to prepare people and all we have to do is knock on doors and find them. Like Travis, we become exposed to a more complex and more powerful view of how the field becomes white and ready to harvest.

Like Travis, Kristin also reported operating at a higher level. Kristin told of teaching a couple in a troubled marriage. Kristin and her companion prayed for them all week. During the discussion, Kristin was praying that something special would happen that the Lord would give her the words she needed. She then said, "I let them finish and then I opened my mouth. When I first started it was me talking. Slowly God took over. I do not mean that in the same sense as I have used it before. I mean slowly, God actually took over. These were not my words."

In Kristin's letter, she went on to share the actual words that she uttered. She indicated that she:

- Uttered bold words that challenged the excuses of the investigators.
- Explained the role of faith and the need to overcome the world and live in peace.
- Expressed love.
- Provided a challenge to pray.

As she said these things, the power of God permeated the room. She said it was the most powerful she ever felt.

Afterwards a number of things happened. When they reached the street, Kristin broke down crying and she and her companion offered another prayer for the couple. When God begins to speak through us, we see people differently. We love them as God loves them. We become like Nephi, and "[our] eyes water [our] pillow" for them (2 Nephi 33:3). We yearn for their spiritual well-being and we begin to suffer over them.

Then Kristin said, "Every time we talk about what happened, we learn something new from the experience and realize just how powerful it was." When God actually takes over, it means we are seeing people as God sees them, we are speaking to them as God speaks, and we have desires for then that God has. This experience is an experience of "pure knowledge, which shall greatly enlarge the soul without hypocrisy, and without guile" (D&C 121:42). Such revelation is intense. We continue to unpack its meaning and learn from it for the rest of our lives.

The Spirit stayed with Kristin for days. She said,

> I honestly feel like a new person. I do not know if I have ever felt so humbled in my whole life. I really do not know how the Lord used me to do that. I have been struggling my whole mission to be a pure conduit for Him and I still have far to go. I do not know if I have ever felt so small in my whole life.

Moses spoke to God face to face. He was shown the entire world. After the vision, he fell to the ground and took hours to recover. When he did, his first words were, "I know that man is nothing, which thing I never had supposed" (Moses 1:10). When we teach with the power of God, our perspective is altered. Our ego is no longer the center of the universe. We no longer crave the honors of men. We begin to see as God sees.

Upon further reflection, Kristin realized that she had been praying for help. She wrote, "I did call upon the powers of heaven. That is what prayer is. I called upon the powers of heaven." Kristin had purified herself and in the service of others and she pled for divine intervention. The divine intervention came.

When we are on a mission, we tend to pray continually. Often it appears that nothing happens. Then we reach a certain point and our prayers start to get answered more frequently and more dramatically. Why is this? Did God change or did we? As we become increasingly purified and focused on others, we change and our prayers change. Just as she reported above, Kristin was becoming confident in the presence of God. She was becoming confident in calling down the powers of heaven.

When missionaries become confident about their ability to move into the presence of God and teach with the power of God, they change. It is natural for a missionary to bemoan the bad area in which no one has any interest in the gospel. It is accurate that areas can differ and some are much harder than are others. Some entire missions, for example, can be much harder than others. Yet the confident missionary tends to go into a "bad" area and has more impact than other missionaries. He or she creates interest. Soon there are more good things happening than normally do not occur in that "bad" area. Reaching the uninterested person is a big part of the challenge.

Teaching, No Greater Call contains material on "interesting the uninterested." The discussion focuses on Jesus and the woman at the well. Jesus was traveling through Samaria and sat down by Jacob's well. The Jews and the people of Samaria were not on good terms. An uninterested and probably very distrustful woman came to the well. Jesus boldly intruded into her life: "Give me to drink" (John 4:7).

Why did Jesus do this? He did it because he wanted to start a relationship. His statement was a pebble in her mental pond. It was intended to disrupt and bring a reaction. He did not know what the reaction would be, only that there would be one. That is all He needed, because He had unconditional confidence that He could move the conversation to a higher level.

The woman expressed what appears to be some offense. She asked why a Jew would ask such a thing. How did Jesus answer this question? He did not. He violated the expectation of an answer. Instead he said, "If thou knewest the gift of God and who it is that saith to thee, Give me to drink; thou wouldest have asked of him, and he would have given thee living water" (John 4:10).

Now notice the shift. Jesus not only avoided the expectation of an answer; He further disrupted her expectations. He implied that He is someone special and suggested that He can do extraordinary things. This meant that the conversation would likely take a more intimate turn. This conversation was not going to be about the weather or about sports. It was going to become more meaningful. Jesus had structured the situation so that the conversation might move to a deeper level. He accomplished all this with a single statement.

The woman, however, questioned his ability and authority. She pointed out that He had no tool with which to draw, and asked if He is greater than their father Jacob who dug the well. On the surface this response was saying, "I am ready to challenge you." At a deeper level, it was saying, "I am interested in challenging you because you seem different and I want to find out if you have anything valuable to say." Jesus next made a bold claim about His living water. She, in essence, said, "Fine, give me some." She was basically telling him to "put up or shut up."

Since Jesus had no liquid substance to give her, he had to move the conversation to a still different focus. He did this by replacing her request with a request of his own. He told her to go get her husband. She said she had none. (Notice how his request overrode hers. She did not go back to the request for water but responded to the new request. When we ask questions, they become powerful tools for shaping conversations.) Next Jesus told her she had five husbands. This prophetic statement stunned her and she perceived that He was a prophet. It was a bold stroke that had a transforming effect. She was now very ready to listen. Later, this once uninterested person went into the village and testified of Him.

Most readers get to this part where he tells her that she has five husbands and they then psychologically distance themselves from the story. They see a supernatural act and they assume Jesus could do that but they cannot. This is a big mistake. In the above case, Kristin claims, "I let them finish and then I opened my mouth. When I first started it was me talking. Slowly God took over. I do not mean that in the same sense as I have used it before. I mean slowly, God actually took over. These were not my words." As missionaries, you may be able to identify a few times when you have said inspired things during an important point in a discussion. When that happens, you are being "given" what you should say "in the very hour" (D&C 84:85).

You might respond, "Yes, but not like the prophetic statement Jesus made." Actually, they are like the statement Jesus made. Perhaps they are not as strong, but they are from the same source. This gift of revelation can increase in frequency and in strength. Travis and Kristin have provided numerous examples in previous letters. What we need to do is call on it more and more. If we do, our confidence will grow.

When I consider the story of Jesus and the Samaritan woman, I recall a story that took place when I was a young missionary. I had developed the same kind of confidence that Travis writes about at the start of this letter. I expected everyone to be baptized. In my area, there was a young woman who lived with some members. She had a strong personality and she had expressed opinions against the Church. The people around her made it a point not to discuss Church-related issues.

One day, she was standing near us. I started a conversation by asking her something challenging. I no longer remember the exact words. Yet the tone was like the conversation Jesus had at the well ("Give me to drink."). Like the woman of Samaria, she responded with a challenge of her own. Towards the end, I became bold and told her she needed to take the discussions. She matched my boldness, indicating that she would not take the discussions. I told her I would meet her in that same spot on Thursday afternoon at 4:00 PM. She said "no way." I said, "You can stand me up if you want but I want you to know that I will be here waiting for you." I then took out my appointment book and wrote the time down and walked away.

My companion later told me the conversation was a waste of time. She would not show up. I told him I was certain she would show up. I knew that despite all her strong statements, she had interest.

Like the conversation at Jacob's well, communication was happening at two levels. On the surface, we were challenging each other. Below the surface, we were getting to know each other, forming a relationship. In saying the things that I said, I was creating an excuse for her to show up. I was confident that she would; I was even confident that we would baptize her. I could see it and feel it.

Two days later I was transferred. I last thing I told my companion was that he had to be sure to be in that spot on Thursday. He again said it was a waste of time. I made a big deal of it. He said "OK." On Friday, I got a call from the people the young woman lived with. They were furious because she went to the place and we were not there. She told them she would never talk to another missionary. I was deeply upset. Sometime later I was able to seek her out and explain what had happened. It was too late. The window had closed. She was in a different place. Forty-five years later I still believe she would have been baptized if the missionaries had had the confidence to show up.

The story has an unhappy ending, but I think it illustrates a key point. We can have conversations like Jesus did at the well. Such conversations require confidence. As we grow in our faith, we can acquire the kind of confidence illustrated by Travis, by Kristin, and by Jesus.

There is one more thing to know about the story of Jesus and the woman at the well. As the initially uninterested woman left the well and went into the village to testify of Jesus, the disciples arrived. Perhaps pointing to the woman, Jesus taught them a very important concept: "Lift up your eyes, and look on the fields; for they are white already to harvest" (John 4:35).

This is a lesson for every missionary who lacks faith in the promises of chapter nine in *Preach My Gospel*. The field became white and ready to harvest because Jesus sought out an uninterested investigator. He then, in a very short conversation, plowed the field, planted the seed, and nurtured its growth. Because he taught with the power of God, the barren field became white and ready to harvest.

As we begin to gain faith in God, we will begin to see that the readiness of our field is a function of who we are. The whiteness comes from holding ourselves accountable to the expectations of God. When people do not respond to the expectations of God, we hold ourselves accountable and use the experience to discover the changes we must make for God's will to unfold. It is an orientation of high personal responsibility. As we gain the orientation described by Travis, we are more likely to speak with the power described by Kristin. As we do so, we will become further purified and gain increased faith and exercise more personal accountability. As we do, our field will become white and ready to harvest.

I love each one of you.
Be extraordinary in Christ,
President Quinn

Challenge 13

WRITING THE THINGS OF THE SPIRIT

My Dear Fellow Servants,

The challenge in this letter is illustrated by an experience. We once had a pair of relatively new missionaries come to our home for regular dinner appointments. These were two impressive young men who were diligent and sincere. In compliance with a mission program, they asked if they could teach us the discussions for practice purposes. We agreed. We played the role of honest investigators and therefore asked hard but fair questions about the basic things they were teaching. When we reached the end of the lesson, they taught us that investigators are converted when they feel the Spirit. They tried to explain. We asked questions. They greatly struggled. In my role as an honest investigator, I was greatly troubled by the inconsistency. I thought, "If the Spirit is the very key to my conversion, why can't these two missionaries help me understand and feel this thing they call the Spirit?"

Afterwards they asked for feedback. I raised my concern in a kind way and they were interested in exploring it. I suggested that if they wanted me to understand the Spirit, the answer was not for them to *tell* me about it. The answer was for them to teach with the Spirit in such an unmistakable way that I could *feel* the Spirit. They could then teach me to recognize what I was feeling. They asked how they could best learn to teach with the Spirit. I suggested that the process begins in daily study. Study should not be passive; it has to have purpose or real intent. What might that purpose be? It might be an effort to become experts in the process of feeling and pondering the Spirit.

If we become experts in the art of feeling and pondering, then we can become more expert in teaching with the Spirit. As we invite and testify with conviction, we can expect the Spirit to confirm our words. We can then call attention to the Spirit and teach people what it is that we want them to seek so that they can move closer to Jesus Christ. In other words, we must learn to do what it is we ask our investigators to do: focus our hearts and minds on the Spirit of God.

The first personal study box in chapter two of *Preach My Gospel* turns our attention to Joseph Smith. It asks how his reading and pondering of James 1:5 led to the receipt of revelation. That verse in James indicates that if we lack wisdom, we should ask of God. Joseph then writes,

> Never did any passage of scripture come with more power to the heart of man than this did at this time to mine. It seemed to enter with great force into every feeling of my heart. I reflected on it again and again, knowing that if any person needed wisdom from God, I did; for how to act I did not know, and unless I could get more wisdom than I then had, I would never know; for the teachers of religion of the different sects understood the same passages of scripture so differently as to destroy all confidence in settling the question by an appeal to the Bible.
>
> At length I came to the conclusion that I must either remain in darkness and confusion, or else I must do as James directs, that is, ask of God. I at length came to the determination to 'ask of God,' concluding that if he gave wisdom to them that lacked wisdom, and would give liberally, and not upbraid, I might venture." (Joseph Smith—History 1:12–13)

This passage suggests that Joseph had a purpose. He read the Bible with real intent; that is, he hungered to understand what it was that he should do. As Joseph read the verse in James, an experience occurred. It was an emotional reaction. It was something that Joseph could *feel* in his heart. Once he had this feeling, then his mind was drawn back to the verse "again and again."

The emotional reaction was something we call the prompting of the Spirit. We speak of *feeling* the Spirit. The process of having his mind drawn back again and again is called pondering. Pondering is deeply focused contemplation. When we have real intent, when our mind is deeply focused on the written word of God, we tend to *feel* the promptings of the Spirit, and we have an enlightening experience with the scriptures. In such experiences, we are guided by the "still small voice" (see 1 Kings 19:12; D&C 85:6; 1 Nephi 17:45). The still small voice usually helps us come to some kind of understanding or conclusion. *Preach My Gospel* suggests that we need to become experts in the art of pondering. Doing so will help us to teach with conviction and declare the truth with power.

In this case, Joseph's conclusion was that he should venture forth to pray. Years later, he still remembered this episode with the Spirit because it had become one of his "core experiences." A core experience is a very important event in our lives, one of deep meaning, an experience that helps to define who we are. The above event was a core experience in the life of Joseph, and even years later, he could write the story and do so with great conviction. Long after it happened and was recorded, many of us read the story and we feel the conviction of Joseph. When we read or hear someone's core story, we may also feel the same still small voice witnessing that the story is true. If this happens, it means we are now having an experience of our own. We are having an episode with the Spirit. The original experience or story becomes part of our core story. We can now bear testimony of the spiritual impact of the original story in our own life. Telling our personal story with conviction may then lead to the repeating of the entire process in the life of someone else.

Elder Richard G. Scott of the Quorum of the Twelve explained how to bring the Spirit into our lives. He indicated that in life we learn by hearing, seeing, and feeling. Yet most people pay attention to what they learn by hearing, seeing, and thinking—not by what they feel. He further suggested that there is a link between learning from what we feel and writing down what we feel. Please read and carefully consider each important sentence. This is advice that can change our lives:

> You can learn vitally important things by what you hear and see and especially by what you feel, as prompted by the Holy Ghost. Most individuals limit their learning primarily to what they hear or what they read. Be wise. Develop the skill of learning by what you see and particularly by what the Holy Ghost prompts you to feel. Consciously seek to learn by what you see and feel, and your capacity to do so will expand through consistent practice. Ask in faith for such

help. Live to be worthy of it. Seek to recognize it. Write down in a secure place the important things you learn from the Spirit. You will find that as you write down precious impressions, often more will come. Also, the knowledge you gain will be available throughout your life. Always, day or night, wherever you are, whatever you are doing, seek to recognize and respond to the direction of the Spirit. Express gratitude for the help received and obey it. This practice will reinforce your capacity to learn by the Spirit. It will permit the Lord to guide your life and to enrich the use of every other capacity latent in your being.[21]

Elder Scott told us four things that we should do:

1. We should switch our way of learning. We should learn how to learn differently, develop the skill to think about feeling, and become conscious of the Spirit.

2. We should live in a way (asking, being worthy, and recognizing) that increases the likelihood that we will have feelings of the Spirit.

3. We should write what we learn from the Spirit so we will have even more experiences with the Spirit.

4. We should train ourselves to, at all times and in all places, recognize and respond to the Spirit so we can learn more, be enriched of the Lord, and have every other capacity enlarged.

I invite you to become disciplined in the above skill. I invite you to make a daily record of your experiences with the Spirit. I invite you to then make a weekly abridgement of your daily record and write a letter home that conveys the most important things the Lord has taught you this week. There are three reasons for doing this. First, it will help you move your family closer to Christ. Second, it will move you closer to Christ. Third, because you are closer to Christ, you will become more effective in finding and teaching.

Consider a final statement. It comes from my son Ryan, who testifies of the power of pondering and writing as a returned missionary. Notice his claim at the very end:

> The other key to reading the scriptures (including the letters we send) with power is pondering. Many of the most important revelations in all the world came after a person pondered (e.g., Nephi's vision in 1 Nephi 11–14; Joseph Smith's vision of the three degrees of glory in

D&C 76; Joseph F. Smith's vision of the spirit world in D&C 138). President Howard W. Hunter said that we should not read a certain number of scriptures (such as a chapter) every day, but that we should read for a certain amount of time every day. Why? Because it may be more important to read a single verse and ponder deeply about its import than to read a whole chapter of scripture.

I have had many powerful experiences and spiritual insights from pondering. This is one reason why keeping a regular journal has had such impact on my life. It forces me to ponder. I have pages of journal entries that catalog my deep scriptural thoughts. I never write in my journal anymore without having revelation, at the most, or deep gratitude to my Heavenly Father for my countless blessings, at the least.

The claim that when he writes he has revelation is important. When a missionary learns to study revelation, have revelation, and write revelation, the missionary is intimate with the Spirit. Such a missionary can then teach by revelation. They can speak of scriptures and of personal experiences with the Spirit. As they do, the Spirit will testify and investigators will feel the Spirit. We can then call attention to the Spirit and teach people what it is that we want them to seek so that they can move closer to Jesus Christ.

I love each one of you.

Be extraordinary in Christ,

President Quinn

Challenge 14

HUNGERING FOR IMPROVEMENT

My Dear Fellow Servants,

Some missionaries arrive with a wonderful characteristic. They desire to be obedient. They will try and do whatever the Lord wants them to do. Yet this wonderful attribute does not necessarily bring success. Obediently following is crucial but not enough. The challenge is to obey, to do, to ponder, to learn, and to improve. In this letter, I will discuss acquiring the hunger to improve and how it alters our life.

On page ten of *Preach My Gospel* is a discussion of success. In the list of successful characteristics is this statement: "Work effectively every day, do your best to bring souls to Christ, and seek earnestly to learn and improve." On page two, it states that as our understanding of the Atonement grows, our desire to teach the gospel will increase, and we will feel the "great importance to make these things known unto the inhabitants of the earth" (2 Nephi 2:8). As missionaries feel this intensified desire to teach, something else also happens. They hunger to become more effective in their finding and teaching.

As a mission president, this has become so important to me that I have often told you that our purpose is not simply to "invite people to Christ." Our purpose is to *"ever more effectively* invite people to Christ." Every day, our prayers, our study, our finding, and our teaching need to be better than the day before. For this to happen to me, I need think about my purpose and continually examine every practice. Each day, I need to try new experiments and observe the results. If I learn to do this as a missionary, I become skilled in the process of constant repentance. Consider an illustration of a missionary learning this skill.

When she was in the MTC, my daughter Kristin wrote the following paragraph as part of one of her letters home:

> My life has changed. Remember the talks I had with Hermana (Sister) Hansen last week about repentance and listening to the Holy Ghost? I've been trying to apply the lessons I learned to my life and WOW. What a difference! Last night we had a gospel study on repentance and I realized (also, after reading Shawn's letter) how everything comes back to repentance. The way you gain humility, love, charity, faith, and anything is by constantly repenting.
>
> I never realized how much I have to repent for. Sometimes I just do the STUPIDEST things. What am I thinking? I know what's right and what's wrong, but I do it anyway. I'm just grateful that I recognize things now. Before I came here, certain things just didn't seem all that bad—especially telling little lies here and there. Now I realize those are the dumbest ones. Why sacrifice so much for a stupid lie that doesn't make that much of a difference anyway? This is not to say that I don't ever do it, but I'm doing my best to change that and work with the Lord to do so. Through Him, anything is possible. Sometimes it hurts to get there, but IT IS SO WORTH IT. I would pay any price to be in good standing with the Lord.

After declaring that her life had changed, this new missionary made several key points. First, everything comes back to repentance or the need to make continuous positive change. Second, we gain godly characteristics through repentance. Third, we all continually make mistakes. Fourth, as we move closer to Christ, little things that we use to rationalize away now require repentance. Our progress increases our accountability. Fifth, in engaging the challenging process of repentance, we need the help of the Lord ("through Him, anything is possible"). Finally, a missionary who repents feels blessed and rejoices in the Lord. Such a missionary feels willing to pay "any price" to be in "good standing with the Lord."

Now here is an important point: a missionary who hungers to be in good standing with the Lord is a missionary who is fully engaged. A missionary who is fully engaged is also fully challenged and is becoming something more than he or she is at the moment. Over time, a person who lives a life of faith and repentance learns how to live a life of reflective learning. I will explain what this means, but first, consider a story that contrasts with the above story.

At the end of my mission, I was in a leadership position, and I tried to help a missionary who was having some trouble being effective. Because missionary work is hard, he tried to avoid it. He went about wasting time in a number of pursuits that were unrelated to missionary work. He often made the following statement: "I could be a good missionary if I really wanted to; I just don't want to." As his missionary leader, I worked hard to establish a positive relationship while I also challenged him to take charge of himself, to make a commitment to live the rules, to work hard, and become a more effective teacher. In essence, I was inviting him to repentance and more complete conversion. He seriously contemplated this challenge but instead of accepting it, he found a number of new excuses. I suggested that we fast together and have another meeting.

At the end of the fast, we again met. The discussion was long and serious. He was more sensitive than I had ever seen him. After a long exploration, the question of commitment again moved to the forefront. I asked him to commit. He sat quietly for several minutes. I also sat quietly and waited. I could see him anguishing as he contemplated the decision regarding a full commitment to the Lord. Finally he began to cry. He looked up and he asked, "Elder, what if I try with all my might and I fail?"

The missionary's final question provides a powerful insight. He was full of fear. His rationalizations and self-deceptions were mechanisms for covering his fear. The thing he feared was failure. Because he was afraid of failure, he was afraid to commit. He was afraid that if he tried and failed, he might discover that the person living inside his body was a loser, a zero, a worthless entity. Because of this fear, he did not act. It seemed safer to him to say "I could if I wanted to" than to try and thus prove to himself that he could not.

Now note this important point. Meaningful living orbits around the notion of eternal progression, and eternal progression orbits around the principle of faith. The fear of failure at one level often causes us to fail at many levels. We cannot stand still. At any moment, we are either moving closer to Christ or we are moving away (see 2 Nephi 28:30). As missionaries, if we seek to avoid doing the hard work because we fear that we might fail, or because of any other fear, we guarantee descending into a life of inaction, stagnation, and boredom.

Boredom is a condition in which we feel a lack of interest and easily become weary. Even fully engaged missionaries will find themselves having to do seemingly boring tasks that are not challenging. In fact, a mission can be full of repetitive tasks.

The opposite of boredom is a sense of challenge and engagement. Over time, a person who lives a life of faith and repentance learns how to live a life of challenge. This is true because a person who lives a life of faith and repentance internalizes his or her purpose and begins to live from that purpose. A person who does this finds the power to create their own sense of challenge and growth.

By way of illustration, consider a story about a factory worker reported in a book by a prominent psychologist:

> One of the clearest examples I have ever seen was when I did research in a factory where audiovisual equipment was being assembled on a production line. Most of the workers on the line were bored and looked down on their job as something beneath them. Then I met Rico, who had a completely different take on what he was doing. He actually thought his job was difficult, and that it took great skill to do it. It turned out he was right. Although he had to do the same sort of boring task as everyone else, he had trained himself to do it with the economy and the elegance of a virtuoso. About four hundred times each day a movie camera would stop at his station, and Rico had forty-three seconds to check out whether the sound system met specifications. Over a period of years experimenting with tools and patterns of motion, he had been able to reduce the average time it took him to check each camera to twenty-eight seconds. He was as proud of this accomplishment as an Olympic athlete would be if, after the same number of years spent preparing, he could break the forty-four second mark in the 400-meter sprint. Rico did not get a medal for his record, and reducing the time to do his job did not improve production, because the line still kept moving at the old speed. But he loved the exhilaration of using his skills fully: "It's better than anything else—a whole lot better than watching TV." And because he sensed that he was getting close to his limit in the present job, he was taking evening courses for a diploma that would open up new options for him in electronics engineering.[22]

As a factory worker, Rico was not ordinary. He had internalized a sense of purpose and his life was going somewhere. No matter what context he was in, no matter what the others were doing, he made the choice to learn and grow. If Rico had been a Mormon missionary, what would have happened to his prayers, his study, his finding, his teaching, and his relationships with members? Every day he would have more successfully invited people to Christ because every day he would have been better than the day before.

The researcher who wrote the above story tells us that when we live from an internalized purpose, we refuse to be bored because we do two things others do not do. First, we take accountability for ourselves. We recognize that we determine our own freedom and growth. Second, we take whatever task is not challenging and we reinvent it so that it is challenging. If, for example, we are bored when we have to cut the grass, we can ask, "How can I turn this into a challenge? How can I cut the grass better than it has ever been cut in half the time it has ever been cut?" These questions would reinvent the task.

Now think about applying this same principle to missionary work. Here are two examples. First, my wife, Delsa, often tells of her missionary days with her favorite companion. When they were out finding, they often had long, boring periods walking between distant houses. Instead of being bored, they took accountability and they reinvented the task. As they walked down the street, they made up songs about the scriptures they were trying to memorize. Suddenly, the wasted time became productive time. They were making themselves more effective. They were also creating positive feelings about themselves and each other. After all these years, Delsa speaks of that companion as her favorite companion.

The second example comes from Travis. He also thought the finding process was boring. Travis was easily bored and he hated being bored. So, instead of complaining, he took accountability and he reinvented the task. Travis described inventing the game of missionary baseball. He designed the game so that he plays against Satan. A rejection was an out, a conversation was a single, a callback a double, an appointment a triple, and a discussion a homerun. Travis, who hates to lose, said he particularly hated to lose to Satan and so kept going and trying harder until he won.

As missionaries, we may find a task like finding boring, but we may reinvent that task around some personal challenge such as these:

- "Today I will talk to twenty people and in every case I will say something unique and different."
- "Today I will talk to twenty people and seek the Spirit to guide every conversation. I will then write down what the Spirit taught me."
- "Today I will contact more people than I have ever before contacted."
- "Today I will challenge myself to see if there is a way to have a meaningful discussion with one hundred people."
- "Today I will go to the mall and ask twenty people when it is that they experience God."

The point is that we never have to be bored. If we take accountability ("I am bored only because I allow myself to be bored") and we take charge of our tasks, we can live a life that is more fully engaged.

As we repent and embrace the Atonement, our desires will change. Not only will we hunger to teach, we will hunger to be an ever more effective missionary. Our orientation to learning will change. Our life will change. We will progress at an ever-increasing rate.

I love each one of you.

Be extraordinary in Christ,

President Quinn

Challenge 15

My Dear Fellow Servants,

In chapter two of *Preach My Gospel*, we consider what it means to study effectively. When we think of study, we often think of what we did when we were in school. Often study meant reading a book, remembering what was in it, and then taking a test. We did this for so many years that when we come on a mission, we fully believe that what we did in school is the study process we should follow in the mission. It is not! The approach we learned in school is quite passive, and it only involves the mind.

Jesus, in contrast, taught a much more active notion of study and learning: "If ye continue in my word, then ye are my disciples indeed; and ye shall know the truth, and the truth shall make you free" (John 8:31–32).

When we live the doctrines of Christ, we move closer to Christ. As we become more alive in Christ, we are enlightened and we become free of darkness and error. God's approach to study and learning is not passive and head-based. It is active; it is about doing. When we move forward in faith, we change our own heart. When we act so as to elevate our feelings, we automatically elevate our minds. *Preach My Gospel* teaches us to get into this active mode of learning. On page 19 of *Preach My Gospel* is a discussion of living what we learn. It puts an emphasis on the notion of application. It tells us that as we come to understand and live new principles, our faith, knowledge, and testimony will increase. It states, "Acting on what you have learned will bring added and enduring understanding."

My son Ryan once wrote to Kristin and Travis and discussed the concept of application. He referred to a letter I had written about study, writing, and power. He began his discussion of application by telling them of a pattern he observed among missionaries in regards to the Missionary Guide that used to be what *Preach My Gospel* is today. Here is what he said:

> Application takes enormous faith, but it has enormous power. And it is not only the key to understanding the letters you'll receive, but also to understanding the Missionary Guide and the scriptures. At the end of every section of the Missionary Guide, there is a challenge for missionaries to set specific goals to practice the skill for the day in their proselytizing. Missionaries all over the world uniformly ignore the challenge and therefore miss out on the most important part of their study session. And scripture teaches us with the most power only when we apply it. This is why Joseph Smith said that the Book of Mormon is "the keystone of our religion and a man will get nearer to God by abiding by its principles than by any other book." (Introduction)

I am quite taken by his observation that missionaries all over the world skipped the application part. This means they preferred the passive to the active mode of study. It means that it is normal or ordinary to study the way the world taught us to study. Someone who takes application seriously is an extraordinary servant of Christ. The person is extraordinary because application involves agony.

One week, both Kristin and Travis wrote of trying to understand and apply the doctrines of Christ. In their accounts, we find a strange blend of agony and ecstasy. Kristin wrote a letter that was full of agony. She indicated that she was trying to comply with the greater emphasis that her leaders were placing on working with members. She then said that working with members was hard. It did not seem to produce results. She didn't know what she could do to make the process more effective. Nevertheless, she and her companion obediently stopped at each member's home and had prayer. She reported that it was a good experience, but she felt like she was not really working effectively and was therefore not complying with a directive from President Hinckley to double baptisms.

Kristin also described a specific disappointment. She was very focused on a particular family of investigators, and she described praying fervently and then going to teach the family. The family was not there for the appointment. Kristin then described her extreme pain. In all of this, she made it clear that taking the role of a missionary seriously "is a very, very painful thing."

That same week, Travis wrote of listening to a lesson given by his leaders. It was about the Atonement. Each missionary was asked to pray about what they needed to change. Travis said he did and he got an answer but already knew what his problems were:

> The Spirit is all over me when I do things wrong. I made a list of nine things. Some were honors of men, impure motives, not loving missionaries, comparing myself to others, light-mindedness, etc. I have found that I am always seeking the honors of men, and also I do not always stand up to others on what is right. I do not always correct with love. The list goes on.

Here again, we see agony. On a mission, we tend to experience much agony. Given this fact, it is quite curious to read what Kristin wrote after telling us of her pain. She said that in testimony meeting she stood up and told her peers that she loves being a missionary. She has done this so often and with such enthusiasm that one of the other missionaries asked, "But Hermana, why do you love it so much?" Kristin reflected on this. She said she suspected that it was because she had never grown so much as she had in the mission. When we do hard things for Christ, our agony is consecrated for our benefit, and we grow. When we do the hard things of righteousness, we experience the joy of being more righteous, more like God.

Travis told an interesting story about doing hard things. First, he indicated that his new mission president had explained the vision the president has for the mission. Travis was very taken by the president's vision. He then wrote a statement that reflects the same agonizing work and the same joy described by Kristin. Travis wrote:

> I fell in love with the vision. For the next two nights, I struggled with sleep. I was so excited about this vision. I prayed deeply for forgiveness of sins and an understanding of the vision. I felt I should also live it. I love it. I have been more obedient, had honest prayer, and

done my best. I now feel clean as I wake up, I have powerful morning studies, and my day is great. Now I am praying for help to implement "the vision" into my zone.

We had six investigators at church. Everything is so great. I can only see our area going forward. I never want to leave. I feel so close to my Father in Heaven. I love him. I love this work. My testimony grows each time I see someone find happiness through it.

A few days later, Travis asked the president how he could implement the vision in his zone. The president said that Travis could answer that better than he could because Travis had the right to revelation for his zone. This was the answer of an inspired president. He expected the zone leader to get revelation for his zone. Travis said that the president then explained something else. He talked about being clean. The president wanted the missionaries to be clean so they could do "hard things."

What hard things did the president want them to do? He wanted them to think! More specifically, he wanted them to think and plan by the Spirit. He said that missionaries think tracting is hard, but thinking of better things to do is harder. The president was saying that it is easier to fall into a routine that does not work and stay in that ineffective routine than it is to seek revelation and find more effective ways to do the work.

The mission president was saying that we need to do the hardest kind of study. We need to deeply examine everything we do. We need to be focused on the result we seek to create. We need to critically assess the effectiveness of our every act. We need to think of alternative patterns. We need to experiment with ways to become more effective. We need to think and plan by the Spirit. This is a hard thing. The president went on to say that the Book of Mormon is a journal of people doing hard things. He wanted his missionaries to have a journal full of doing hard things.

The same week that their letters came, I was asked to attend a meeting with a regional leader and five stake presidencies. They were also concerned with President Hinckley's challenge to double baptisms. The meeting had a very positive tone. We began in the scriptures and we returned to them often. We talked of dramatically increasing baptisms. Then we turned to administrative issues, like the process of confirming people in sacrament meetings. There was much discussion of sharpening up this procedure or that one. I was very troubled. Making small improvements in what we already know how to do is a good thing. It is also a comfortable thing. It struck me that making minor improvements in existing procedures was not going to double baptisms. Trying not to be disruptive, I said, "I am not sure if it is appropriate for me to do this, but I would like to challenge how we are thinking." They were very positive and invited me to share my thoughts. I said, "The request to double baptisms is a request for a radical result. It is like the CEO of a company standing up and saying, 'Let's double profits.' Who can argue against such a worthy goal? The problem is that radical improvements in results require radical changes in behavior. In corporations, we tend to listen to such challenges and then go back to our desks and do what we have always done in the past. The result is that nothing happens.

"At this meeting, I have heard a number of incremental proposals. We are suggesting that we need to do a better job at what we already know how to do. In others words, we want to continue doing what we have been doing, but we just want to do it a little better. That is good but it is not enough. We are hoping for different outcomes while doing what we have always done in the past. It will not result in doubling baptisms.

"The only way to get radical outcomes is to engage in radical or new behaviors that come from Christ. Doing such things is always hard, painful, or expensive. It is hard to think and behave in a new way. It is painful because if it really is radical, it means something that we do not know how to do. It means learning by faith. It means leaving our routines. Usually, it doesn't happen, because we are not committed enough to learn our way into a new way of being.

"Doubling baptisms is not an ordinary request. It is a radical request. It requires radical change. Yet radical change is a phrase we do not often use in the Church or in any other kind of organization. The word *radical* makes people very uncomfortable because it implies a loss of control.

"Yet we might think about the word *radical*. The word originates with the term root. In algebra, for example, the radical sign tells us to search for the square root. Radical change occurs when we return to the root. In the Church, our root is Jesus Christ. When we return to Jesus Christ, we experience revelation. When we return to the root through revelation, a radical change occurs in our awareness, our level of commitment, and our behavior. If we are moving closer to Christ, we should be getting ideas on how to do what we do not know how to do." This potentially disruptive statement was taken quite well. We discussed it openly. We agreed that we had much difficult work to do.

What I said to the leaders in that meeting applies to missionaries. Recall that the mission president told Travis that he wanted the missionaries to do a hard thing. He wanted them to think and plan with the Spirit. He wanted to them to return to the root, experience revelation, and thus make radical change. He wanted them to transform themselves by changing their level of cleanliness. He wanted them to move closer to Christ. He wanted them to be engaged in the active mode of study and learning.

I think of an example of this process from years ago when I was a bishop. All the bishops in the region were asked to hold a ward missionary open house. I was drawn to the notion of the open house and spent some time praying about it. I started out by asking, "What result do we want to create?" We wanted lots of investigators to come and we wanted them to experience God.

I went into ward council and asked them if open houses worked. They thought they were supposed to say yes and so they did. I challenged them. After a while we agreed that most open houses were ineffective. At best, they brought in one or two visitors. I asked them if they had ever brought their friends to an open house. Most said no. I then asked them to make an honest list of why.

The list went something like this: we have no motivation; we do not trust the seventies to do a good job (note: there used to be a seventies quorum in each ward that was responsible for missionary work); there is nothing at the open house of value; I might be embarrassed; I worry that the people I invite might be harassed; I do not know how to invite them; the list went on and on. It was clear why open houses did not work. We held them because we were supposed to, but almost no one really intended to invite anyone.

I organized the objections into clusters and then asked the people to envision an open house that transcended the problems. They struggled at first and I tried to help. "What if the event was filled with exciting elements like a terrific dinner and great entertainment with a powerful spiritual twist? What if the whole ward council was responsible and not just the seventies? What if the church building became a visitor's center and each organization was responsible for one room with one display? What if the standard was that when any human entered that room, the person would immediately feel the Holy Ghost? What if the members could not challenge the non-members but only answer questions they asked? What if we did role playing and trained the members on how to invite someone to the open house? I continued to list such possibilities. Soon the council took over the discussion.

A few months later, at the open house, we had 80 non-members. The average for all wards in the region was two non-members. Because we planned under the direction of the Spirit and learned by faith, we developed a new vision and new capacity. A radical change had occurred. Our ward had learned how to hold effective open houses.

This ward council learned to think of better things to do. They were fulfilling their stewardship. For a missionary, the challenge is to think of the missionary's stewardship in a similar way. The challenge for each of us, all the time, is to think of better things to do. Today: How might I pray better? How might I study better? How might I plan and organize better? How might I find better? How might I teach better? How might I work with members better? How might I write in my journal better?

I love each one of you.
Be extraordinary in Christ,
President Quinn

Challenge 16

CONTROLLING THE MIND

My Dear Fellow Servants,

In this letter, we will consider a challenge at the heart of the gospel: how to control the mind and become purified in Christ. We will consider the story of a missionary who desired to be virtuous and see what happened. We will learn how to do something that few people on this earth know how to do.

In chapter six of *Preach My Gospel*, under the heading of virtue, we are given an important message about controlling our thoughts: "Your mind is like a stage in a theater; in the theater of your mind, however, only one actor can be on stage at a time. If the stage is left bare, thoughts of darkness and sin often enter the stage to tempt. But these thoughts have no power if the stage of your mind is occupied by wholesome thoughts, such as a memorized hymn or verses of scriptures that you can call upon in a moment of temptation. By controlling the stage of your mind, you can successfully resist persistent urges to yield to temptation and indulge in sin. You can become pure and virtuous."

In this directive are three key notions. First, we entertain one thought at a time. Second, if we do not control the mind, it will go where nature takes it, along the path of least resistance, and it will often end up in places of darkness. Third, by consciously thinking about spiritual things, we control the mind. We block the path of least resistance and open an upward path to places of light. Since our objective is to move closer to Christ so we can more effectively invite people to

Christ, it is important that we understand the notion of controlling our thoughts.

I once interviewed a missionary as he prepared to leave on his mission. He was so mature and so prepared it was as if he were coming home from his mission. When the interview was over, I asked if he had any questions. He indicated that he did. He said he was most concerned about lustful thoughts. I immediately thought of the above notions from *Preach My Gospel*. I prepared myself to respond to his concern when he surprised me. Before I could speak, he went through all of the above *Preach My Gospel* notions and then he asked, "Is there anything else you can tell me?"

I felt embarrassed because I had nothing else to say. Yet I was deeply moved by the real intent of this magnificent young man. So I offered a little prayer and simply began to talk, hoping that the heavens would take over. They did.

I indicated that my entire adult life I have tried to implement the above discipline so as to control my lustful thoughts. I have had moments of victory. Yet the hormones in my body are powerful and I am surrounded by a culture that constantly communicates sexual cues. The thoughts keep coming back. It sometimes seems discouraging.

Yet over the years, I have begun to notice something about the continuous return of lustful thoughts. Because I have tried so often to fight the battle, it is now relatively natural to fight the battle. That last sentence is very important. It means that, over time, a strange and paradoxical change has occurred in me.

When the natural man has lustful thoughts, the natural reaction is not to fight them but to flow downstream with those thoughts to various points of darkness. Since I have so often tried to fight lustful thoughts, it is natural for me to engage in the struggle. Therefore, the constant reoccurrence of lustful thoughts tends to naturally trigger a positive effort, and that effort puts me into the spiritually active state. It is a state of trying to control my mind. So here is the paradox:

The natural occurrence of lustful thoughts has become a stimulant for spiritual self-elevation. The negative thing—lustful thoughts in this case—has become a positive thing: a stimulant to move closer to God. By taking charge of the mind, we can create patterns of response that are not natural. Yet over time, the righteous response becomes more natural. When this happens, we actually become elevated by that experience that would normally pull us down.

Perhaps this is what the Lord means when He tells us that if we are in the proper condition of mind, "all things wherewith you have been afflicted shall work together for your good" (D&C 98:3). I told my young friend that the point is not to be discouraged by the return of lustful thoughts. The return of these thoughts is biologically and culturally determined. They will come back. The point is to be committed to the continuous battle for the control of our own mind and to rejoice in the fact that every time we fight the battle, we are moving closer to Christ and we are also gaining celestial capacity.

I do not know how much value that young missionary found in my observation. Yet since the time of that conversation, I have given the subject of controlling our thoughts a great deal of thought. I have also, in preparing to be a mission president, had some intense experiences with the living God. As result of the experiences, I have taken an expanded view of the notion of mind control. Here I want to share a new perspective and a new method.

First, note that the concept of controlling your thoughts is often taught by prophets. President David O. McKay stated, "The measure of a man is what he thinks when he does not have to think."[23] President Spencer W. Kimball taught that ordinary people react to their environments. He indicated that we should sometimes use our agency to do the unnatural act of "fighting against the current."[24] As we use our agency in this unnatural fashion, we gain the capacity to become actors rather than reactors, and this capacity allows us to shape what happens.

To me, this means that, like Christ, we become creators of ourselves and of the world in which we find ourselves. By turning our thoughts to Jesus, we experience new feelings and gain the power to create and live in a new world. Filled with the merciful love of Christ, we can be perfect in Christ now (see Moroni 10:32–33). Here I am reminded of the first line of a great hymn: "Jesus, the very thought of Thee / With sweetness fills my breast" (Hymn #141).

Here I want to make an important differentiation. The above paragraph in *Preach My Gospel* speaks of controlling our thoughts. It suggests that we need to learn to think about what we are thinking about. I believe this is correct. Yet I want to expand the perspective. I would like to focus not on the monitoring of our thoughts, but on the monitoring of our feelings. I would like to be clear that thoughts and feelings are different. In society, there is a tendency to denigrate feeling and elevate thinking. There is a tendency to ignore and suppress emotion.

In the scriptures we find a different model: there is a great emphasis on feelings. Charity, or the pure love of Jesus Christ, is often discussed as a concept. Yet the concept is not a fixed thing. Charity is a dynamic, elevated state. It is a state in which both feelings and thoughts are elevated. When we are full of charity, we become Christ-like. As missionaries, it is important that we understand charity.

Joseph F. Smith reported what he felt like at the time of his baptism; it is a wonderful description of what it feels like to live in the love of God:

> The feeling that came upon me was that of pure peace, of love and of light. I felt in my soul that if I had sinned . . . that it had been forgiven me; that I was indeed cleansed from sin; my heart was touched, and I felt that I would not injure the smallest insect beneath my feet. I felt as if I wanted to do good everywhere to everybody and to everything. I felt a newness of life, a newness of desire to do that which was right. There was not one particle of desire for evil left in my soul. . . . This was the influence that came upon me, and I know it was from God, and was and ever has been a living witness to me of my acceptance of the Lord. (*Preach My Gospel*, 222)

This is a wonderful description of what it feels like to live in the love of God. As missionaries, we would all be wise if we reflected on and recorded when we have had such feelings. It would serve two important purposes. First, it would help us clarify the fact that our goal is to move ever closer to Jesus Christ so as to more effectively invite people to bathe in the love of God. Second, being able to describe and model the feeling would make us more effective in extending the invitation.

In modern revelation, we are directed to be filled with charity and to "let virtue garnish [our] thoughts unceasingly" (D&C 121:45). When we feel the pure love of Christ, our thoughts are automatically virtuous. Because our feelings are positive, our minds open to the light of revelation and we are filled with "pure knowledge," which greatly enlarges the soul "without hypocrisy and without guile" (D&C 121:42). Our new, positive thoughts then trigger more positive feelings, which further trigger positive feelings and so on.

In the scriptures, we learn that the Light of Christ operates through the realm of feeling. The Holy Ghost does the same (see, for example, Galatians 5:22–23). Feeling is critical. Laman and Lemuel, for example, were told, "ye were past feeling, that ye could not feel his words" (1 Nephi 17:45). It is important to realize that *feelings* are the primary medium of Christ. Responsiveness to the feelings of the Spirit leads to actions and thoughts that result in feelings of charity or the pure love of Jesus Christ.

The merciful love of Christ is a force or condition that envelops us. His love is also a system of communication that opens our mind to celestial understanding. His love is also a mode of expression that saturates the soul and gives power to our words of testimony. His love is also a carrier of revelatory information about His nature and the nature of His kingdom. His love also serves as the channel between the earthly world and the world of spirits. His love also becomes an environment in which we may flourish and grow.

It is important that we become experts in the realm of feelings. Feelings are the primary realm of Christ. It is important that we focus on feelings and learn to work with them in such a way that we can recognize and follow the Spirit and thus ever more regularly bathe in the love of God.

I have spent a lifetime trying to control the problem of lustful thoughts through the above process of thought control. In preparing to be a mission president, I have had some intense experiences with the living God. Like Lehi and like Alma, I have made several journeys into terrifying darkness (see 1 Nephi 8:7–10 and Mosiah 27:29). Each time, I have been driven to beg for mercy. Each time, I have been filled with God's love. From these experiences, I have come to an expanded understanding. The expanded understanding centers on the power of this line: "Jesus, the very thought of Thee / With sweetness fills my breast." In this line, thought is the process and emotion is the outcome. We need to focus on the outcome we want to create.

Here is the key: stop trying to stop the negative; start trying to create the positive. Learn to aspire to live in the merciful love of Christ. To do this, you must be clear about what the love of God is like. Examine your life. Identify clearly what it means to partake of the fruit of the tree of life, to have sweetness fill your breast. Identify the times when you have been filled with the love of God. These should be your most spiritually intense moments, your memories of greatest joy, and the core stories of your life.

Draw from these memories. Rejoice in them and then recognize that your purpose, your aspiration, is to live continually in the love of Jesus Christ. The result you want to create over and over is the joyous *feeling* of being in the presence of God *now*. Once you recognize this, focus your thoughts not on your reactive, negative thoughts, but on the positive feelings you continually want to experience. If you do this, you are more likely to feel the feelings of Christ and think the thoughts of Christ. You will become more alive in Christ.

As you more frequently experience the love of God, you will nevertheless encounter experiences that generate negative emotions. Yet, because you are spending extended periods in the love of God, the negative emotions will be a stark contrast. You will be immediately attuned to the emergence of these negative emotions. You can then use your mind to return to positive emotions.

Here is a suggestion. Any time you have any negative feeling, program yourself to repeat the following phrase: "Jesus, the very *thought* of Thee, with *sweetness* fills my breast." Notice that I said, "*any* negative feeling." I did not refer only to the issue of lust and physical virtue. Negative feelings include jealousy, lust, embarrassment, self-consciousness, depression, sadness, unhappiness, anxiety, fear, distaste, scorn, irritation, anger, hate, boredom, humiliation, shame, guilt, and a long list of others.

When any negative feeling comes, repeat the above phrase. Then sing your favorite song of Jesus. Recite the scriptures that tend to transform your soul. Consciously control your mind. Block the path of least resistance. Create a new channel of thought and feeling. As you do, you will move towards your purpose, which is to bathe in God's love and to be more alive in Christ.

As I indicated, I have spent my adult life trying to control lustful thoughts. The endless battle has served me well, because it has transformed and elevated me. I no longer focus on fighting lustful thoughts. I focus on living in the love of God. I focus not on using my mind to control thoughts; rather, I focus on using my mind to do what Alma advised his son Shiblon to do: I try to "channel" my passions or feelings (see Alma 38:12). As I do this, lustful feelings become a smaller concern. They are now just a subcategory of the many negative feelings. My objective is not only to control lustful thoughts but to live in the love of Christ. I pray that you always will.

I love each one of you.

Be extraordinary in Christ,

President Quinn

Challenge 17

PURIFYING THE HEART

My Dear Fellow Servants,

When we were in the MTC seminar for mission presidents, we were told that some missionaries reach a point when they have a transformational experience. They fully surrender to Christ and become purified in Him. Afterward, you can put them in any area and they will succeed.

I believe this claim for two reasons. First, as a young missionary, I had this experience. Second, as a mission president, I watched some missionaries have similar experiences. In this letter, I share with you my own sacred account. If you value and internalize it, your confidence may begin to "wax strong in the presence of God" (D&C 121:45).

On page six of *Preach My Gospel*, we read that through the first principles, we "can experience healing, forgiveness of sins, and complete conversion to the Savior and His gospel." As the Book of Mormon comes to a close, Moroni teaches this notion of complete conversion. It is the final or crowning doctrine of the entire book:

> Yea, come unto Christ, and be perfected in him, and deny yourselves of all ungodliness; and if ye shall deny yourselves of all ungodliness, and love God with all your might, mind and strength, then is his grace sufficient for you, that by his grace ye may be perfect in Christ; and if by the grace of God ye are perfect in Christ, ye can in nowise deny the power of God.
>
> And again, if ye by the grace of God are perfect in Christ, and deny not his power, then are ye sanctified in Christ by the grace

179

of God, through the shedding of the blood of Christ, which is in the covenant of the Father unto the remission of your sins, that ye become holy, without spot. (Moroni 10:32–33)

So the crowning doctrine of the Book of Mormon is to become completely converted or perfected in Christ—not after we die, but right now. Many people have difficulty understanding this. They believe that infinite perfection is a final state requiring a resurrected body. They fail to understand that Christ invites us to a state of finite perfection that can occur here and now. Examine again the invitation of Moroni:

- Come unto Christ
- Be perfected in Him
- Deny yourselves of all ungodliness
- Love God with all your might, mind, and strength
- Then is His grace sufficient that you may be perfect in Him
- Then you cannot deny His power
- You will be sanctified through His blood
- You can have your sins remitted and become holy and without spot

The message of this letter is that we can do what *Preach My Gospel* suggests: we can become completely converted to Christ. I believe that Moroni meant what he wrote, and a missionary can respond to Moroni's invitation. When they do so, they become endowed with power and find the capacity to more effectively invite others to be perfected in Christ. In this letter, I will explore one way in which this might come to pass.

Over the course of a mission, if we choose to engage the work, we continually grow. At the end of such a mission, we have very different desires and capacities. To understand how our desires change, consider a statement written by Travis near the end of his mission:

I stopped running and lifting because of the spiritual effects. Every time we go over to the weight room, someone is watching TV. You do not realize how TV affects you spiritually until you are away from it for a while. They usually have it on MTV or some other station with swearing or half-naked women running around. I found these images getting stuck in my head. So finally, after fighting it for too long, I decided I could not go anymore.

This passage illustrates how much Travis changed over the course of his mission. Before he left, having a TV on such programming would not have bothered him much. At the end of his mission, it bothered him enough that he changes his behavior rather than continue to be exposed to it. Why the difference?

By the end of his mission, Travis had made many efforts to move closer to Jesus Christ. Because he succeeded, his feelings were more sensitized to the Spirit. Being around that TV drove away the Spirit. Since he valued the Spirit and monitored himself, he knew when he was losing the Spirit, and he was willing to sacrifice exercising rather than be injured spiritually. The statement suggests that he wanted to control his context so he could maintain his relationship with Christ. Controlling context and controlling routines does much to insure such a relationship.

With this image in mind, I would like to share a story that provides a method for moving closer to Christ. On my mission, I spent the first nine months learning to become more and more obedient. Then I had an amazing experience. I engaged in a process that led to my complete conversion and the conversion of many others. I share this precious experience with the hope that it might facilitate your own complete conversion lead you to understand and internalize the invitation of Moroni.

As a junior companion, I experienced some missionary success, but it was limited. As a senior companion, I committed to work harder than I had ever worked. Initially this brought no success. Then I paid deeper attention to the scriptures. I worked hard to become a better teacher. In finding, I worked at being an enthusiastic actor and not someone who was acted upon. I thus began to move closer to Christ and suddenly, my appointment book began to fill. I was excited to finally have people to teach. Finally I was going to be successful.

Then the phone rang. The mission president was transferring me. It seemed inconceivable that at this moment I would be transferred. On the other hand, I was being transferred to the most attractive area in the mission. It was not until later that I would understand that going to the new area would be a critical variable in my spiritual development.

I went to the new area and continued to work. In terms of spiritual things, I was starting to understand more deeply—but there was still something missing. I began to read the scriptures even more thoughtfully. More accurately, I began to search the scriptures. As I did, I began to sense that there was still something missing.

One day, a member informed us that he had an investigator that was ready to be taught and he volunteered to attend the first discussion. The discussion went along as usual. At the conclusion, my companion and I bore witness of Joseph Smith and then turned to our friend. He paused for a moment, looked at the young lady, and said, "I know that Joseph Smith was and is a prophet of God." The room filled with the Spirit. The investigator started to cry.

As we walked home, I was baffled. That man said the exact same words that we had said but the result was dramatically different. When he spoke, he had an influence that we did not have. There was no question that the influence was the Holy Ghost, but this man seemed to have it in a different way. There was still something to be learned. I had to find out what the secret was, so I returned to the scriptures. It seemed like we were so close to being effective and yet we just could not make it happen.

After several weeks of searching and praying, we attended a meeting and heard an inspired man speak. He spoke about the scriptures as a source of strength and about the process of spiritual influence. His words caused a burning in my soul. When he finished his address, I intentionally lingered behind. When I finally had the chance to speak with this man, I explained my desire to be effective. I told him about the lessons I had learned. I told him that something was still missing. Finally, I asked him if he could tell me what it was.

He looked into my eyes and said nothing. Nearly a minute went by, and I began to feel very uncomfortable. Finally he spoke. He said, "Elder, when these pretty young ladies pass you on the street, what do you think about?"

Before I could answer, he asked, "Do you ever speak sarcastically to your junior companion?"

"Do you get up at 6:00 a.m. every morning?"

"Do you keep every mission rule?"

His list of questions grew longer. Finally he said, "These are things that keep the Holy Ghost from being your companion. If you want the constant companionship of the Holy Ghost, then you must purify yourself. I will tell you how to do it. Go home and fast for a day. In the attitude of fasting and prayer, make a list of every behavior that pokes at your spirit. Once you have made your list, then go to the Lord. Covenant with the Lord that you will fast from the things on that list for forty days. In other words, for forty days you will do nothing that appears on that list.

"You cannot just stop the old behaviors and start the new ones. You need the help of the Lord. So each morning go to the Lord and specifically promise him that you will avoid or start each item on the list. Ask for His help so you can have extra strength, and then at night go over your list with the Lord. If you failed on some items, figure out why. Tell the Lord. Ask for more strength the next day.

"Go through the process for forty days. If you do, you will find that your most basic desires will change. Your spirit will flourish and the Holy Ghost will become your constant companion. You will become an effective tool in the hands of the Lord."

I thought I had become an obedient missionary, but this man was raising the standard. He was taking the notion of exact obedience and complete conversion very seriously.

We went home determined to make the concept work. We began to fast and make a list. It proved much harder than we assumed it would be. I would pray and then I would feel impressed to write down some item. Then, arguing that there was nothing wrong with that particular thing, I would fight the impression. For example, I felt impressed to put golf on the list. My response was, "There is nothing wrong with golf. We only play on preparation day." I ignored the fact that on the other six days my mind continually dwelled on how to play better. I wrestled with the Spirit and then finally wrote golf on the list.

It is interesting that from the moment I wrote it on the list, I experienced the most intense desire to play golf. Everywhere I turned there was some reminder, some temptation to break the commitment. So it was with each item on the list. Each day, I had to fight all my natural inclinations and turn to the Lord for the help necessary to overcome myself. Sometime between the 30th and 40th day, I suddenly realized that my desire for the things on the list had disappeared. It was as if a great anchor had been cut from me.

The last morning, my companion and I knelt in prayer and then started out the door. I was impressed to go back and pray again. With unusual confidence, I addressed the Lord: "Father, these are thy children. We are now doing everything within our power to live the gospel. We turn the burden over to thee. Please carry us the rest of the way and the glory be unto Thee forever." This was a profoundly important sentence. We were giving all we had. We were comfortable in the presence of God. We were now surrendering ourselves. We hungered only to think the thoughts of Christ, to speak the words of Christ, to do the work of Christ.

We went to our first appointment. Halfway through the discussion, our investigator began to make an excuse that he could not be baptized because he did not believe that Joseph Smith was a prophet of God. I interrupted him: "That is untrue. You do know that Joseph Smith is a prophet. Your real fear is that your mother will disapprove if you join the Church. In the name of Jesus Christ, I promise you that your entire family will embrace the gospel because of your courageous example. The Lord wants you to be baptized now and it is necessary that you comply."

I never before had done anything like that. In fact, I knew nothing about his mother. He had hardly mentioned her. While I could hardly believe what I had said, the Spirit filled the room. This brother began to weep. He committed to be baptized the following Saturday.

The experience repeated itself. At our very next meeting with each investigator, there was a celestial manifestation and every one of them was committed to baptism. Between Thanksgiving and Christmas, we baptized at least two people every week. It was an unusual number of baptisms for our mission.

While the number of baptisms was large, the truly impressive thing was the change in my companion and me. We were different people. Our most basic desires and motives had been altered. Credit and recognition were no longer of any consequence. For the first time in our lives, the things of God were more important than the "things of this world" and "the honors of men" (D&C 121:35). We were completely converted, truly working for the glory of God. We were perfected in Christ.

In this process, our sensitivity deepened. We noticed how often we would cry. Several times a day, we would be brought to tears by a prayer, a talk, a discussion, a scripture, or almost anything. Our concern was continually focused upon others. For the first time, we could understand Nephi's claim: "For I pray continually for them by day, and mine eyes water my pillow by night, because of them" (2 Nephi 33:3). We could understand this statement because for the first time, we could understand Nephi's motives. We were filled with the pure love of Jesus Christ. The Lord could trust us because our motives were His motives.

An ironic thing followed. The phone rang. The mission president extended a call for me to serve as one his assistants. Months before, this would have been a personal thrill, an external manifestation of progress and recognition. That day, I did not feel so thrilled. There was a long silence. I began to weep. Leaving that area and those people was one of the most difficult things I ever did.

Over the years, I have shared this story with others in search of godly power. Many have engaged the process. The Spirit invites each person to repent in some unique way and each person progresses in some unique way. The invitation to complete conversion and perfection in Christ is a highly personalized process. For missionaries, the process is important because it is difficult to invite investigators to be perfected in Christ when we are not striving to be perfected in Christ ourselves.

I love each one of you.

Be extraordinary in Christ,

President Quinn

Note: In 2011, the author gave a devotional address based on the experience in this letter. It can be viewed at https://devotional.byuh.edu/media110301.

Challenge 18

INTERNALIZING THE PURPOSE

My Dear Fellow Servants,

In a talk given to mission presidents, Elder D. Todd Christofferson indicated that it is very difficult for missionaries to internalize the missionary purpose.[25] To internalize a purpose is to fully commit to it, to make it a part of one's identity, to naturally hunger to do the thing, and to do it with love. He suggests that many missionaries become focused on the means instead of the end. So they concentrate on studying or planning or finding or teaching or inviting. These are all good and necessary things, but Elder Christofferson suggests that when a missionary actually internalizes his or her purpose, a transformation takes place. Here are some indicators.

- Study is no longer "an obligation" or "time devoted to getting smart"; instead the missionary has a hunger to feast on the words of Christ so he or she will be filled with the revelation necessary to conversion.

- A planner is no longer seen as a scheduling tool but as a mechanism to ensure that the right things "happen to produce conversion."

- Finding is no longer a required task done out of duty but a desirable activity in which one discerns by the Spirit and "recognizes the potential for conversion."

- Teaching is no longer an instructional activity but a process of "offering salvation." It becomes an exercise in "deep listening and response" and it is done with "humility, boldness, and love."

- Instead of inviting people as a required routine, invitations are issued with "urgency, feeling, and persuasive power."

These statements are descriptions of transformation. Imagine a missionary who studies to be filled with revelation; who plans so that he or she can produce conversion; who actually desires to find and recognizes the potential for conversion while finding; who teaches to offer salvation and does it with deep listening, humility, boldness, and love; and who offers invitations with urgency, feeling, and persuasive power. This image seems intimidating. It is natural for me to conclude that no normal human being could ever do this.

Yet, on page three of *Preach My Gospel*, we read that the gospel must be taught by the power of the Holy Ghost. The scriptures promise that the Holy Ghost will lift a missionary to new levels of influence and impact. The Holy Ghost will "teach you new truths," "give you words to speak in the very moment," "carry your message to the hearts of the people you teach," "testify of the truthfulness of your message and confirm your words," and "help you discern the needs of the people you are teaching." On page four, there is a directive: "You are to teach with the power and authority of God." These notions are also transformational.[26]

In the Book of Mormon, we read of two men who did this:

> And it came to pass that Nephi and Lehi did preach unto the Lamanites with such great power and authority, for they had power and authority given unto them that they might speak, and they also had what they should speak given unto them—
> Therefore they did speak unto the great astonishment of the Lamanites, to the convincing them. (Helaman 5:18–19)

The power of Nephi and Lehi is hard to comprehend. They taught with a level of power that is rarely seen. Because we rarely see it, we may not believe that such teaching is possible and therefore we will not aspire to teach in such a fashion.

In many of my previous letters, we have read of Kristin and Travis. As new missionaries, they were committed to do the right things, yet like all new missionaries they faced the challenges inherent in missionary work and they struggled greatly. In this letter, we see them move to a new level of desire. They want to move to a higher spiritual level. Please pay great attention as you read and ponder on this question: is it possible for me to ever become the kind of missionary that is described by Elder Christofferson?

Travis wrote of an interview with his mission president. In the interview, the president asked Travis how he was going to move to the next level of progress. Travis gave him an answer consistent with the principles taught by Elder Christofferson:

> I told him that I want to be able to teach with such power that people can't turn me away. My plan to do that was by studying by myself and with others. I need both the skills and spiritual awareness. I've been studying every teaching opportunity that I've had lately, whether it's in district meeting, a discussion or a talk. It doesn't matter. I am especially paying attention to the way I follow promptings. I'm trying to listen to the Spirit in every situation. If a missionary asks me if they can do something, I try to listen to the Spirit. Last night I gave a spiritual thought and I felt it was good but I made a number of mistakes. One was that I went too long. I needed to be more direct and brief. I find myself talking too much.

The first thing to note is that, at the latter stages of his mission, Travis believed it was possible to teach with the power of God so that he could touch every person. He also developed the desire to have such power. Finally, he had a plan for acquiring it. How was Travis going to become so powerful no one could turn him away? He was going to:

- Engage in diligent study
- Acquire new skills
- Acquire increased spiritual awareness
- Study his own teaching tendencies
- Pay attention to how he follows promptings
- Listen to the Spirit in every situation
- Assess his every mistake and repent
- Talk less and listen more

This was not the Travis we had dropped off at the MTC. He had grown. Here he was, desirous to move to an advanced level of spiritual maturity and willing to engage in extensive personal discipline and learning. It suggests that Travis had evolved, he was internalizing the purpose of his mission, and he hungered to be a revelatory missionary who taught continually by the power of God.

If a missionary remains faithful, it is possible to learn to live by prayer and by revelation. Towards the end of her mission, Kristin shared an account that illustrates this growth:

> So I had a lot of really great days and then Tuesday hit. I have been kind of sick and I was feeling it on Tuesday. Also we weren't having any success. We have lunch at 1:00 and don't start working until 2:30 because everyone is napping. Usually we're not anywhere near our house, but when we are we can go back and rest for a half hour.
>
> This happened on Tuesday. When I woke up I lay there and I did NOT want to go back out and work. Immediately I began to pray. I don't know, it's cool, it's like praying is just a reflex for me now. I begged Heavenly Father to PLEASE give me the desire to get up and go. It was so tempting to just lie there. The thing is I know I could say the word and my comp would be like, "okay, let's stay here." Anyway, I did it. We got up and went. It didn't end up being a great day or anything, but I KNOW I would have been miserable if I hadn't gone out and worked.
>
> I love Heavenly Father so much. I feel like I'm forming a real, almost tangible relationship with Him. While we walk, I pray. I ask to know what to do with or say to the investigators.

In this passage, Kristin was having a day without success. She was anticipating immediate activity that held little hope for success and her natural reaction was to stay home. She also knew that her companion would immediately agree if she suggested staying home; there was no social pressure to do the work, so Kristin felt a substantial temptation.

This pattern is normal and it is reactive. What happened next was not normal. She prayed. Why? "Praying is just a reflex for me now." Kristin had evolved spiritually. She had moved so much closer to Jesus Christ that she had internalized new characteristics. Prayer had become an automatic response when the Spirit of Christ told her she was not doing the right thing. Also, note how she prayed. She did not offer a passive set of words; instead, she "begged" for the desire to do the right thing. She then got up and went to work.

What was the outcome? There was no success. So what had she accomplished? We find a clue in this sentence: "I KNOW I would have been miserable if I hadn't gone out and worked." Kristin learned to choose the pain of doing the work over the pain of not doing the work.

Because she learned to do this, she in fact achieved success. That success was not external but internal.

Notice the line regarding how she felt about God: "I love Heavenly Father so much. I feel like I'm forming a real, almost tangible relationship with Him." Because she had such a relationship, it shaped her desire. For what did Kristin pray? "While we walk I pray. I ask to know what to do with or say to the investigators."

When we overcome our natural desires and do the will of Christ, we become pure. Our desires turn outward to our investigators. We hunger for revelation and the power of God.

In the first story above, Travis expressed his desire to be a revelatory missionary and to have the power of God so no one can turn him away. In the second story, Kristin provided a basic illustration of making revelation a part of her nature or identity. A short time later, Travis made an unusual claim:

> I've had a lot of time to ponder this week. I've learned quite a bit. I find myself receiving revelation more and more often. I think that is it a skill. You have to be worthy to receive the revelation, but then it becomes a skill. Once you receive it, recognizing, interpreting, and acting on it are skills.
>
> Revelation is always there for us to receive. If our state of mind is right, we can learn from on high all day. I feel that I receive revelation as I talk with people, whenever I choose. God is always willing to give, but it is my choice to receive.
>
> For example, this week we stopped by Larry's auto shop to make calls. He has been a member for two years. We ended up having a good conversation about his conversion. It lasted about one hour. I learned so much from him. As I have learned to have deep conversations with almost all who I talk to, I receive revelation. I could learn more from talking to new members all day than from working all day.
>
> From Larry, I learned that maturity is essential to conversion. He had two opportunities to receive the gospel in his life. He accepted the second time because of his maturity. I learned of the importance of members finding those who are "mature" enough to accept. We cannot know hearts the way friends can. We must teach the members to find those who are "mature" enough to act on the Spirit. I learned much more from him. I am struggling to put it into words.

What I realized was that deep conversations open our minds to prepare us for revelation. They stimulate our thinking, our pondering. I guess that is why Dad always complained about our shallow conversations. I wish I had more time to write other thoughts. I truly learned a lot this week. I'm finding myself in a state of receiving revelation more and more as my mission progresses.

Receiving revelation is the process of learning from the Holy Ghost. A skill is an ability that one develops. Travis claimed that a missionary can master the art of receiving revelation. What follow is a list of his key points:

1. He was receiving revelation with increasing frequency
2. One must be worthy to receive revelation
3. Receiving revelation becomes a skill
4. Revelation is always there to receive, one can have it all day
5. Revelation can be received by choice as one talks to people
6. Deep conversations provide revelation
7. Deep conversations open our minds and prepare us
8. Members are a source of revelation
9. What is learned in deep conversation can be applied at once

Many of us assume that revelation is something that occurs infrequently. Travis offered a different perspective. He indicated that he was having revelation with increasing frequency. The scriptures suggest that when we purify ourselves and bask in the love of Christ, our confidence increases and the Holy Ghost can become our constant companion (see D&C 121:33–46).

Travis indicated that we can learn by revelation all day long, and he was particularly prone to experience it in conversations. Christ taught the doctrine that supports this position: "I stand at the door and knock" (Revelation 3:20). Travis was telling us that we can become skilled at opening the door and holding it open. It could always happen because Travis was hungry to learn and was always searching. It even happened when he walked into an auto shop. In the auto shop, he asked questions that gave rise to spiritual conversations. His hunger to learn of Christ drove conversations of Christ. In those conversations, he listened deeply and, because he did, the conversations became even richer. Such conversations accelerate learning and the skill to start them is a hallmark of a mature missionary.

In his evolution as a missionary, Travis also developed another skill that accelerates learning. At the end of his mission, I had the opportunity to chat with his mission president. The mission president was greatly appreciative of Travis. He listed many wonderful accomplishments. Yet there was one thing that impressed him the most. The president talked about the weekly letters that Travis wrote. He said; "Every week Elder Quinn writes an excruciating self-assessment, indicating all the mistakes he made that week and explaining what he is going to do differently, yet never, never has he ever pointed a finger at anyone or anything else but himself." Travis had learned the art of repentance, which is the art of self-monitoring, personal accountability, and self-change. Travis had become the master of one of the engines that propels us ever closer to Jesus Christ. Imagine if every mission president could utter that sentence about every missionary.

Travis was not a perfect person. He still experienced failure, as we saw in many of these letters. Yet this imperfect person, like his sister Kristin, learned how to open the revelatory door on a regular basis. The two of them were beginning to internalize their purpose and they were becoming revelatory missionaries.

As a natural man, I read the words of Elder Christofferson, I feel intimidated, and I naturally conclude that no normal human being could ever do what he describes. Actually, my conclusion is correct. No normal human could ever do it. Yet two of my own precious, struggling, mortal children teach me that it is possible. They can do this because they are not normal. Because they are faithful missionaries with an increasingly intense desire to serve Jesus Christ, they are internalizing their purpose and becoming unnatural servants of their master. They inspire me to want to do the same.

I love each one of you.

Be extraordinary in Christ,

President Quinn

Challenge 19

MAKING DIVINE CONTACT

My Dear Fellow Servants,

When missionaries go to another country, they often learn a new language. This is hard work. They have to reprogram their brains. Yet when they succeed, they experience exhilaration and rejoice in their new capacity to communicate. Here we discuss a very similar challenge: learning the language of God so we can make divine contact and change lives.

The second chapter of *Preach My Gospel* is about effective study. Moving closer to Christ is the foundation of effective study and effective teaching. The very first statement is "to teach effectively you need to obtain spiritual knowledge." The immediate objective is to learn the language of God, the language of the "still, small voice." In this letter, I will explore the notion of the still, small voice and how listening gives rise to the art of establishing divine contact.

In the MTC, Travis wrote about the scriptures.

> I have really found unbelievable excitement in reading and studying the scriptures. I realized it is because I just want to do anything to be able to touch people. It makes me want to know the scriptures inside and out so that in any way possible I will be able to touch the investigator. I want to be able to answer any question that Heavenly Father wants me to answer at any time. I want the knowledge so that I can do this. I love learning from my teachers about how to do things better. Every time I leave to go anywhere I find myself thinking that I can't wait to be in Oakland.

In early morning seminary, Travis read the scriptures but I never remember him expressing excitement. In the MTC, he claimed that he found "unbelievable excitement" in studying the scriptures. Because Travis was internalizing the purpose of a missionary, because he was moving closer to Jesus Christ, he had a desire to touch the lives of others and it influenced how he studied.

To understand the role of study and revelatory teaching, I often refer to an analogy that I call "the moment of divine contact." Johnny Miller is a BYU graduate and a famous golfer. He once made a video to teach people how to play better golf. In introducing the video, he said something unusual. To explain it, I need to explain something about the golf swing. It has three parts to it. A golfer takes the club backwards (backswing), moves it forward and hits the ball (contact), and then follows through. Most golf teachers spend their time focusing on how to stand, how to grip the club, and how to execute the backswing and the follow-through.

Johnny Miller takes a different approach. He explains that during the swing, the head of the club is traveling at approximately 90 miles an hour. The moment of contact is when the head of the club actually touches the ball. It is a period measured in thousandths of a second. It is hardly noticeable. Most teachers do not mention it.

As a young boy, Miller became preoccupied with the moment of contact. He spent thousands of hours observing and thinking about the moment of contact. In fact, he spent so much time and claims to know so much about this brief moment that he believes someone should give him a PhD in the moment of contact. Because of his great knowledge of the moment of contact, his approach to teaching golf is very different from other instructors. In this sense, he is extraordinary in his teaching. Because of his deep understanding of the moment of contact, he can do things other teachers cannot do.

The story is an analogy for doing missionary work. I believe that in our study efforts we should each become obsessed with understanding the moment of divine contact. Divine contact is when God makes contact with human beings and when human beings make revelatory contact with other human beings. The scriptures are a record of God's revelations. We can study the scriptures looking for historical and theological facts. This is fine. I would suggest, however, that missionaries would do well to search for moments of divine contact. We should pay particular attention to the moments in the scriptures when God gives revelation to humans and when humans convey revelation to other humans.

As we read, for example, the first chapter of the Book of Mormon, we might read every verse looking to learn about divine contact. In the very first verse, we might pay attention to the phrase "having been highly favored of the Lord." We might ask what it tells us about divine contact. In verse three, Nephi states that his record is "true." In verse five, we learn that Lehi prayed "with all his heart, in behalf of his people." In the next three verses, Lehi sees "a pillar of fire," he is "overcome with the Spirit" and he sees "the heavens open." We might read each of these phrases and ask ourselves what they teach us about the moment of divine contact. The reason we do this is that our purpose is to move ourselves and others closer to God. We want to make divine contact. We want to become experts in the moment of divine contact.

While we study the scriptures, there is another form of divine contact that we should consider. It is the divine contact that God is making with us as we study. We should pay attention to our feelings and our thoughts and we should record these moments of divine contact. We do this because we want to become more effective in the art of making divine contact with God and, as missionaries, we particularly want to become more effective at making divine contact with our investigators.

Reconsider an example, an account from a letter written by Travis:

> Mom, your letter also had a tremendous effect on me. We were teaching a guy named Rich. He wasn't contentious, but I don't think he was very interested. I would give answers to his questions and he would pick the answers apart. We got on to the topic of judging people. He asked if I judge anyone or anything. I told him that I loved all my friends to death and I would have done anything for them, even though they had different standards. I told him that anyone who really understood our church and believed in it feels the same way about judging. I then bore my testimony to him in tears. I was bold, plain, and simple. It was not drawn out. It was simply what I knew to be true and how I felt. That's when the miracle happened. Rich had no more questions. He was quiet for the first time. I invited him to read and pray. His answer was, "I invited you guys over here today not to try to help me, but I wanted to change you. I wanted to

open your eyes to other things. I wanted to see if you believed what you taught. That's why I questioned you so much. When you just told me that, I knew you weren't changing. I saw it in your eyes, that you know it's true." He would not read, but there was a dramatic change in his attitude, and it was because I bore pure testimony.

This is a moment of divine contact. What can we learn? Travis learned something from his mother. She must have written something sacred that he could apply. Travis must have taken it seriously. Travis then found himself with a troublesome investigator. In facing a challenging question, Travis first told a core story (an account of his friends), and then he bore a powerful testimony. At that moment, the investigator felt the Spirit and was moved. He did not accept the gospel, but his outlook was changed. He knew that Travis knew.

In the last sentence, we got a hint of what his mother must have taught. It must have been about the art of bearing a "pure testimony." Travis learned something from his mother, he experimented with it, and he experienced an outcome. He could now evaluate the process and further refine his capacity to bring about the process of divine contact.

I use this story to illustrate that our study of divine contact should not stop at the end of our study period. It should go on all day, every day. We should study every interaction, looking to understand divine contact. We should particularly pay attention to any interaction that is supposed to be spiritual.

This study may include deep attention to a talk being given by a three-year-old in Primary. Is she inspired? Is she making divine contact with the audience? Why or why not? What can I learn from watching her? This means I should probably takes notes on every talk in church, from Primary to sacrament meeting. Suddenly both the boring and the interesting talks should become interesting because they have something to teach me. We should more particularly pay attention to every finding and teaching effort made by any missionary. Like Johnny Miller, we should be totally absorbed in the study of divine contact so that we can learn the language of God. If we do, we become experts in the language of the still, small voice and we will be better able to achieve our purpose.

To more fully consider the notion of study, please consider a story from the biography of Monty Roberts called *The Man Who Listens to*

Horses: The Story of a Real-Life Horse Whisperer. For thousands of years, men have been breaking horses. Over time, there has been an evolution of techniques. These techniques are time-consuming. Breaking a horse often takes many days of hard work. The work is both complex and dangerous. The techniques of horse breaking tend to reflect a common assumption: the horse must be dominated. Given this assumption, the techniques often involve savage abuse. The techniques represent the weapons in a war between man and animal. The object of the war is the eventual subjection of the "broken" horse.

Monty Roberts had a father who broke horses. The father was a hard man, and he treated his son much like he treated the horses. There were a number of times when his father brutally beat him. The relationship was always strained.

As a little boy, Monty became a champion rider. As he grew older, he longed to understand horses better. As an early teenager, he had to opportunity to go to Nevada and study horses in the wild. This was not casual study. He spent long hours with binoculars observing the every move of each horse in the herd. He did this in the heat of the day and in the cold of the night. He did it over two summers.

Like Johnny Miller in his study of the moment of contact in golf, Monty began to note something astonishing about the contact between horses. The horses used their bodies to communicate. They would use body language to exchange meaning and shape behavior in the herd. Monty became more and more convinced of his discovery. Soon he wondered if he could use this same language to communicate with the horses. He experimented with ways to use his own body to send the same signals to the horses. Eventually he taught himself how to do an amazing thing. He would bring a wild horse into a corral. He would read the horse's body language, and he would then send messages to the horse. At one critical moment, he would use his eyes in a certain way. At another critical moment, he would turn his body at a certain angle. At another critical moment, he would place his fingers in a particular position. At each moment, the horse would respond as he expected. He found that in thirty minutes, he could "gentle" a horse. In thirty minutes, he could have a rider safely on the back of a horse that was no longer wild. He further discovered that he could do this with all horses, even those considered hopelessly crazed.

Imagine his excitement. As a teenager, he had made a discovery that overturned thousands of years of human learning. He had developed a process that was faster, safer, simpler, and more effective. As the years passed, Monty accomplished miraculous things with horses. He was asked to work for the Queen of England and other famous people. Because he had learned a new language and he could use it to shape the moment of contact, he had great impact on the world. We can do the same.

There are many things we should note about this story. One is how Monty gained his knowledge. He learned the language of horses by an extraordinary commitment to study. In his study, he was willing to do things others were not willing to do. He lay on his belly in the heat of the day and cold of night, carefully observing every detail of behavior. He thought about every move. He asked himself questions. He took notes. He developed informal hypotheses and looked for data to test them. Gradually he developed his own personal theory of how horses communicated. Then he further tested his theory by trying to employ the language. As he did this, his experiments led to greater and greater knowledge and effectiveness.

I believe that a missionary can and should do the exact same thing. Our challenge is to learn the language of the still, small voice, to study the moment of divine contact, and learn how we can become ever more effective in creating moments of divine contact. When we say that a missionary should study, we usually mean he or she should read and learn what is in the scriptures. This is very, very important. We must do this. Yet this is not sufficient to bring extraordinary results. Extraordinary results require extraordinary study. We need to study all day long by observing everything that occurs. Our study should be active. We need to observe divine contact and then experiment by applying our observations and then evaluate our experiments and refine them while making further observations. What Monty did with horses, we need to do with the Spirit of God.

Although I did not know the stories about Johnny or Monty at the time, I tried to do what they did as a missionary. I became obsessed with the notion of teaching with power. When I read the scriptures, I read them looking for insights on how to make divine contact. As I read, I continually asked myself what I was feeling and what new ideas were unfolding. I asked myself how I could apply these ideas.

My study time never ended. I was always in study. When I went to church, I took notes on every talk, always asking myself, *Is this person making divine contact? Why or why not? How can I learn from their success or failure?* I would evaluate every presentation I made and every presentation made by other missionaries. I did this to find new principles upon which to experiment, and I wrote the principles down.

Every week, I reread the principles and tried to reduce them to a smaller set of principles. I tried to get clearer and clearer about the process of making divine contact, of understanding the language of the still, small voice, of more effectively fulfilling my purpose as a missionary. As I did, I—like Johnny and like Monty—gained new capacities. I was able to see and do things others were not able to do. I became more expert in the art of divine contact.

I invite you to become an expert in the art of divine contact and the language of God. Make it a point of focus. Keep a written record of your knowledge. Begin by making a list of all the times you have made divine contact or have seen it made. Realize that it happens with investigators at key moments in discussions, with companions, with members. It happens in meetings.

List all the examples you have seen. What do they share in common? What does it take to make divine contact happen? Continually evaluate your efforts to make it happen. Ask other missionaries about it. Get them to verbally describe their list. Ask them what is common across their experiences with the phenomenon. Read the scriptures looking for the moment of contact. If you do this, you will be doing something that is good (and not natural). You will be making yourself into an extraordinary servant of God. You will become more alive in Christ and more able to effectively invite others to move closer to Christ. Your time in the scriptures will be precious and you will learn to love to study.

I love each one of you.
Be extraordinary in Christ,
President Quinn

Challenge 20

Becoming a Visionary Influence

My Dear Fellow Servants,

Faithful missionaries learn skills that create success on their mission, and the same skills contribute to success after their mission. A key skill throughout life is the ability to formulate a vision. Elder Richard J. Maynes once said, "I have yet to meet a businessman, educator, artist, or athlete who has attained a high level of excellence in their chosen field who has not successfully been able to connect the vision of their future to their everyday life."[27]

Chapter eight of *Preach My Gospel* suggests that we need to have a vision. On page 146, it tells us, "Goals reflect the desires of our hearts and our vision of what we can accomplish. Through goals and plans, our hopes are transformed into actions." In this letter, we will consider how to become more visionary missionaries who can lead themselves and others.

In my letters to Kristin and Travis, I often wrote of the importance of vision. At first, they did not respond much to the notion. Then Travis wrote me a wonderful letter. He said that he had prayerfully developed two visions. The first one was for himself:

> My vision for myself is to be the most effective tool that I can be for my Lord Jesus Christ. I can see myself bringing every person that I talk to the gospel of Jesus Christ. I can see my gospel understanding continue to progress every day. I have a vision of myself not being able to sleep at night because I would rather be working to bring souls to Christ. I see the Spirit guiding me in every word I say. I

see my relationship with my Heavenly Father and His Son growing stronger every day. I see myself changing my area, my district, my zone, my mission, and the world.

Travis's vision was very vibrant and very concrete. I like the line: "I have a vision of myself not being able to sleep at night because I would rather be working to bring souls to Christ." This reminds me of Nephi when he yearned for the eternal welfare of those who did not accept Christ. Nephi says; "Mine eyes water my pillow by night" (2 Nephi 33:3). Travis envisioned himself as a fully converted missionary, one who was no longer a natural man but was alive and constant in Christ. The following two lines are also striking: "I see the Spirit guiding me in every word I say. . . . I see myself changing my area, my district, my zone, my mission, and the world." These lines impress me because I believe that once a missionary becomes more fully alive in Christ, that missionary actually acquires the power to change the world.

Not only did Travis develop a vision for himself, but also as a district leader, he developed a vision for his district. He did this by asking the members of his district to write their own personal visions. Then he asked them to share their visions. Based on their personal visions, he then asked them what they thought he should put into his vision for the district. He listened to their inputs. He prayed. He rewrote the document over and over until he felt it was right. Then he shared it with his district. Shortly thereafter, he wrote of a most unusual account of an interview with his mission president.

> We talked shortly about the district. I brought up some things and focused on what has brought about change. As this finished I know the president expected an ordinary interview, but instead I explained my challenge to my district to do their visions and I told him I would like to go first. I read my visions and said, "President, what advice do you have and what can you do to help in this?" I had a notebook and pen in my hand and waited. The response came, and it was a very ordinary answer. He gave me no new suggestions. I thanked him and asked him to encourage other district members.

Travis continues:

> Now you get my analysis on this. President was blown back. He didn't have an answer. He is so used to the same old interviews that he didn't expect to have an extraordinary interview. I think he knew

this and was disappointed in himself. I believe these interviews will make him examine himself and he will be prepared for an extraordinary interview next time. I know of at least two other elders who went to him with visions. I believe that by being extraordinary missionaries in our district it will force a change in our areas, in our mission, and in every aspect of life. I believe being extraordinary makes all of those around you work towards being extraordinary.

This surprising statement deserves some examination. The conversation began with an explanation of what "brought about change." Shortly after Travis became the district leader, the district began to progress. Later, when he was called as a zone leader, he again developed a vision with the zone, then he took the vision seriously, and again there was progressive change.

Travis says the president expected an "ordinary interview." What is an ordinary interview and why was this one extraordinary? It was extraordinary because Travis had a vision and he was going somewhere. He was an actor, not a reactor. He shared his visionary purpose and then he asked his priesthood leader for advice. With a pen in hand, he obediently "waited" for direction. Notice that at this moment he was both powerful because he had direction and humble because he as ready to be led.

The mission president gave no significant advice. Travis accepted this fact with love and thanked the president. He asked the mission president to listen to the visions of his district members and to encourage them. What a great and mature request! Visionary servants are leaders who love the people they serve. Travis loved his missionaries and wanted the president to support them.

Later, Travis made an analysis of what happened. He believed the mission president was surprised. He wrote, "I believe these interviews will make him examine himself and he will be prepared for an extraordinary interview next time." Travis then made this profound observation: "I believe that by being extraordinary missionaries in our district, it will force a change in our areas, in our mission, and in every aspect of life. I believe being extraordinary makes all of those around you work towards being extraordinary."

A missionary who becomes more alive in Christ becomes more constant in Christ. The constant missionary is constantly a missionary.

In every interaction, the constant missionary seeks to invite "all" people to move closer to Christ (see Matthew 28:19–20; 2 Nephi 26:33). This means the missionary has one purpose: to elevate family, other missionaries, mission leaders, members, and investigators. Such a person is not ordinary. Such a person is an extraordinary, visionary servant of Christ who is in constant pursuit of a righteous purpose.

After doing the above, Travis worked hard to implement his vision. Eventually he was transferred. On transfer day, he wrote about his feelings. I was moved by his account and went back to find several passages from his earlier letters that told the story of his time in that area and district. I was able to pull out passages that captured some of the ways he developed over a six-month period. On a mission, we sometimes evaluate ourselves on a weekly basis, but this does not help us to see what happens over a longer period. Please read the following passages carefully. As you do, look for the concepts of vision, hope, goals, discipline, action, and success. Also, notice how things are changing over time.

Perspective 1: The Early Days in the Bleakness of Brentwood

August 24, 1999: "As expected, later that night I got a call. I was to be a senior companion in Brentwood, a spread-out town with lots of farms. I'm also kind of training because my companion has only been out a month. I was told to be at the Visitor's Center at 7:20 AM. I truly love each of the people I worked with in Oakland and I miss them. I feel empty inside and I am trying to deal with it because I know it is part of the mission. I also am scared of all the new things that are happening, particularly being senior companion for the first time in a new area. I don't know how to handle it. I am just praying for the Lord's help."

August 31, 1999: "Let me explain my situation. I am a new senior companion. I do not know what I am doing. My companion has been out one month. There were difficulties that limited his training. Second, I came into the area and there is nothing going on. We had one family of three that had taken one discussion but the missionaries had barely taught that because the last six months appointment after appointment had fallen through. Third, it is 100 degrees every day or close to it and tracting is tough. Fourth, we are living with a companionship that hate each other. Yesterday they were cussing at each other and it was out of hand. Dad, I had one of them read your letter on getting along with your companion and it helped. I guess they talked for a long time last night. Fifth, our members do not help much, at least so far. Every dinner appointment has resulted in no referrals and no one seems to be working on it. Well, the list goes on and on but I may be exaggerating because I am dealing with it but this is how it feels.

"I told myself at the beginning of the week we were going to get this area going but it is not coming really fast and it is hard on me. I guess I like instant success. First, I did what Ryan said, I went straight to the bishop and said 'What do you want me to do?' He basically said 'go to my counselors—they usually have good ideas.' So we both acted very excited but did not act on it. So we went to the Relief Society president but she was out of town. On Sunday we did talk to her counselors and they gave some ideas.

"Now, I understand that bishopric is busy so I do not blame them, but it is hard on me. I was struggling with what to do to get it going. We started to just tract and check anyone who we thought looked less active on the ward list. This was very difficult because the area is growing fast and a lot of streets are not on the map. To make a long story short on the whole thing, the work is progressing slowly with hard work but it is coming along. We have begun working with a couple of inactives."

Travis found out he is going to be a senior companion in a new area and he was scared. I think most of us can identify with that feeling. He arrived in the new area and found that his companion was new, no work had been done in his area, the climate was hostile, he lived with missionaries who hated each other, and the members were not helpful. This was discouraging! The normal reaction would be to withdraw. Travis, instead, committed to get the area going, but it was not so easy. He went to the ward leaders, but the ward leaders were not really responsive. He was left to himself and he found the process of finding to be very difficult. It was at this time that Travis developed the vision we read above.

Perspective 2: Looking Back at Abundance of Brentwood

February 21, 1999: "I am being transferred. I am very pleased with the results we have had in this district. Every companionship has baptized. Every companionship has dates set except one. Most of all, every person in the district has grown and is converted. Everyone knows who they are and who they represent. I have grown to love each district member deeply. Everyone in the district has grown to love each other. It brought tears to my eyes as I listened to each missionary read their vision and explain that they wanted to be extraordinary and how they planned to achieve it. I love these people. It brings tears to my eyes to think of leaving them.

"We have taught more standard discussions this week than I have my whole mission. Mostly all of them were firsts and then a couple seconds. That goes along with all of the other investigators we have been working with. Instead of being lazy my last week in the area, we had maybe my best week in the area. I am leaving the area now with seventeen teaching units, twenty-five investigators, and five baptismal dates. This is not including the three or four more dates we should set this coming week. This is opposed to the ten teaching units, fifteen investigators, and two dates we had set at the beginning of the week. The Lord has blessed us for our work. I really believe. We had everything go right this week.

"I feel good about myself. I gave this area all I had. The thing that makes me happiest is that the missionary that is filling my spot is the missionary I would have picked if I could have chosen one from the whole mission. I'm happy about that.

"Well, I'm really struggling with leaving this area and my companion. I truly love the people. As I took pictures today, tears have filled my eyes. I've grown to love these people. I feel like they are my family. I would do anything for them. It pains me to think of anyone sleeping. I want so badly for every person I've worked with to have the happiness the gospel brings. I mean that. I can't imagine leaving; this is my home.

"I do look forward with excitement to my new opportunity. I see new challenges. I'm just grateful that God is mindful of what I need in order to progress. I need different challenges. I plan to search for His guidance and help. I know He lives. He is active in my life. I rejoice in His goodness. He is my Father. I love all of you. Please know that."

Here the indicators of collective success are many. The companionships had and would continue to baptize, individual missionaries had grown and been converted, and they knew who they represented. Each one was loved by the district leader. The members of the district loved one another. Each one had a vision and a plan. Could there be a much more positive description of a district?

Yet it did not end with the area. Travis reported extraordinary numbers, but the numbers were less impressive than what he said about his own condition. Travis said he "felt good" about himself. Notice that in his last week he refused to get lazy, and his last week was his best. He gave the area all that he had. He left it in a better condition than he found it. He loved his companion and the people. He wanted them all to be alive in Christ. Travis then went on to rejoice in Christ. Could there be a more positive description of a missionary? Now note what happens next.

Perspective 3: Entering the Tri-Valley Zone

February 28, 1999: "I was overwhelmed, a new area, zone, district, companion. I knew I wanted to be an extraordinary zone leader but I was not sure how to go about it. So I just asked questions about the zone and the area. My companion is great. Our personalities don't match, but they will. He is obedient, but I knew he needed to be excited to work. I want him to catch fire."

Travis was overwhelmed as he had been before. Yet this time he knew what to do. He simply went about asking questions, gathering data, looking for the signs that told him about the conditions that exist. As he made his analysis, he gave us one important clue about what he wanted to do. It concerned his companion. He wanted him to "catch fire."

We can safely guess that Travis was going to attempt to set a vision and then set out to more fully convert his companion, the missionaries, the members, and the leaders. Sometime later, his mission president told me this is exactly what happened.

In the above passages, we find a story of a missionary who found himself in a most discouraging situation. Many of us experience this. Yet he committed to follow the directive we find in *Preach My Gospel*: "Do all you can to leave your area stronger than you found it" (p.137). He did this by setting a vision, deriving goals, and attacking his goals with discipline. Through this process, he transformed his hopes into actions, results, and successes.

You may feel very discouraged about your current situation. You may be quite justified is doing so because missionary work is hard. Yet to remain in the reactive state of discouragement will only lead to unhappiness. I hope that from reading this letter, you may begin to see a way out of discouragement. I pray that it will help you feel the Spirit of Christ inviting you to a more proactive life stance. I hope you will follow it, develop a vision, and set and attack goals so that you might become alive in Christ and feel good about yourself. I will end with some guidelines on how you can create a personal life vision.

Guidelines

Step 1: If you have one, read your patriarchal blessing. Look for sentences that tell you about your life purpose and how you are to pursue it. Write a short abridgement of your blessing just as Book of Mormon prophets wrote abridgements of larger, inspired records. The focus should be on your purpose. You will know you have it right when you read it and you feel revelatory power telling you how to move forward in becoming who you really are.

Step 2: Think about your purpose as a missionary. Read the first page of *Preach My Gospel*. Pray about the essentials that are necessary for you to effectively accomplish your purpose.

Step 3: Pray about your stewardship (area, district, zone). Develop a personal vision for how you would like to see it change. Think about how you must change the way you relate to companions, investigators, members, leaders, and your own family. Think about how you must change the way you relate to your family through the letters you write.

Step 4: Talk with others. Share your impressions of your desire future. Invite them to share their own. Listen carefully. Explore what would be necessary for them to bring about their desired future.

Step 5: State the nature of your commitment. Specify the central commitments of your soul. Do not write a word that you do not deeply feel. When you read your life statement, it should be authentic. It should inspire you and direct you. When you read it, you should be able to say, "These are my real values and this is the world I truly aspire to create. This is worth living for and worth dying for. It is who I am, a child of the living God, trying to move closer to Christ to continually bathe in the love of God."

Do not try to write it all at once. The first day, write down whatever thoughts come to mind. Do not worry about getting it right. The next day, prayerfully rewrite what you did. Repeat this every day. Your life statement will evolve every day. It will polish itself. It will become a document written by revelation. It will help you to be more alive and more constant in Christ. It will help you to "act" and not "to be acted upon" (2 Nephi 2:13–14; 26–27). It will therefore bless the lives of others.

I love each one of you.

Be extraordinary in Christ,

President Quinn

Challenge 21

TEACHING BY LISTENING

My Dear Fellow Servants,

In the conventional perspective, the word teach is equated with words like instruct, educate, train, tutor, lecture, impart, explain, clarify. Each word suggests that the teacher is an expert who pours information upon a passive student. By the time we graduate from high school, we have spent thousands of hours in experiences that reinforce this view. It is most difficult to consider any other view.

On page 185 of *Preach My Gospel*, Elder Holland suggests a radically different approach to teaching. He suggests that we teach by listening. He says we need to ask investigators "what matters most to them. What do they cherish, and what do they hold dear? And then listen. If the setting is right, you might ask what their fears are, what they yearn for, or what they feel is missing in their lives. I promise you that something in what they say will always highlight a truth of the gospel about which you can bear testimony and about which you can offer them more. . . . If we listen with love, we won't need to wonder what to say. It will be given us—by the Spirit and by our friends."[28]

I once read the above paragraph in front of a seminar for mission presidents. I told the many leaders present that I considered this paragraph to be one of the very most important in *Preach My Gospel*. Most people looked at me as if I were crazy. Thankfully there was one man in the room nodding his head. He was a member of the Quorum of the Twelve Apostles.

How do we teach by listening? In a conversation, it is natural to be thinking about what we need to say next. It is not so natural to listen deeply. An effective missionary has one purpose, to bring the other person closer to Christ. When we truly embrace this purpose, we change how we communicate. We honestly hunger to know the deepest feelings of the other person. When we succeed, we come to love them.

This ability to feel what the other is feeling is called empathy. When we come to empathize with the feelings of another, God will more readily inspire us to express our feelings in such a way that our words will reach their heart and give them a new view of self, of God, and of the world (see Bible Dictionary, "Repentance"). Divine contact happens as we communicate from heart to heart.

When Kristin first arrived in the mission, she noticed that she and her companion taught many first discussions. This seemed like a good thing. Then she noticed there was usually little progress towards Christ. She observed:

> Teaching here is totally different than how we learned at the MTC. . . . My companion told me it's because no one will listen if we take longer. But it just doesn't seem right to me. We never ask find-out questions. I get frustrated that they don't pray and read, but how can I really get them to do that when I haven't found out if they have any concerns or if I haven't really prepared them before inviting them?

Kristin realized that teaching to change lives requires listening and love. We all need to learn how to connect with each investigator by learning to how to help them express their deepest feelings. Our object in visiting them is to maintain the relationship so we can move the relationship to trust and authentic communication. If we learn to listen with love, the Spirit will inspire us and we will link the people to God.

In the next paragraph, *Preach My Gospel* gives us another key to authentic communication:

> People also communicate by the way they sit, their facial expressions, what they do with their hands, their tone of voice, and the movement of their eyes. Observe these unspoken messages; they can help you understand the feelings of those you teach. Also be aware of your own body language. Send a message of interest and enthusiasm by listening sincerely.

When we think of communication, we think of words that convey thoughts. Yet 90% of all feelings are conveyed through non-verbal communication, through body language. If we say things we do not feel, others know. We may say something positive while we have anxiety in our voice, or we may say some kind word while we show irritation by making some quick gesture. People consciously or unconsciously recognize these signals and note that they cannot trust what is being said.

When our feelings and our words match, our communication is said to be congruent. When we listen to someone speak with low congruence, we tend not to trust their words. It's difficult for us to be positively influenced by them. When we listen to someone with high congruence, someone who is speaking what they truly feel, we tend to trust the person and we are more influenced by what they are saying.

This concept is very important for missionaries. We cannot entice or invite people to change unless we can establish trust. People will not trust us unless our communication is congruent. We need to live to have positive feelings and we need to learn to communicate them. Another way to say this is that we need to do three things: learn the word of God, say the word of God, and be the word of God.

When we become a direct reflection of God, people notice. Our words are signals of truth because our words and our feelings are congruent or one. The message is logically and emotionally true. The listener feels that they have just received a pure signal. They can trust what we say.

Preach My Gospel advises us to ask questions of others. I would point out that we also need others to feel they are free to ask us questions. Yet sometimes this is not the message we actually send.

There was a man who ran ten weeklong group sessions every summer. In these groups, strangers came together at the beginning of the week. They then engaged in intense and intimate communication. By the end of the week, they were close friends. In these groups, all topics were open for communication and exploration. One year the man who ran the groups had an accident and one of his arms was cut off. He had a great deal of difficulty coping with his loss. During the next five years, he ran fifty groups, and not one person asked him what happened to his arm. The next winter he did some work with a counselor and came to a psychological resolution around the loss of his arm.

In the years that followed, there was always a time when one of the group members asked him about the loss of his arm.

During those first five years after the accident, he was sending a message in some unconscious way. His behavior said, "The loss of my arm is a source of considerable pain. It is a taboo subject. If you ask me about it, you are entering personal territory where you are not welcome." He never said these words, but he clearly communicated the message and people did not ask. Later, he behaved differently. After changing himself, he was sending a message that said, "I am at peace with the fact that I have one arm; feel free to talk about it."

Sometimes as missionaries, we are like this one-armed man. While we're teaching, we convey an unspoken message that says, "Do not ask me questions—especially the hard ones." We feel insecure and want to complete the assigned task to say the words we are supposed to say.

An effective missionary sends a different message. An effective missionary learns to feel confidence in the presence of God (see D&C 121:45). He or she is no longer afraid of "looking bad." He or she sends the implicit message, "I am at peace with the truthfulness of the gospel and the revelatory power of Jesus Christ. I am filled with the love of God and I am not interested in the honors of men. If I do not know an answer, and if I am not given it by revelation, I will simply tell you I do not know. I will go home and study and learn the answer and return and tell you. Even better, we can sit down and find it together. So please, feel free to ask me any question. I want you to ask."

It is important that we grow into such confidence. In fact, it is important that we go even further. We need to learn to surface rather than suppress objections and concerns. If we do not know what our investigators are feeling and thinking, we cannot connect with them in a meaningful way.

I believe that the discussions are an excuse to be with a person and to explore issues of deep concern. As missionaries, what we are really looking for is the "open window." The open window is the time we need to establish enough trust that we can connect both logically and emotionally. The window opens when the investigator begins to feel safe in surfacing their deeper concerns. They trust the conversation to go deeper and deeper without fear of the questions that will emerge.

The objective is not even to answer the questions but to make the trusting and loving relationship possible. We might get asked a question that we have no idea how to answer. So we might say with great confidence, "I do not know how to answer that particular question for you, and I will get an answer, but what I sense is that there is an even deeper concern that is under that question. Do you feel comfortable telling me about it? What is it that leads you to ask that question?" Such responses keep the conversation flowing. The key is to keep the conversation flowing until the moment the Spirit says, "Express your love and bear your prophetic witness of this." If we learn to perform in this manner, our confidence will become unconditional. We will not fear having the investigator tell us what they really fear because our object is not to be an expert but an inspired representative of Jesus Christ.

All of this also applies to how we work with other missionaries. We cannot lead someone unless we understand and love that person. We still may need to be bold. Boldness and love may seem to be opposites, but when we work by revelation, we find that boldness and love can operate at the same time.

Travis described a situation in which his leadership position required him to deal with some disobedient missionaries. He and his companion held a meeting. On the surface, everyone said everything was fine. Yet the words were not congruent with the feelings expressed and Travis knew that everything was not fine. One of the missionaries involved was particularly polished in the art of rationalizing, or externalizing. The meeting ended, but Travis was frustrated with the outcome. The next day, Travis found himself back in the apartment and the same missionary was not out working. Travis wrote:

> I didn't want to deal with it, but I went in, sat down, and talked to him. I asked him what he thought about the day before. He acted like it was great. He asked me what I thought. At first I didn't want to be honest, but I left the comfort zone. I said, "Elder, I love you." I then explained that I developed that love through prayer. I made this clear and told him that he could believe it if he wanted to or not. Then I told him I was going to be completely honest. I know he thought he had me convinced that he was doing great. I told him it made me sick to watch him cry about how hard he has it and make excuses. I told him to change his motives and quit playing his ten-year-old games. Then I explained that until he learns to do so, he will hate his mission and never progress. He started crying. I don't think anyone has ever seen through him or told him how it is. I told him again that I loved him and walked out. I felt very good because I left

my comfort zone. I was guided by the Spirit and enabled to ask bold stroke questions. The situation changed things. He sat in his room for a while and came out, got his companion, and went out to work. That night one of the other elders called and told us they worked all day. I don't know if he'll change long term, but I know it hit him.

Note some key points. First, Travis did not want to "deal with it." He did not want to confront the conflict that existed. This was natural. Travis then asked a question and got words and feelings that did not match. Then, even though he did not want to deal with the conflict, Travis chose to leave his comfort zone and to speak with loving boldness. He began by declaring his love. Then he boldly told him the truth as he saw it. When he was done, Travis reconfirmed his love.

Why did it work? First, Travis was pure. His motive was not anger, but love. He wanted to attract the missionary to move closer to Christ. Second, Travis had to do what he didn't want to do: he had to leave his comfort zone. He had to exercise faith to say the words of revelation. This act of loving boldness became a signal of love. The missionary could hear the painful message because it was truly wrapped in love.

Now, the very most important part of this story comes next. Travis wrote, "Afterward, I sat studying, receiving revelation. It was incredible. I realized so many things. I offered a prayer for that elder. It is the first time I've had to do something like that. I learned some incredible things about how to work with elders more effectively. I also learned a valuable lesson on teaching. I just felt at peace."

When we go outside our comfort zone in the service of Christ and we stop and reflect, the learning is almost always intense. We are filled with revelation. I believe this would have happened to Travis even if the above missionary had rejected him. The outcome does not matter. People have their agency. It is the exercise of faith and love that matters. When we speak with the heart and mind of Christ, we will be filled with the Light of Christ, and the confirmation of the Holy Ghost will give us peace and increased understanding.

As we mature as missionaries, our communication matures. We learn to teach by listening. We learn to speak with loving boldness. As we do, people encounter the Spirit of God and lives change.

I love each one of you.

Be extraordinary in Christ,

President Quinn

Challenge 22

Speaking in Church

My Dear Fellow Servants,

When a missionary speaks in church, he or she is standing and waving a flag. The flag sends one of two messages:

- I am a normal young man or woman and you shouldn't trust me with referrals because I am not going teach your friends with the power of Christ. Instead I will communicate normally and thus push them away from the Church.
- I am extraordinary in Christ. When you hear my words, you hear the words of Christ. Because I speak with the power of God, you know I am a dedicated servant of my Master, and you can trust me with your friends. When they are with me, they will be taught by Jesus Christ.

Members, consciously or unconsciously, recognize which flag you are waving and they respond accordingly. In every act at church or in the home of members, you are waving your flag and they are receiving your message. They respond to you according to your faith.

In this letter, I will share with you a message from Elder Bruce R. McConkie. In it, he explains how to give a "perfect" talk. Before I do, I will share two other important stories. The first is about Nephi and how he transformed himself. The second is from my son Travis, who applied the teachings of Nephi and thus prepared himself to practice the teachings of Elder McConkie. If you embrace the message, you will stand at the pulpit and speak with power. Members will recognize the flag you wave and they will know they can trust you with their most cherished friends.

On page 18 of *Preach My Gospel*, we are told that our gospel study will be most effective when we are taught by the Holy Ghost: "For he that diligently seeketh shall find; and the mysteries of God shall be unfolded unto them, by the power of the Holy Ghost" (1 Nephi 10:19).

The words come from Nephi. The same man also tells us: "When a man speaketh by the power of the Holy Ghost the power of the Holy Ghost carrieth it unto the hearts of the children of men" (2 Nephi 33:1). When we study effectively, the Holy Ghost will give us revelation. When we teach effectively, the Holy Ghost will carry our inspired words to the hearts of others.

Reconsider chapter four of Second Nephi. Nephi's parents had just passed away. Immediately there was another confrontation with Laman and Lemuel. In this experience of loss and contention, Nephi got discouraged and depressed. In this state, he first told of his method for pondering and then he told something quite out of character with all the other things he had ever written. He writes, "O wretched man that I am! Yea, my heart sorroweth because of my flesh; my soul grieveth because of mine iniquities. I am encompassed about, because of the temptations and the sins which do so easily beset me. And when I desire to rejoice, my heart groaneth because of my sins" (2 Nephi 4:17–19).

On the one hand, Nephi was no longer a natural man. He delighted in the scriptures and in the things of God. Yet he had a discouraging experience. In this negative state, his sins weighed upon him. He was discouraged just like you and I sometimes get discouraged.

The ordinary thing to do when we feel this way is to do nothing. Nephi took a different, extraordinary route. He consciously shifted his mind. He moved from a focus on his past problems to a focus on his past moments of divine contact, his core stories with God. He said, "Nevertheless, I know in whom I have trusted. My God hath been my support." God has:

1. "Led me through mine afflictions in the wilderness"
2. "Preserved me on the waters of the great deep"
3. "Confounded mine enemies, unto the causing of them to quake before me"
4. "Heard my cry by day"
5. "Given me knowledge by visions in the nighttime"
6. "Sent angels down to minister unto me"

7. "Carried my body away upon the wings of his Spirit upon exceedingly high mountains"

8. "Shown mine eyes great things, yea, even too great for man." (2 Nephi 4:19–25)

This is a list of Nephi's core stories. To make such a review is to examine the history of God in his own life, the history that cannot be denied because he knew the events occurred. To review such events is to be certain that God lives and the Atonement is real.

As soon as the depressed Nephi made this review, it had an impact. A remarkable shift occurred. Nephi said, "Awake, my soul! No longer droop in sin. Rejoice, O my heart, and give place no more for the enemy of my soul. Do not anger because of mine enemies. Do not slacken my strength because of mine afflictions. Rejoice, O my heart, and cry unto the Lord, and say: O Lord, I will praise thee forever; yea, my soul will rejoice in thee, my God, and the rock of my salvation" (2 Nephi 4:28–30). In this verse, Nephi applies his father's advice. He chooses to stop being acted upon (see 2 Nephi 2). How does he do this? Nephi tells himself to take charge of his own emotions, to originate rather than react. He tells himself that since his core experiences are real, since God really does live, there is no need to live in anger or other negative feelings.

Nephi taught us that we have to learn to control our mind and transform ourselves. Nephi chose to control and author himself, to have positive feelings, to be alive in Christ. Through this counter-normal work, Nephi moved himself closer to Jesus Christ, felt the love of Christ, and was elevated out of the ordinary, reactive state. Nephi joined with Christ in the re-creation of Nephi.

What exactly does it mean to re-create yourself? Please open your Book of Mormon and read 2 Nephi 4:29–35. As you do, note the punctuation marks. As the sentences go on, the punctuation marks tend to shift from periods to exclamation points. Exclamation points are indicators of great feeling. In these verses, we are reading something called the Psalm of Nephi. Nephi has moved from depression to rejoicing in Christ.

Preach My Gospel tells us that "learning from a good teacher is important, but it is more important for you to have meaningful learning experiences on your own" (17). In the process of effective study, we can reflect on our core experiences. In the process of effective study, we can record our core experiences. They thus become available to our conscious mind. Like Nephi, in times of discouragement, we can return to these core experiences and ask, "Did this really happen to me?" Because these events did happen, they witness to us that God really lives. Because we have that witness, we can become more alive in Christ, more filled with enthusiasm, and more effective in our finding and teaching.

When my children were in the early weeks of their missions, I tried to teach the principles that I have explained in the last few letters. At one point, I wrote to Kristin and Travis about 2 Nephi 4. I taught them that having meaningful experiences with the Spirit is important. I taught them that writing down their spiritual experiences is like making deposits in a spiritual bank account. When we are conscious of our spiritual experiences, we can draw on them like Nephi did to transform ourselves. I then also taught them about the topic of this letter. We can use our core stories to teach more effectively. A few weeks later, Travis replied, "After I received your letter I made a list of stories that meant something to me. Then I went through and found scriptures for each one. I had noticed I had fallen into a habit of giving meaningless spiritual thoughts and the letter was a big help. I have been really trying to apply it every day."

Towards the end of Travis's mission, I reviewed some similar notions. He wrote home and made some very important observations about the letter:

> As I read Dad's letter this week, I received some indirect revelation on some things. It was triggered as I read your spiritual experience account. I was given some thoughts through the Spirit. First, I felt inspired to take my spiritual bank account a step further. Through the first few months of my mission, I gathered spiritual thoughts. I took experiences I had, added scriptures, and made them into lessons. They are powerful because they are meaningful experiences. I have used the same list for spiritual experiences my whole mission. They have become part of me. I can rehearse the experiences and the scriptures any time. They have become a cornerstone. If I ever struggle, I go back to them.
>
> When I got to a certain point on my mission, I stopped adding to my list. I continued to write experiences in my journal, but I

wasn't retelling them. I believe that these latter experiences are not as much a part of me. By constantly retelling experiences to people, they become part of you. So I have decided to go through my journal and add to my list and turn them into lessons. This way, they will never fade. Also, it will make me more powerful because I will have a lesson for any topic. I will be able to teach any time with greater power. I will also be able to learn more things from the stories each time I tell them. I don't believe it has been good enough to just record; it is my responsibility to retell.

I love the fact that Travis understood and applied what Nephi teaches us. I love his declaration of revelation and the fact that it happened while Travis was reading a letter. As we write the things of our soul to our parents, and as they write the things of their souls back to us, we teach each other and Holy Ghost can carry our words to each other's hearts (see 2 Nephi 4:15). We can more fully convert each other.

It also thrills me to know that early in his mission, Travis learned to develop lessons in which he was able to integrate his thoughts and experiences with the scriptures and testify with power as we saw in the recent letter in which he transformed the antagonistic investigator. Because Travis was conscious of his core experiences, he could return to them, like Nephi. Travis wrote, "If I ever struggle, I go back to them." Travis learned how to transform himself by reviewing his moments of divine contact in the same fashion that Nephi did.

Travis further indicated that he needed to return to his former practice and reengage the process of integrating the things he has "seen and heard" with the scriptures (see 2 Nephi 4:16). He said this would allow him to teach with "greater power." He also indicated something else that was very important. He said, "I will also be able to learn more things from the stories each time I tell them." This is a very mature insight. Each time we read the scriptures, we can learn new things from the Holy Ghost. The same is true of our core experiences: each time we consider them or teach them, the Holy Ghost can teach us new things about what our core experiences actually mean.

Elder Bruce R. McConkie was a serious student of the scriptures. He once gave a particularly important talk titled, "The How and Why of Faith-Promoting Stories." In it, Elder McConkie encourages us to begin our presentation by identifying and declaring an eternal principle. He then encourages us to identify and tell a story that illustrates the principle. He tells us to first find a story from the scriptures. He indicates that these stories are important because they illustrate the workings of God in ancient times. Since "God is no respecter of persons" (Acts 10:34), these ancient stories give us clues on what to expect from God today. Their purpose is "to create faith in our hearts so that we will trust in the same Lord who blessed our forebears and thereby inherit the same blessings that he poured out upon them."

However, he does not stop there. He suggests that a second story also be told. He calls it "a modern faith-promoting story" and tells us three places where we may go to find such stories.[29] I see an important progression in the movement from one place to the next; you might watch for this progression carefully.

Source One: Elder McConkie says the first place to go for modern stories is the history of this dispensation. Such stories demonstrate that the things that were happening in the lives of the ancient saints are happening in our time. It shows that "our religion is a living thing that changes the lives of people." I love that sentence. I think we should be careful to look for all indicators of our religion being a living thing that changes lives. We pay attention to all stories in the history of the modern Church that enlarge our soul. We should record these and use them to illustrate the principles we teach. We might, for example, teach the principle of prayer and then tell the story of Joseph Smith going into the grove.

Source Two: Elder McConkie tells us that we should also teach stories from the lives of people "whom we know, whose voice we know and whose spirit we can feel." This suggests that the stories of those around us are important because they are even more familiar to us and to our audience.

Such stories have more immediacy and more intimacy. As teachers, we are likely to tell such stories with greater feeling. The audience is more likely to recognize and identify with the story. They are, therefore, likely to connect both emotionally and logically.

In these letters, I often share stories from my family members. These stories are very important to me. I have strong feelings about the missionary experiences of my family members, and when I use them in my teaching, I do so with great feeling. In an earlier letter, we saw a case when President David O. McKay included in his testimony the story of his father getting revelation in a cave. As we read his words, we can tell that President McKay taught this story with great feeling.

Source Three: Elder McConkie tells us that the most "perfect" source is our own stories, our own accounts of our own experiences with the living God. When we tell these stories, we apply the "seal of living reality" to our teaching. The story testifies to us—like Nephi's stories testified to him—that God is real. As we tell these stories, the Holy Ghost gives witness. People feel the witness and are more likely to recognize that God operates in the present as He did in the past.

Our challenge is to conduct our daily study so that we that we are seeking diligently to have the mysteries of God unfolded to us by the power of the Holy Ghost. We are to prepare so that when we teach, the Holy Ghost will carry our words to the hearts of the children of men. We can do this by learning to integrate the scriptures with our own moments of divine contact. We can do it by teaching eternal principles, illustrating them from the scriptures, and applying the seal of reality by testifying with conviction from our own experiences with the living God.

If you practice doing the things in this letter, when you are called to speak in church or in any other setting, you will speak with power. You will wave the flag of Jesus Christ and people will know that His power flows through you. They will be attracted to you and will be more likely to bring their friends to you so they can be taught by Jesus Christ.

I love each one of you.

Be extraordinary in Christ,

President Quinn

Challenge 23

Transforming Units

My Dear Fellow Servants,

It is often assumed that the job of a missionary is to invite individuals to Christ and facilitate their conversion. This is a very intimidating notion for a new missionary to contemplate. But what if we raised the bar? What if the challenge was to convert an entire ward of members?

Some might respond that the ward is the stewardship of the bishop and not a missionary. Yet *Preach My Gospel* suggests that a ward is our best resource for finding people to teach (170) and one of the best ways to move the work forward is to gain the trust of the members (161). On page 161 is a wonderful story of a sister missionary who was able to transform the attitude of an entire ward. In this letter we will consider how to do this seemingly impossible thing. It is one of the most important things you can learn to do.

Travis shared a story about a family he taught. He wrote about challenging Tammi (the mother) to move her baptism up a week. She said yes, and Travis wrote what she said after agreeing to the challenge.

> She then said something that touched my heart and brought tears to my eyes. She said, "I want you guys to know that you have literally saved my life. Please don't ever feel discouraged with what you are doing. You have saved my soul. Three months ago I had no desire to live but then you knocked on my door. Now I have found true happiness. Thank you so much."

Travis then writes something important: "I do not think I have ever felt that good in my life."

Later, Travis describes Tammi's baptism. The next day the testimony meeting focused on missionary work. It went over by thirty minutes, and in the next meeting, people continued to get up and bear testimony of missionary work. They asked Travis to share his testimony. He wrote:

> Then I was asked to stand up. In tears I told them that six months ago I left Brentwood thinking nothing could top it. It was my home. Then I went on to talk about how much I love Pleasanton and how much the Lord had blessed me. I felt the Spirit very strong. I remember one time Shawn [Travis's brother] saying he would have spent his whole mission working to find Bob [a man who joined the Church]. I told them I would have spent my whole mission working to find Tammi and her family. As the class ended I wanted to stay in the room.

Travis expressed how much he loved Tammi's family, as well as missionary work. He followed that up with an important statement connecting his feelings about missionary work, to the ward and their feelings about missionary work. As you read it, think about the claim I made earlier about transforming a whole ward.

> I cannot explain how much the two wards love us right now. I do not say that out of pride but to prove how big of a difference trusting and loving the missionaries makes. The singles ward is the same as the family ward. Tonight they want us at a family home evening to bear our testimonies. Things are unreal right now and are only going up.

Travis then wrote from his heart:

> So as you can tell, I am loving life. I have never felt so good in my life. I truly am in the business of saving souls. That is not just a phrase. It is real. God is real. He is doubling baptisms. I am just glad to be a part of it. Jesus Christ lives. He is our literal Savior. The plan of Salvation brings happiness. The ultimate happiness is exaltation with your family. I love you all.

Those are not the words or experiences of a normal person. They are the words and the experiences of a transformed person who has now become an effective servant of God. The power of God is burning within the missionary, and individuals like Tammi are being converted. But note that it is not just Tammi who is being changed. Please again ponder these words: "I cannot explain how much the two wards love us right now. I do not say that out of pride but to prove how big of a difference trusting and loving the missionaries makes. The singles ward is the same as the family ward. Tonight they want us at a family home evening to bear our testimonies. Things are unreal right now and are only going up."

The two wards are on fire with missionary work. Why? One reason is that they trust and love the missionaries. They were not on fire when Travis first arrived. A few months before, when Travis entered this new area, he visited ward leaders and they brushed him off. He was just one more missionary who would be hanging around for a few months. They expected, like many other missionaries, that he would come and go and nothing much would change.

It would have been natural for Travis to be offended by the ward leaders. He could have pointed his finger at them and used them as an excuse for not engaging the work. Indeed, this is the normal thing to do. Pointing fingers at ward leaders, companions, mission leaders, and so forth is natural behavior. It leads to normal outcomes.

There is another way. As missionaries, we can move closer to Jesus Christ and thus live in the endowment of power. When we do, members begin to change. Trust goes up. Here is a great illustration from my daughter, Kristin:

> The most important thing is trust of the members. Last night Elder Leavitt and Elder Inistroza had a charla [discussion] with the mom of a member. She's had tons of missionaries teach her. This mission was so numbers-oriented before that the missionaries always tried to pressure her. Elder Leavitt said they just taught her the doctrine and let the Spirit come and she was like, "I want to be baptized." They told the daughter's best friend (the bishop's wife) and she was like, "Whaaat? Are you serious? Elders, I have a BUNCH more referrals to give you now."

Time and again, we see this pattern. When members feel the power of Jesus Christ operating and bringing success, it becomes contagious. It is then that they begin to respond. This means missionaries can change members and entire wards if they first change themselves.

Jesus taught this as one of the central themes of his earthly minis-
try: "And why beholdest thou the mote that is in thy brother's eye, but
perceivest not the beam that is in thine own eye? Either how canst thou
say to thy brother, Brother, let me pull out the mote that is in thine
eye, when thou thyself beholdest not the beam that is in thine own
eye? Thou hypocrite, cast out first the beam out of thine own eye, and
then shalt thou see clearly to pull out the mote that is in thy brother's
eye" (Luke 6:41–42). Here Jesus suggests that how we see and how
effectively we act is predicated upon how we are on the inside. When
we are filled with hypocrisy, we can see the hypocrisy in others but not
in ourselves. We tend to be ineffective in our efforts to change the other
person. He suggests that we first remove beam that is in our own eye,
that is, reduce our own hypocrisy and then we will be in a different
state. In that different state, we will see more clearly how to best change
our brother.

Jesus goes on to point out that the heart, or our motives, determine what we say and the goodness of the impact we have: "A good
man out of the good treasure of his heart bringeth forth that which
is good; and an evil man out of the evil treasure of his heart bringeth
forth that which is evil; for of the abundance of the heart his mouth
speaketh" (Luke 6:45). Here Jesus is telling us that what we bring forth
in the world is a function of the condition of our own heart. If we allow
God change our heart, we are then able to help God change the world.
This is why obedience, sanctification, and unification are critical. If we
become more pure, we acquire power to do things we are currently sure
we cannot do.

Joseph F. Smith said,

> We want young men . . . who have kept themselves unspotted from
> the world. . . . Where you get men like this to preach the gospel to
> the world, whether they know much to begin with or not, the Lord
> will put his Spirit into their hearts, and he will crown them with
> intelligence and power to save the souls of men. (Gospel Doctrine,
> 1938, p. 356)

Here President Smith is suggesting a rather astounding claim.
Each of us has power beyond our normal understanding. We can
have extraordinary impact. We can facilitate the conversion of other
human beings. Wards can be transformed. The earth can be altered. An

ordinary person can do these things if they simply choose to look inside and pull the beams from their own eye. The notion is not sensible to the normal mind, only to the person filled with the Spirit of God.

Jesus is teaching us that we are in control. If we pull the beam from our own eye, we will have enormous power. We change how we see by purifying what is in our heart. If we pray for our hearts to be open, if we pray with all energy that we be filled with the pure love of Jesus Christ, we will be transformed (see Moroni 7:47–48).

In their weekly letters, Kristin and Travis were continually looking within. They went through a grinding search for their own hypocrisy. They moved closer to Christ, and then bishops changed, wards caught fire, and people got baptized.

When we first arrived in Australia, we taught you this concept. The whole process began with a simple step: seeing members and seeing yourselves in a new light. You committed to obedience, diligence, sanctification, and unity. You worked to bring the spirit of prophecy to every interaction with every member. After only a brief time, a sister called the mission office and she said, "These missionaries have really changed, I do not know what got into them, but it is very impressive."

That was the beginning of a trust-building process. Later, some missionaries were able to transform entire wards. It was from those wards that a great river of baptisms began to flow. I encourage you to continue this work.

I love each one of you.
Be extraordinary in Christ,
President Quinn

Challenge 24

Transforming Leaders

My Dear Fellow Servants,

In the previous letter, I referred to the words in *Preach My Gospel* on gaining the trust of the members. We read of how Travis and his companion accomplished this difficult feat. In this letter I would like to focus on influencing the bishop and other key ward members.

Here I share an impressive story of a sister missionary who believed that humility gives rise to confidence that you can accomplish "whatever the Lord requires of you" (*Preach My Gospel*, 120). Because she did, she was able to transform an angry and uncooperative bishop. To be a truly effective missionary, you must be able to transform uninterested or antagonistic ward leaders into interested ward leaders. You can only accomplish this through Christ, but you can accomplish it.

We begin with an observation made by Travis. He had been on his mission only a few weeks when he wrote home and indicated that he had some important insights. The first occurred to him while he listened to his companion pray. Here is what he wrote:

> The first is something Elder Tanner said in a prayer. He said, "Help us to always be worthy to call ourselves Christians." I had never thought about that before but it is so important. We hear people say that they are Christian all the time but they are not. To be a Christian means to take upon yourself the name of Christ. This means you follow His example and do your best to be like Him. If you don't do this, you are not a Christian. If you look at how many people actually do it, there are not many true Christians around.

According to Travis, a Christian recognizes Christ, takes the name of Christ, follows the example of Christ, and strives to be like Christ. This suggests that being a Christian does not mean claiming a philosophy. It means engaging in the constant work of self-change. It means constantly listening for the Spirit of Christ and then doing what is necessary to move closer to Christ. If we do this, we experience a change in nature. We take on new attributes. Among the attributes we take on are humility, confidence, and strength. By way of illustration, consider the story of Kristin and her bishop.

After a few months, Kristin was made a senior companion. As she labored, Kristin had great difficulties with her local bishop. Previously the bishop had had some negative experiences with the missionaries assigned to his ward. This is common. Missionaries often fail to realize that when they fail to serve effectively or live in a disobedient way, they often leave a negative legacy. Sometimes for years after the missionary leaves, the local members and leaders still carry anger and refuse to work with the missionaries in the unit. In such situations, it is likely that many people are not baptized because of what some missionary did a long time ago. It is a terrible legacy.

This particular bishop was angry at past missionaries, and he often acted as a barrier to the work. Kristin shared an incident in which she met with the bishop:

> We had an interesting talk with the bishop this week. He started telling us all this stuff we needed to do differently with Iris's family. He was already upset about some other stuff so he wasn't being too tactful. He kept throwing all this stuff out about how we need to teach them as a family, not as individuals. Everything he was saying was true, but I had excuses for each thing. I thought about Ryan's letter and just acted like a pillow and only responded to things I had reasons for.

Kristin had been working hard. She felt like the bishop had not been supportive. Now he was giving her direction that felt like criticism. What is the natural reaction? What would most missionaries do? What would you do?

Kristin said that in the midst of the experience, she reflected on a letter from her brother Ryan. In that letter, Ryan had discussed the art of listening. He spoke of being like a pillow and just absorbing things that would normally make a person angry. With this thought in mind, Kristin "bridled" her "passions" (Alma 38:12). She chose not to have a natural reaction. Instead of lashing out or withdrawing, she took control. Even though she was feeling offended, she responded with purpose. She was feeling such pain she only wanted to escape, but first suggested that they read a scripture. She said,

> I had no idea what to share and just opened up my scriptures. I don't even remember what it was—something in Nephi, but it talked about being humble. I started to talk and tears just came pouring out. I thought about the humbling experience I had the week before and I told them—if we want to progress in anything, we have to humble ourselves. Sometimes we have to pray for experiences to be humbled and this is hard, because it means something painful is going to come; but if that is all it takes, I'm willing to do it because all I want is to be as close to the Lord as I can be.

Here there are a number of points worth noting. First, because she monitored her feelings and bridled them, she did not feel upset or angry. She had other feelings instead, feelings of sadness. Second, she just wanted to get out of there but instead, wanting to be diligent, she asked if she could share a scripture. As she engaged in this unnatural act of discipline, note what happened next. She "happened" to open to a scripture on humility. Third, she didn't know what to say but she just started talking. As she talked, tears began to flow. They flowed because Kristin spoke from the center of her soul. She was completely authentic. Her words and her feelings were congruent. Fourth, she told of a core experience from the week before that illustrated the notion of humility discussed in the scripture. Fifth, she taught the principle with power. Sixth, she bore the following witness: "I'm willing to do it, because all I want is to be as close to the Lord as I can be."

At this point Kristin met the requirements of a Christian as outlined by Travis. She was therefore a living witness of Christ. She was a living example of the attribute of which she was bearing testimony. She not only talked about humility, she lived in humility. She was in an extraordinary state, a condition that we seldom witness. She was filled with humility, confidence, and strength. Now, how do people react when a missionary is in such a Christ-like state?

His poor wife didn't know what to do I was crying so hard. She was just like, "Oh, yes, yes, we know." The bishop didn't say anything at first and then he closed the door where there was noise coming. We had this great talk about the difference between missionaries that come out. We all knock on the same doors but there is a difference in missionaries and in their investigators. We talked about what we can do to get the ward more excited about missionary work. What a turnabout in the conversation. It was amazing!

Please note the miracle that occurred. The bishop had been angry with the missionaries for a long time. Because of past negative experiences, he had lost faith in the missionaries and provided little support. Then he encountered a missionary who was living and teaching from a Christ-like state. It was like encountering an angel—because that was what he was actually encountering. When a missionary is filled with the love, light, and power of Christ, the missionary is an angel of God.

Such an encounter is a moment of divine contact. The bishop was converted. He repented. He took a new view of himself, of God, and of the world (see Bible Dictionary, "Repentance"). What was his new view? First, he noted that not all missionaries are the same. This was a dramatic recognition. Previously he assumed that they were all the same and that they could not be trusted. He moved from this topic to how he and Kristin could work together to get the ward more excited about missionary work. I would suggest that this qualified as a miracle, a miracle brought about by a missionary who had been out a relatively short time.

I think the above story is of great importance. Doesn't every righteous missionary hunger to have a sincere conversation with a bishop about how to get the ward more excited about missionary work? Yet how often does this happen? Not often. Missionaries often have a meeting with a bishop, note that he is not excited, and then go off complaining to each other about the fact that the bishop does not seem interested.

My question is this: why should the bishop be interested? He has a thousand things on his mind. He has probably encountered numerous missionaries who wanted to talk to him about what he could do for them. It is natural, normal, and ordinary for a bishop to not be excited about missionary work. We may even meet a bishop who is negative about missionaries, as was the above bishop. If this is so, it is usually with good reason.

If what I have just said is true, then what hope is there? For a missionary who lives in the passive state, for a missionary who is "acted upon," there is no hope. The bishop and ward are not going to change.

For a Christian missionary, there is endless hope. A Christian missionary is an extraordinary missionary, someone who is overcoming nature to move closer to Christ. A Christian missionary is alive in Christ and is filled with Christ-like attributes, an angel who realizes that his or her purpose is to make divine contact, to convert and elevate everyone, including all members of the Church and particularly leaders of the Church. A Christian missionary goes to visit a bishop, expecting to do the spiritual work necessary to attract the bishop closer to Christ; then the Christian missionary goes to each member home expecting to do the work necessary to attract the member closer to Christ.

How do extraordinary missionaries do this? First, they continually clarify purpose. In every interaction, they ask, "What result does God want me to create?" They then let go of their own ego needs and engage in selfless service and obedient submission. Then, like Nephi, they move forward in faith trusting the Lord to give then what is needed in the very hour. As they interact with bishops and other ward leaders, they engage in acts of love and they thus invite the leaders to Christ.

I love each one of you.
Be extraordinary in Christ,
President Quinn

A Final Note

I once led a discussion in a church class. We were talking about purpose. A woman shared that there were many aspects of her role in life about which she felt unsettled or maybe even bitter. One day she asked, "What is the most important thing I will accomplish in this life?" She felt a potent answer emerge from within, "Raising your children to be faithful followers of Christ." She said that after that experience everything changed. Her activities stayed the same but she lived a more positive and meaningful life.

I think her discovery applies to me and to others. I hunger for that same outcome. So do the prophets. In the midst of his very active life, Nephi explained that "he wrote for the profit and learning of his children."

As we reach the end of this book, the image that comes to me is that we all have the opportunity to lead in such a way that our children are more likely to be faithful followers of Christ. When they are on their missions, we have a window when we can teach them more effectively than at any other time. If we have a meaningful message, they are hungry for help. If we speak to them from our most meaningful life experiences, they will listen and learn. It is my prayer that this book will inspire someone to write for the profit and learning of their children.

Notes

1. "Called to Serve," *Hymns*, no. 249.
2. *My Soul Delighteth in the Scriptures*, H. Wallace Goddard and Richard H. Cracroft (Eds) (West Valley City, UT: Bookcraft, 1999), 4.
3. Virginia H. Pearce, *A Heart Like His* (Salt Lake City: Deseret Book, 2006), 80.
4. *New Era*, July 1978; emphasis added.
5. Reverend Dr. Howard Thurman, *Meditations of the Heart* (Boston: Beacon Press, 1953), 54.
6. *Preach My Gospel* (Salt Lake City: The Church of Jesus Christ of Latter-day Saints, 2004), 89.
7. Ibid, 3.
8. David O. McKay, *Gospel Ideals*, 22.
9. Richard G. Scott, "Realize Your Full Potential," *Ensign*, Nov. 2003, 41.
10. *Preach My Gospel* (Salt Lake City: The Church of Jesus Christ of Latter-day Saints, 2004), 13.
11. David O. McKay, in Conference Report, Oct. 1969, 8.
12. Sheri L. Dew, *Go Forward with Faith: The Biography of Gordon B. Hinckley* (Salt Lake City: Deseret Book, 1996), 64–65.
13. John Groberg, "The Power of God's Love," *Ensign*, Nov. 2004.
14. *Teachings of Spencer W. Kimball* (Salt Lake City: The Church of Jesus Christ of Latter-day Saints), 547.

15. *Preach My Gospel* (Salt Lake City: The Church of Jesus Christ of Latter-day Saints, 2004), 198.
16. David O. McKay, in Conference Report, Oct. 1969, 8.
17. *Preach My Gospel* (Salt Lake City: The Church of Jesus Christ of Latter-day Saints, 2004), 13.
18. Ibid, chapter 6.
19. Ibid, chapter 4.
20. Ibid, chapter 2.
21. Richard G. Scott, "Realize Your Full Potential," *Ensign*, Nov. 2003, 41.
22. Csikszentmihalyi; *Finding Flow: The Psychology of Engagement with Everyday Life* (New York: Basic Books, 1997), 105–6.
23. David O. McKay, in Conference Report, Oct. 1951, 92–98.
24. Spencer W. Kimball, "Ocean Currents and Family Influences," *Ensign*, Nov. 1974.
25. "Our Missionary Purpose," Seminar for New Mission Presidents, 2008.
26. *Preach My Gospel* (Salt Lake City: The Church of Jesus Christ of Latter-day Saints, 2004), 3–4.
27. Richard J. Maynes, "A Celestial Connection to Your Teenage Years," *Ensign*, Nov. 1997, 30.
28. *Preach My Gospel* (Salt Lake City: The Church of Jesus Christ of Latter-day Saints, 2004), 185; emphasis added.
29. Bruce R. McConkie, "The How and Why of Faith-Promoting Stories," *New Era*, July 1978.

About the Authors

Photo credit: Shauri Dewey

Robert E. Quinn holds the Margaret Elliot Tracy Collegiate Professorship at the University of Michigan and serves on the faculty of Management and Organization at the Ross Business School. He is one of the co-founders and the current Director of the Center for Positive Organizational Scholarship. Quinn's research and teaching interests focus on leadership, organizational change and effectiveness. He has published 18 books on these subjects.

He is a fellow of the Academy of Management and the World Business Academy. He was a co-recipient of the Academy of Management's 2010 Martin Trail Blazer Award for opening new directions in the field of organization theory. He is also the recipient of the 2011 Marion F. Gislason Award, presented by the Executive Development Roundtable for life-long contributions to the field and practices of leadership.

Hc has thirty years of experience in assisting large organizations in the transformational process. He has also served as a mission president for the Australia Adelaide Mission.

Photo credit: Traci Rampton

Shauri Quinn Dewey is the in-house editor and marketing manager for Robert E. Quinn. She has worked in media for the last 15 years. She wrote and produced Public Service Announcements, as well as the children's Internet show: Ready, Set, Internet! for the National Center for Missing and Exploited Children. She also worked as a consultant for Root Learning, writing and producing digital e-learning modules and video projects, and eventually created and led their video department.

After marrying her husband, James, she began to follow him on various posts around the world where he works as a U.S. diplomat. In 2011, on their first posting to Baghdad, she ran the US Embassy's TV studio and had the opportunity to not only work with 4-star Generals, traveling dignitaries and national media personalities, but also to dodge incoming rockets on a regular basis.

Shauri received an undergraduate degree from Brigham Young University, and a graduate certificate from Georgetown University. She currently lives in Alexandria, VA with her husband, James and their daughter, Cora. She served in the Anaheim, CA, Spanish-speaking Mission of the Church of Jesus Christ of Latter Day Saints.